TENCH COXE

A STUDY IN AMERICAN ECONOMIC DEVELOPMENT

A Da Capo Press Reprint Series

THE AMERICAN SCENE
Comments and Commentators

GENERAL EDITOR: WALLACE D. FARNHAM
University of Illinois

TENCH COXE

A STUDY IN AMERICAN ECONOMIC DEVELOPMENT

BY HAROLD HUTCHESON

DA CAPO PRESS · NEW YORK · 1969

A Da Capo Press Reprint Edition

This Da Capo Press edition of *Tench Coxe: A Study in American Economic Development* is an unabridged republication of the first edition published in Baltimore in 1938 as New Series, No. XXVI, of the Johns Hopkins University Studies in Historical and Political Science.

Library of Congress Catalog Card Number 75-87441

Copyright 1938, The Johns Hopkins Press

Published by Da Capo Press
A Division of Plenum Publishing Corporation
227 West 17th Street
New York, N. Y. 10011

Printed in the United States of America

TENCH COXE

A STUDY IN AMERICAN ECONOMIC DEVELOPMENT

LONDON: HUMPHREY MILFORD
OXFORD UNIVERSITY PRESS

TENCH COXE

A STUDY IN AMERICAN ECONOMIC DEVELOPMENT

BY

HAROLD HUTCHESON

Instructor in Economics, Connecticut College

BALTIMORE

THE JOHNS HOPKINS PRESS

1938

330.0924
H91π
9/221
Dec.1974

PRINTED IN THE UNITED STATES OF AMERICA
BY J. H. FURST COMPANY, BALTIMORE, MARYLAND

TO MY MOTHER AND FATHER

PREFACE

The work of the members of the so-called American Nationalist School in creating an " industrial conscious- ness " on the part of Americans during the first half of the nineteenth century has been set forth. Little attention, however, has been paid to the precursors of this group of writers. Instead, Hamilton's masterly *Report on Manufac- tures* has often been referred to as the fountain-head of their ideas. That several contemporaries of Hamilton thought and wrote as he did is not generally known. One such figure was Tench Coxe. As an advocate of a national economy, exponent of an American cotton culture and manufacture, and an economic adviser to important political figures of his day, Tench Coxe undoubtedly is worthy of more attention than he has hitherto received. This study is presented as a modest contribution to an understanding of his life and thought.

In the preparation of this account of Tench Coxe the writer has first relied upon those published writings of Coxe for which identification could be had; and second, upon that body of manuscript material of or pertaining to Coxe, which has been available. These sources, it is believed, have enabled him to present a reliable account of Coxe's economic opinions and activities.

Repeated efforts to gain access to the main body of Coxe manuscripts (containing upwards of 60,000 pieces and preserved by his descendants at their estate at Drifton, Pennsylvania) have proved fruitless. Mr. Daniel Coxe of Philadelphia, as the representative of the family, was approached on numerous occasions by the writer with the hope that some arrangement could be effected for the use of the manuscripts. Among other things, it was suggested to Mr. Coxe that the collection be deposited with the Librarian of The Johns Hopkins University, and that following the preparation of this study, the writer should edit the manuscripts for publication by the University Press. Unfortunately, Mr. Coxe was either unwilling or unable to agree to this suggestion; nor were others more acceptable to him. Several interesting episodes in the life of Tench Coxe could not, therefore, be treated with the desired attention to detail. In particular, the part played by Coxe in the formulation of Hamilton's *Report on Manufactures* cannot, upon the basis of available material, be definitely ascertained. This is to be regretted, especially since there is much in the *Report* that suggests the influence of Coxe, who when it was prepared served Hamilton as an assistant. According to information supplied by Dr. Julian P. Boyd, the Secretary of the Historical Society of Pennsylvania, and the only outsider who has been fortunate enough to examine this collection of Coxe manuscripts, it contains several letters which passed between Hamilton and Coxe concerning the *Report,* as well as a copy of the *Report* itself, in the handwriting of Coxe.

For having first directed his attention to the usefulness of a study of the life and thought of Tench Coxe, the writer is indebted to Dr. Broadus Mitchell, of the Department of Political Economy of The Johns Hopkins University. At every stage in the preparation of this work, Dr. Mitchell has offered encouragement and advice. Responsibility for the sins of omission and commission, however, rests entirely upon the writer.

For a liberal grant to enable him to carry on research in Philadelphia, the writer makes grateful acknowledgment to the Lessing Rosenthal Fund for Economic Research. He also wishes to express his appreciation for the generous assistance accorded him by the staffs of the Library of Congress, the Historical Society of Pennsylvania, the Library Company of Philadelphia, the Virginia State Library, the Maryland Historical Society, the Carnegie Library of Pittsburgh, the Library of the American

Philosophical Society, and last, but by no means the least, the Library of The Johns Hopkins University. To Misses Angela and Lilly Lavarello, he expresses thanks for expert typing of the manuscript.

HAROLD HUTCHESON

CONTENTS

CHAPTER I

THE LIFE OF TENCH COXE

Were Tench Coxe alive today, one can well imagine that he would be conspicuous amongst those who are seeking solutions to the many and complex problems which our current economic arrangements present. An untiring readiness to serve in the promotion of the national interests is the clue to his life. He is to be ranked among the first in a long line of economic experts who have served the national government in an advisory and administrative capacity.

Born on May 22, 1755, in Philadelphia, Tench Coxe was the second of the thirteen children of William and Mary Francis Coxe.[1] The mother was the daughter of Tench and Elizabeth Francis. Tench Francis, originally of Ireland, had emigrated to this country while a boy, settling in Talbot County, Maryland.[2] Seeking a better field for his talents as a lawyer, he removed to Philadelphia. There he very soon rose to fame, serving as Attorney-General of the Province of Pennsylvania from 1742 to 1754. He was also Recorder of the City of Philadelphia from 1750 to 1755. He died in August, 1758.[3]

On his father's side, Tench Coxe's family background was illustrious. Colonel Daniel Coxe, III, paternal grandfather of Tench, came to this country from England in

---

[1] See genealogy of the Coxe family by William Nelson, *New Jersey Biographical and Genealogical Notes* ("Collections of the New Jersey Historical Society," IX), 81 ff.

[2] Oswald Tilghman, *History of Talbot County, Maryland, 1661-1861,* I, 7. The family connections on his mother's side are best set forth here. R. H. Spencer, *The Thomas Family of Talbot County, Maryland, and Allied Families*, p. 124, states that Tench Francis was "probably" born in Ireland.

[3] *Ibid.*, p. 124; Tilghman, I, 7.

1

1702.[4] Enormous tracts of land in the possession of the family furnished him opportunity as a politician and promoter of settlements upon those lands.[5] His father, Dr. Daniel Coxe, II, was a graduate of Cambridge and a member of the Royal Society. He enjoyed a reputation for his voluminous writings on chemistry and medicine, as well as for his services as personal physician to Charles II, and afterwards to Queen Anne.[6] These court contacts doubtless assisted him in extending his land holdings in the new world, which at one time included all land between 31° and 36°, from the Atlantic to the Pacific Ocean.[7] This particular tract was called " Carolana." To encourage a settlement upon it Colonel Daniel Coxe wrote an interesting pamphlet, entitled, *A Description of the English Province of Carolana, by the Spaniards called Florida, and by the French la Louisiane* (first edition, 1722).[8] As we shall see later, certain novel ideas were incorporated in the pamphlet, which render it of more than passing interest.

William Coxe, the father of Tench, does not appear to have been particularly interested in the settlement of the family lands;[9] rather he chose to follow the calling of a

[4] Nelson, p. 82.

[5] Frank Monaghan, " Daniel Coxe," *Dictionary of American Biography,* IV, 484-485; Nelson, pp. 82-83.

[6] Monaghan, p. 485; Nelson, p. 81; G. D. Scull, " Biographical Notice of Doctor Daniel Coxe, of London," *Pennsylvania Magazine of History and Biography,* VII, 317-337.

[7] For an account of the land holdings of Dr. Coxe, consult: Monaghan, p. 485; Nelson, p. 82; Verner W. Crane, *The Southern Frontier,* pp. 49, 50, 59; F. E. Melvin, " Dr. Coxe and Carolana," *Mississippi Valley Historical Review,* I, 257-262; Clarence W. Alvord, *The Mississippi Valley in British Politics,* I, 96; John Clement, " Coxe Hall," *Proceedings of the New Jersey Historical Society,* Third Series, IX, 27, 29; and Scull, pp. 327-337.

[8] Crane, p. 339.   A reprint of this pamphlet, minus the preface, is to be found in the *Historical Collections of Louisiana,* ed. B. F. French, II, 221-276.

[9] By will of his father, Col. Daniel Coxe, he received several hundred

merchant in Philadelphia. This he did in partnership with Moore Furman, subsequently a stockholder and official of the New Jersey Society for the Encouragement of Useful Manufactures.[10] Trade in Philadelphia must have been brisk and profitable for them. The city had a population of nearly nineteen thousand by 1760 and surpassed Boston as the greatest trading center in the Colonies.[11] Its merchants, however, in common with those in other ports, had to face the more stringent regulations of the new colonial policy of Britain after 1763 and the reaction of the colonists thereto. The firm of Coxe & Furman on October 25, 1765 joined other merchants and traders in a non-importation agreement.[12]

That the father was a man of some prominence in the community is attested by the fact that he held at various times minor offices in the municipal government. Twice he refused the mayoralty.[13] On July 11, 1759 he was elected a Trustee of the College of Philadelphia (now the University of Pennsylvania); twelve years later he entered as a law student in that institution his son, Tench.[14]

---

acres of land, together with a three-fourths interest in an iron works and grist mill near Bordentown, New Jersey. *New Jersey Archives*, First Series, XXX, 118-119.

[10] Joseph S. Davis, *Essays in the Earlier History of American Corporations* (" Harvard Economic Studies," XVI), I, 391, 402. Nalbro Frazier was also at one time a member of the firm. *Ibid.*, p. 141 and note 2.

[11] Arthur M. Schlesinger, *The Colonial Merchants and the American Revolution, 1763-1776* (" Columbia University Studies," LXXVIII), p. 27.

[12] J. Thomas Scharf and Thompson Wescott, *A History of Philadelphia*, I, 272-273. Wm. Coxe also refused the office of Stamp Distributor for New Jersey in deference to popular clamor against it. Nelson, p. 87. Later, 1776, he was a part owner of three privateers fitted out in Philadelphia. *Journals of the Continental Congress* (1776), VI, 700.

[13] Nelson, p. 87.

[14] Thomas H. Montgomery, *A History of the University of Pennsylvania, 1749-1770*, pp. 343, 535, Appendix F; Henry Simpson, *Lives of Eminent Philadelphians*, p. 259. Montgomery erroneously states Tench's entry as of 1761.

What use young Tench made of attendance at the College is not known. Also of his other activities at this time our knowledge is scanty. We do know, however, that on November 8, 1775, he subscribed for one share of ten Pounds Sterling in the newly formed United Company of Philadelphia for Promoting American Manufactures.[15] This event, measured in terms of his later interests, is exceedingly important. It may well be said to have given direction to his future career, which was hardly true of his collegiate work.

Coming of age in May, 1776, Tench Coxe gave up his formal educational pursuits to enter the mercantile firm of his father. The latter, who had been stricken with paralysis, immediately placed the management of the business in the hands of his son. Though the name of the firm was changed to Coxe, Furman, & Coxe, the business was in reality conducted by Tench after his father's withdrawal from active direction, since Moore Furman was absent most of the time.[16]

Coxe had scarcely become absorbed in the activities of the firm when he, as a merchant, was faced with the task of deciding his probable conduct in the event of a revolt on the part of the colonies. The invasion of Philadelphia by the British in 1777 determined him on a course of neutrality. Inasmuch as this decision proved in later life a continuous source of annoyance to him, especially in his public activities, and since the exact nature of the course which he adopted in 1777 has been a matter of some doubt to those interested in his life, it seems advisable to examine this episode. It appears that Coxe was the victim of circumstances.

As Professor Arthur M. Schlesinger has pointed out, the movements that lie back of the American Revolution were

[15] Coxe's certificate of admission into the Company is reproduced in George S. White, *Memoir of Samuel Slater*, p. 48. See below, chap. v.
[16] Simpson, p. 259.

as much an expression of social discontent within the colonies as they were one of opposition to a narrow colonial policy on the part of Britain.[17] Put otherwise, the prospect of 1775 was a revolution within a revolution. This was particularly true as regards Pennsylvania. Political power in that state in 1775 was centered in the hands of the wealthy people, especially those of Philadelphia and adjacent counties.[18] It thus came about that " taxation without representation " was a local as well as an imperial issue. In short, the disenfranchised saw in the revolutionary movement not alone the possibility of separation from the Mother Country but also of a reform in the government of the state.[19] Merchants, as men of property and influence, were thus placed in the horns of a dilemma. Greater attention on the part of British ministers after 1763 to the enforcement of imperial statutes governing colonial commerce damaged their interests; [20] but participation in the movement for independence on their part added so much fuel to the flames of the movement for reform in the state government. In the Boston Tea Party, an outgrowth of the merchants' policy of a middle course by non-importation agreements,[21] they had a concrete example of what the masses might do if aroused. Moreover, separation from Britain meant pos-

[17] Arthur M. Schlesinger, *New Viewpoints in American History*, chap. vii.

[18] Samuel B. Harding, *Party Struggles over the Pennsylvania Constitution* (" Annual Report of the American Historical Association, 1894 "), p. 371; W. Roy Smith, " Sectionalism in Pennsylvania during the Revolution," *Political Science Quarterly*, XXIV, 209; Charles H. Lincoln, *The Revolutionary Movement in Pennsylvania, 1760-1776*, p. 53.

[19] Chas. J. Stillé, *Pennsylvania and the Declaration of Independence* (reprint from *Pennsylvania Magazine of History and Biography*, January, 1890), p. 27.

[20] Schlesinger, *New Viewpoints*, p. 171; see also his *Colonial Merchants*, p. 48.

[21] The firm of Coxe & Furman in 1765 subscribed to a non-importation agreement in order to obtain repeal of the Stamp Act. Scharf and Wescott, I, 272.

sible total exclusion from customary markets.[22] The position of the merchants, then, was such as not to permit them to join whole-heartedly in the movement for revolt. Progress of the revolutionary movement only added to their fears.

The unprivileged orders in Pennsylvania, when they found the Assembly under the Charter government slow in advancing the patriot cause, concluded that it might be well to adopt a new constitution then and there. Belief that the existing state government was derived from British attachments reinforced this conviction.[23] As the reform movement progressed, the confusion and uncertainty of the ruling order was naturally intensified. During the early part of March, 1777, a new constitution was forced upon this well-to-do class, whereby its power and influence in the politics of the state were considerably curtailed.[24] Thus circumstanced, its support of the American cause in the Revolution was not readily forthcoming; British entry into Philadelphia in September, 1777, was for many of them an occasion of joy.[25]

While there is no positive evidence of the fact, it seems probable that Tench Coxe was induced to become a neutral because of the above circumstances. There is no indication that he actively sided with the British.[26] He was a mer-

[22] Schlesinger, *New Viewpoints*, p. 166.
[23] Harding, p. 374.
[24] *Ibid.*, pp. 374-375; Allan Nevins, *The American States During and After the Revolution, 1775-1789*, pp. 149-156, 249-267.
[25] *Ibid.*, pp. 250, 252; Lincoln, p. 38; Alexander Graydon, *Memoirs of His Own Time, with Reminiscences of the Men and Events of the Revolution*, ed. J. S. Littell, p. 117.
[26] As he himself later expressed it, he entertained "speculative opinions upon the probable event of the measure of Independency." Coxe to Madison, September 17, 1789, MS, Madison Papers, XII. Lorenzo Sabine, *Biographical Sketches of Loyalists of the American Revolution*, I, 341, states that "unless I am misinformed, his [Tench Coxe's] sympathies were on the side of the Crown." Simpson, p. 260, declares that Coxe's mercantile operations forced him to be neutral, which version agrees

chant and, as we shall see, a friend to property interests. It is hardly probable that he viewed without fear the leveling process then in operation in his native state.

Our knowledge of how Tench Coxe passed his time in the presence of the British forces is scanty. The little available, while it does not show that he refrained from the entertainments of the British, does show that he was alert to the suffering of many of his fellow citizens. We find that he was among those who signed a petition to the British commanders in the city praying that they permit the circulation of the old colonial paper currency.[27] The blockade of the city by the Americans had occasioned high prices for provisions; there ensued the inevitable cry of a scarcity of money. The reasoning lying back of the petition was obviously spurious.

On the morning of June 18, 1778 the British army completely evacuated Philadelphia.[28] They were followed by some 3,000 Tories who feared certain death at the hands of the patriots were they to remain in the city.[29] The

with our own. Two cousins of Coxe actively interested themselves in the struggle. Tench Tilghman served as an aide to Washington. See Tilghman, I, 10-11, 40. Daniel Coxe, fifth, on the other hand was ardently pro-British. See his letter of July 4, 1775, to Courtland Skinner, *New Jersey Archives,* First Series, X, 654. For his associations with the British cause in an official capacity, see Nelson, p. 86; *New Jersey Archives,* Second Series, V, 161.

[27] Scharf and Wescott, I, 366. Another illustration of young Coxe's sympathy for his fellow countrymen, in this case more tangible, is to be found in the Diary of Josiah Smith, an exile from South Carolina. It happened that in 1780-1781 many South Carolinians sought refuge from the British fury in their native State by going to Philadelphia. Much suffering was incurred in the mass movement northward, especially amongst the poorer people. To assist these people a subscription list was adopted with the support and authorization of Congress. Tench Coxe is listed by Smith as among those deserving of " lasting remembrance." He donated thirty dollars. See " Josiah Smith's Diary, 1780-1781," annotated by Mabel L. Webber, *The South Carolina Historical and Genealogical Magazine,* XXXIII, 78-84; *ibid.,* XXXIV, 139-146, for list of those who subscribed or donated.

[28] Scharf and Wescott, I, 384.

[29] Nevins, p. 255.

Americans' hatred was intensified when they returned to find their once lovely city now " filthy, ruinous, dreary." [30] That those who had remained in the city as neutrals or Loyalists during the occupation might get their due, a list of persons attainted of treason was made on May 21, 1778, before the British departed. The name of Tench Coxe (listed as a merchant) was included.[31] They were ordered to present themselves for trial. With Thomas McKean presiding, the Court of Oyer and Terminer sat at the College of Philadelphia, September to December, 1778. Tench Coxe was discharged by proclamation, there being no one to appear against him.[32] Two years later he was listed as a member of the Philadelphia militia.[33] Writing later of his course during the Revolution, Coxe had to admit, however, that " the impression of this circumstance was not to be removed in a day. . . ." [34]

Details of the domestic and business interests of Coxe during these trying times are few. We know that he was saddened by the death of his wife, formerly Catherine McCall of Philadelphia. She died on July 22, 1778.[35] There were no children by the marriage. Later, probably

[30] Scharf and Wescott, I, 386.

[31] " Proclamation by the Supreme Executive Council of the Commonwealth of Pennsylvania," *Pennsylvania Archives*, Fourth Series, III, 676 ff.

[32] " List of Persons against whom Proclamations were issued by the Supreme Executive Council & who surrendered themselves to be tried for high Treason," *Pennsylvania Archives*, Sixth Series, XIII, 475.

[33] " A General Return of the 2D, 3D, and 4th classes of Philadelphia militia, August 10, 1780," wherein Tench Coxe is listed as " paid 25th Sept. 1780." *Pennsylvania Archives*, Sixth Series, I. In the militia rolls, 1783-1790, *ibid.*, III, 985, his name appears on the 1787 muster roll of the 7th Company, First Batallion, Philadelphia militia. In 1788 he is listed as a private in 2nd Company, 2nd Batallion. *Ibid.*, p. 1045.

[34] Coxe to Madison, September 17, 1789, MS, Madison Papers, XII.

[35] Gregory B. Keen, " The Descendants of Jöran Kyn, the Founder of Upland," *Pennsylvania Magazine of History and Biography*, V, 458. Her father had numerous business connections in Philadelphia. *Ibid.*, pp. 451, 457.

at the end of 1781 or the beginning of 1782,[36] he took as his second wife Miss Rebecca Coxe, by whom he had several children. Her death occurred in 1806.[37] As to business, there is reason to believe that Coxe continued as a merchant.[38] In December, 1780, however, for reasons unknown, the old partnerships of Coxe & Furman, and Coxe, Furman & Coxe were dissolved.[39] The father was a member of the first; the second included his son, Tench. Other arrangements were no doubt made by the latter to continue in the business, possibly in partnership with someone else.[40]

Following the Peace of Paris, economic conditions in the states presented a sorry spectacle of confusion and uncertainty. In the chapter which follows we shall examine this subject. For the present, it is to be noted that Tench Coxe interested himself in the problem of reform. In this manner he was offered an opportunity to reëstablish himself in the esteem of his fellow citizens. Self-interest, too, no doubt prompted him. Accordingly, we find that in 1783 he was appointed to a standing committee of Philadelphia merchants, which included "Messrs. Morris, Clymer, Fitzsimons, Pettit [and] others."[41] Its purpose was to assist in the ordering of the trade of that

[36] On December 29, 1781, he bought a large amount of furniture from David Evans, Cabinet-maker. "Excerpts from the Day-Books of David Evans, Cabinet-maker, Philadelphia, 1774-1811," *Pennsylvania Magazine of History and Biography*, XXVII, 50.

[37] Nelson, p. 88.

[38] In the Effective Supply Tax levy for the City of Philadelphia, 1779, Coxe is listed as a merchant and put down for £25. *Pennsylvania Archives*, Third Series, XIV, 487.

[39] *Pennsylvania Journal*, December 20, 1780.

[40] The *Pennsylvania Packet* of 1785 contains several advertisements of two mercantile firms which include the name of Coxe. See, for example, April 6, 1785, Donnaldson & Coxe; June 6, 1785, Coxe & Frazier. Harrold E. Gillingham, "The Philadelphia Windsor Chair and Its Journeyings," *Pennsylvania Magazine of History and Biography*, LV, 320, lists Coxe among those shipping chairs in 1783.

[41] Coxe to Madison, September 17, 1789, MS, Madison Papers, XII.

city. The opportunity to participate in this work pleased Coxe. He was, he later wrote, " the youngest member by many years. I was again elected till the restoration of some degree of order to our trade superceded the necessity of this Comm.'' [42]

Further recognition came in 1785 when he was appointed a member of a committee of merchants to work for reform in the tariff system.[43] More notable, however, was his appointment during the following year as a delegate to the Annapolis Convention.[44] Thereafter public affairs engrossed a considerable portion of his time and thought.

As one interested in stability and order in government, Coxe's attention was by no means confined to the vexing problems of inter-state commercial relations. Local politics in Pennsylvania, as we have seen, were very much deranged by the forced adoption of a new constitution in 1777. A violent factional struggle ensued, during the course of which the conservative element of the state made repeated efforts to get into power. In 1781 this rather small group managed to gain control of the Assembly, and during the following year secured the issuance of a charter to the Bank of North America. In itself, this was a proper measure to advance the economic welfare of the state, certainly its important mercantile interests. But the small farmers and mechanics did not see it that way. Their objections were three in number.[45]

---

[42] *Ibid.*

[43] *Pennsylvania Packet,* June 2, 1785.

[44] He was appointed April 11, 1786, by the Council, and on September 20, 1786, submitted a report of the Convention's work. *Minutes of the Supreme Executive Council of Pennsylvania,* XV, 5, 86. His pay amounted to £14-12-6. *Ibid.,* p. 135. While attending this Convention Coxe began an intimate acquaintanceship with James Madison which lasted until his death. Coxe to Madison, June 11, 1801, MS, Madison Papers, XXII. He probably also met Hamilton for the first time.

[45] Harding, pp. 389-391; Lawrence Lewis, *A History of the Bank of North America,* pp. 55-62.

In the first place, the limited ability of the Bank to supply currency was deplored, it being charged that a high rate of interest resulted from this. In the second place, the power of the Bank, supposedly because of its large capital (ten million dollars), small directorate, and unlimited duration, was feared. In the third place, it was thought that the Bank's only function would be to facilitate and not augment the circulation—that is to say, it was to favor the anti-paper or commercial classes.

Using these arguments the poorer classes were able to reinstate themselves in power in the elections of 1785. On September thirteenth of the same year they revoked the charter of the Bank.[46] It is probable that the successful objections of the Bank to an application made to the Assembly of 1784 for the formation of another bank, of which Tench Coxe was to be a director,[47] served to dispel all doubt in their minds as to the monopolistic nature of it.

The repeal of the charter constituted a severe blow to the commercial interests. Aware of its disrupting influence upon commerce, Tench Coxe lost no time in siding with Thomas Paine and others in opposition to the measure.[48] This he did in a pamphlet published in 1786 and entitled, *Thoughts concerning the Bank of North America, with some facts relating to such establishments in other countries, respectfully submitted to the honorable*

[46] The Act repealing the charter is printed in the *Pennsylvania Packet,* September 22, 1785.

[47] This bank, the name of which was to be the Bank of Pennsylvania, was to have a capital of £280,000, divided into 700 shares. To forestall its formation an agreement was reached whereby its subscribers were permitted to share in the privileges of the existing Bank of North America whose capital was for that purpose increased. See Scharf and Wescott, I, 436; J. T. Holdsworth, *Financing an Empire: History of Banking in Pennsylvania,* I, 55; Lewis, pp. 51-53. The firms of Coxe & Frazier and Donnaldson & Coxe subscribed to the new issue to the amount of two and twenty shares respectively. *Ibid.,* p. 144.

[48] Coxe, it is to be acknowledged, had a personal interest in the bank, having been an original subscriber to the extent of four shares at $400 each. *Ibid.,* p. 133.

the General Assembly of Pennsylvania, by one of their constituents.[49]

In this pamphlet Coxe discussed the issues in a dispassionate manner. To his point of view it was not a matter of denouncing the dissenters as stupid and ignorant; rather it was the necessity of educating them. Banks "wisely and justly constituted" are to be defended, he averred.[50] Their origin is to be found in national distress, particularly as they assist in the funding of the public debt. Examining the situation in Pennsylvania, he found that the control of the Bank of North America was in the hands of a few persons.[51] Favoring one vote to each shareholder, he further suggested that the practice obtaining in England of prohibiting proxy voting be adopted. In general, he appears to have desired that the Bank be re-chartered after the fashion of the Bank of England.[52] Regulation, not destruction, was the plea of Coxe.[53]

The interest of Tench Coxe in reform also extended to spheres other than those purely economic. The year following the publication of his pamphlet on the bank, he participated in the formation of the Philadelphia Society

[49] A copy of this pamphlet may be found in the Library of Congress, Miscellaneous Pamphlets, vol. 1092. Another notable defence of the Bank was written by Pelatiah Webster, a gifted student of economics. See "An Essay on Credit: in which the Doctrine of Banks is considered, and some remarks are made on the present state of the Bank of North America," *Political Essays*, pp. 427-464. *Inter alia*, Webster praises the use of checks which the Bank made possible. *Ibid.*, p. 434.

[50] Coxe, *Thoughts concerning the Bank of North America*, p. 1.

[51] The promoters of the Bank of Pennsylvania in their petition to the Assembly for a charter had accused directors of the Bank of North America of "haughtiness and partiality in their method of conducting business." Holdsworth, I, 55.

[52] Coxe, pp. 3, 5, 7, 14.

[53] After repeated petitioning and explanations of good intentions, the Bank was re-chartered on March 17, 1787. Holdsworth, I, 58 ff.; Lewis, p. 73. Later, it again ran into trouble when it sought a renewal of this charter. Coxe, it appears, again came to the defence of the Bank with an essay entitled, "Facts Respecting the Bank of North America." The style of this essay suggests the pen of Coxe.

for Alleviating the Miseries of Public Prisons.[54] Conditions prevailing in the prisons of that city as well as elsewhere, amply justified this step.[55] As formally organized, the Society had an "Acting Committee," which, it was declared, "shall visit the public prisons, or such other places of confinement, or punishment as are ordained by law, at least once every week." Tench Coxe was made a member.[56] In 1788 he was also placed on the Electing Committee of the Society.[57] In 1790 the Society succeeded in obtaining passage of an Act by the Assembly whereby the penal code of the state was favorably revised.[58]

Slavery was another problem of social reform which claimed the support of Tench Coxe.[59] In 1787 he was made a Secretary of the newly reorganized Pennsylvania Society for promoting the abolition of slavery, and the relief of free negroes, unlawfully held in bondage.[60] As such it was his duty to further the aims of the Society through correspondence with other persons and groups

[54] Its charter is reprinted in *The American Museum*, I, 384-385. See also Nevins, p. 460; Scharf and Wescott, I, 444. An earlier Society, formed in 1776, was dissolved when the British entered Philadelphia. Nevins, p. 460. Coxe in 1780 enclosed a paper for publication in a letter to Thomas Bradford, Commissioner of Prisons of Pennsylvania. Whether it dealt with prison reform is not known. It does not appear to have been printed. See Coxe to Bradford, March 27, 1780, MS, Autograph Collection, Historical Society of Pennsylvania.

[55] For a description of conditions in prisons, particularly those of Philadelphia, see John Bach McMaster, *A History of the People of the United States* (2d ed.), I, 98-102.

[56] *The American Museum*, I, 385.

[57] *Pennsylvania Gazette*, January 16, 1788.

[58] McMaster, I, 100; Scharf and Wescott, I, 444.

[59] His father, on the other hand, in 1761 was among a group of merchants petitioning the State Legislature not to enact a duty of £10 on every slave imported into the state, protesting that slaves were needed to keep down the wages of labor. Wm. Renwick Riddell, "Pre-Revolutionary Pennsylvania and the Slave Trade," *Pennsylvania Magazine of History and Biography*, LII, 16-17.

[60] A copy of the charter of the Society is to be found in *The American Museum*, I, 388-389. Founded in 1774, the Society was reorganized on April 23, 1787.

interested in the movement. His letters to Benjamin Franklin, the Society's President, show that he took his work seriously.[61] Later in life, he was again to direct his attention to the great question of slavery.[62]

Worthy as were these efforts of Tench Coxe to further the public interests, they are insignificant compared with the valuable work which he at this time undertook in order to promote American manufactures and, above all, to secure a more effective national government. Convinced of the necessity of this country developing a national economy, he henceforth never failed to advocate all measures having that result in view.

The fundamental step in this direction was, of course, the adoption of the Federal Constitution. Though a member of the Annapolis Convention, Tench Coxe was not present among those who assembled in Philadelphia in May, 1787 to draft the Constitution. None the less, he absorbed himself in the problems which gave rise to the occasion, particularly in their economic aspects. Appearing on May 11, 1787 before the Philadelphia Society for Political Inquiries, assembled in the home of its President, Benjamin Franklin, Coxe read a paper entitled, " An Enquiry into the Principles on which a commercial system for the United States should be founded; to which are added some political observations connected with the subject." [63] In this he examined the economic status of the country with a view to proposing certain reforms to be embodied in the new Constitution. The paper was pub-

[61] Coxe to Franklin, June 9, 1787, MS, Franklin Collection, American Philosophical Society, XXXV, Part I; Coxe to Franklin, n. d., *ibid.*, XL, Part II.

[62] See below, chap. v.

[63] Coxe, *View of the United States*, pp. 4-33. See below, chaps. ii and iii. The Society consisted of fifty resident members who met every fortnight, the summer months excepted, to discuss political and economic questions. Scharf and Wescott, I, 445; Jedediah Morse, *The American Geography*, p. 326.

lished in Philadelphia " and inscribed to the members of
the convention at an early period of their business." [64] The
extent to which his ideas gained acceptance will be examined in the chapter which follows.

Aside from its relation to the movement to reform the
national government, this paper of Coxe is also noteworthy because of the lucid exposition it contains of his
idea of a national economy. It will be examined later.[65]
For the present, we need only point out that his discourse
brought him immediate recognition as a student of that
question. On August 9th of the same year he was called
upon to repeat his arguments before a meeting of friends
of American manufactures, held at the University of Pennsylvania. This event was notable in that it gave rise to
the organization of the Pennsylvania Society for the Encouragement of Manufactures and Useful Arts, of which
Coxe became and remained one of the more active
members.[66]

Following promulgation of the new Constitution, Tench
Coxe worked incessantly in favor of its ratification. Essay
after essay came from his pen; they were widely circulated.
As in the Bank of North America controversy, he never
failed to give calm and careful consideration to all points
of view; and his arguments, though not showing great
competence in the realm of political science, were at any
rate productive of favorable results.[67]

In the meanwhile Coxe was appointed to the Continental Congress (1788),[68] at this time a body representative

[64] Coxe, *View*, p. 4, note 1.

[65] Chap. iii.

[66] See below, chap. v. In the election of officers held on January 21,
1788, Coxe was made a member of the Board of Managers. *Extracts
from the Diary of Jacob Hiltzheimer, of Philadelphia, 1765-1798*, ed.
Jacob Cox Parsons, p. 143.

[67] Coxe's part in the movement for the new Constitution is developed
at length in chap. ii.

[68] In a letter to Madison, October 22, 1788, Coxe informed him of the

of the states more *de jure* than *de facto*. His nomination to this office was made by George Clymer, the purpose being to give Pennsylvania "a mercantile representative."[69] The advent of the new government in 1789 terminated his services, for which he received the sum of £113.[70]

Once the new government was assured of acceptance, Tench Coxe took the occasion of residence in New York to participate in a clever bit of vote juggling. The consensus was that General Washington would be the first and only choice of the electors for the office of President. The choice for the office of Vice-President, however, was uncertain. The general sentiment appeared to be in favor of John Adams. But against him there had arisen a strong opposition group, centered in New York, and characterized by a penchant for paper-money and State Rights theory. This group sought the election of their idol, George Clinton.[71] Having nothing in common with the political theory of Coxe at this time, their efforts were opposed by him. In a letter to Dr. Benjamin Rush of Philadelphia, he wrote:

---

proposed appointment, which he appears not to have desired. MS, Madison Papers, XI. For the appointment, see Richard Peters to Coxe, n. d., in White, p. 48. The work of Congress at this time was next to nothing, as witness Coxe's letters to Thomas Mifflin, President of the Supreme Executive Council of Pennsylvania. In one, written January 26, 1789, Coxe could only speak of the status of certain Pennsylvania lands and the precarious health of King George. *Pennsylvania Archives*, First Series, XI, 539-540. In another, February 1, 1789, he wrote that very few members were present. *Ibid.*, pp. 542-543. Coxe, it may be noted here, was also appointed a Commissioner to open roads in Pennsylvania, April 3, 1788. *Minutes of the Supreme Executive Council*, XV, 445.

[69] Coxe to Madison, September 17, 1789, MS, Madison Papers, XII.

[70] See *Minutes of the Supreme Executive Council of Pennsylvania*, XVI, 10, granting Coxe £90 for attendance to February 16, 1789; also, voucher in Gratz Collection, Historical Society of Pennsylvania, case 2, box 33, covering his pay from that date to March 5, 1789, the amount being £43. Each amount included the mileage allowance.

[71] McMaster, I, 526-530.

John Adams' friends are taking pains to secure his election. Whatever appears in his favor should be now very sensible and moderate—not calculated for popular impression. I wish to be *perfectly unknown* & unobserved, but I shall not omit to promote him.[72]

To Madison, too, he wrote in praise of Adams, declaring him to be " a friend to property." His election was most probable.[73] A few clever moves on the part of Hamilton secured the desired result, thus bringing into office with the hearty approval of Coxe a man whom he later, 1796, came to despise as an enemy to democratic government. The political faith of Coxe, as we shall see, was to shift.

Tench Coxe was not blind to his own personal interests. He had worked laboriously for a new political order, in the meanwhile sadly neglecting his private business.[74] There was no reason, therefore, why he, too, should not seek a reward for his work, his sacrifices. He was a competent student of economic affairs, and could rightly infer that his services would be of value in getting the new government into operation.

Accordingly, on April 5, 1789 we find him addressing a long letter to his friend, James Madison, beseeching support for appointment to an office.[75] Calling attention to the fact that the election of Messrs. Morris, Clymer, and Fitzsimons to Congress represented a loss to finance, customs and other offices where " some men of assiduity, reading and the proper experimental knowledge will be

[72] Coxe to Rush, January 13, 1788, MS, Correspondence of Dr. Benjamin Rush, XXVII, Library Company of Philadelphia (Ridgway Branch). (Underscoring in original.) In another letter to Rush, February 2, 1789, Coxe deplored the lack of knowledge among the people and declared that more free schools were needed. *Ibid*.

[73] Coxe to Madison, January 22, 1789, MS, Madison Papers, X; see also, Coxe to Madison, January 27, 1789, *ibid*.

[74] Coxe to Rush, February 12, 1789, MS, Rush Correspondence, XXVII.

[75] Coxe to Madison, April 5, 1789, MS, Madison Papers, XI.

necessary," Coxe inferentially begged consideration of his talents along these lines. In more direct terms, he wrote:

I am sensible that you have no official right to interfere in these matters, and that no man will more delicately refrain from steps, which he cannot with propriety take, yet as your opinion must have frequently weight and *as I would sincerely wish for no employment which you might consider as improper for me,* and at the same [time] as there is often an uncertainty about the dispositions of professional men to leave private life, I have thought it not improper under the above circumstances to communicate to you what happened [and] my not being averse to the ideas suggested to me. My private property and [inheritances] from my wifes family [and] my own will prove I trust (and this naturally is in entire confidence) about £30,000, chiefly in landed estate in New York, Pennsylvania, Jersey [and] Delaware. The improvements of this from its own income would be a profit quite equal to my desires if the exertions of my best abilities in the public hire were to produce a compensation that would maintain my family in the way you have seen me live. . . . From 1776 when I came of age to the present time I have been engaged in private business, in commerce and the purchases and improvements of land. I have held four employments under the State of Pennsylvania, and many private associations for purposes of policy or profit in which bodies of my fellow citizens have been engaged. *I shall be unhappy, if this letter extracts from you any answer.*[76]

[76] *Ibid.* In place of "inheritances" used here, the manuscript reads apparently "exputations." The underscored words occur in the original. Details of the business activities of Coxe to which he refers in this letter are, as before noted, fragmentary. Nor is much information concerning his dealings in land available. Joshua Gilpin in his "Journey to Bethlehem," an account of travels in western Pennsylvania in 1802-1803, stated that Coxe had "purchased many thousand acres at 4/6 per acre," which Gilpin apparently thought was a foolhardy undertaking. *Pennsylvania Magazine of History and Biography,* XLVI, 141. See also, *Pennsylvania Archives,* Third Series, XXIV, 198, 655; XXV, 113, 482; XXVI, 53, 59. Tracts of land totaling 2,608 acres and situated in several counties are here listed as surveyed for Coxe between 1784 and 1794. In a letter to John Nicholson, January 11, 1788, MS, Roberts Collection,

This letter, which suggests that Coxe had in mind an appointment to the Treasury Department, produced no immediate action in his behalf. Yet hopeful, he wrote again to Madison the following September.[77] This time he referred to the proposed removal of the Postmaster-General, and declared that he would not object to being mentioned for that office. His record in behalf of the public interests was recounted, with an amusing addition to the effect that he had been " twice appointed to the general convention of the church in which I was born, which is perhaps of the most moment as it is testimony of the private character of [an] individual, who tho a sincere friend to genuine religion is but little of a church-going man." [78] Messrs. Morris, Maclay, Clymer, and Fitzsimons of the Pennsylvania Congressional delegation were, he believed, favorable to his appointment. Finally, for Madison's benefit he set forth his conception of the duties of the office:

In regard to the office I do not consider it a mere regulation of mails, and distribution of letters. But it is intimately blended with the connexion of the members of the union and particularly of the Atlantic and western territory. It may be made to aid considerably the advancement of internal commerce and territorial improvement, and expedite the sudden operations of the Executive department.[79]

But again Tench Coxe had no success. The Postmastership, then an office of minor importance, went to Samuel Osgood. In a letter thanking Madison for any effort he

Haverford College, Coxe spoke of the desire to develop lands in Northumberland County.

[77] Coxe to Madison, September 17, 1789, MS, Madison Papers, XII.

[78] *Ibid.* Coxe had been a pew-holder in St. Peter's Church. C. P. B. Jefferys, " The Provincial and Revolutionary History of St. Peter's Church, Philadelphia, 1753-1783," *Pennsylvania Magazine of History and Biography*, XLVIII, 355.

[79] Coxe to Madison, September 17, 1789, MS, Madison Papers, XII.

might have expended in his behalf, Coxe pursued no further his quest for office.[80]

Thereafter, it appears, someone continued to work in his favor. He had perhaps been given assurances of a Treasury appointment, his first choice as we have seen. At any rate, on May 3, 1790, Senator Maclay wrote as follows in his diary:

There is a prospect of Tench Coxe succeeding Duer in the assistancy of the Treasury. His character was spoken of with great asperity by Fitzsimons, Morris, and Wilson. Clymer rather supported him.[81]

William Duer, to whom Maclay here refers, was the original appointee to the office. He was well known as a financier, a land speculator, and later, as a promoter of the New Jersey Society for the Encouragement of Useful Manufactures. Pressure of his many private business interests and the fact that these were not deemed compatible with the holding of public office, especially in the Treasury, account for his removal after a term of not more than seven months.[82] His successor was, as Maclay suspected, Tench Coxe, who on May fourth wrote Madison to inform him of the appointment by Hamilton.[83]

To avoid difficulties similar to those encountered by Duer, and, of course, to act within the law, Coxe transferred his commercial connections to his brother, Daniel

---

[80] Coxe to Madison, September 28, 1789, MS, Madison Papers, XII.

[81] William Maclay, *The Journal of William Maclay, 1789-1791*, p. 249.

[82] Davis, I, 174, 371-372. Davis writes that Hamilton in appointing Duer was not above criticism. *Ibid.*, p. 176.

[83] Coxe to Madison, May 4, 1790, MS, Madison Papers, XIII. His certificate of appointment is reproduced in White, p. 182. It is dated May 10, 1790. In accordance with the Act creating the Treasury Department, it was made by Hamilton. See Section 1, Act to establish the Treasury Department, 1st Cong., 1st sess., chap. 12, *U. S. Statutes at Large*, ed. Richard Peters, I, 65. The office paid $1500 per annum. *American State Papers, Finance*, I, 34.

W. Coxe.[84] On May seventh he arrived in New York to assume office. Writing of his arrival on that date, Maclay put this into his diary:

Tench Coxe came this day in order (as he said) to enter on the assistancy of the Treasury. He was deeply affected with the literary itch, the *cacoethes scribendi*. He has persevering industry in an eminent degree. These are the qualities that have recommended him to this appointment. Hamilton sees that the campaign will open against him in the field of publication, and he is providing himself with gladiators of the quill, not only for defence but attack.[85]

The attack upon Coxe's character, of which the Senator earlier wrote, was not carried further. In fact, Coxe does not appear to have known of it. On June fourth he wrote Dr. Rush that, "I am of the opinion that the unimportance deemed to belong to the appointment was one principal cause of silence. It seems probable now that little will take place concerning it, and it therefore rests with me to impress the public with favorable ideas of my usefulness and proper deportment in it." [86] To accomplish this, he intended to collect all information obtainable on the United States; this was to be preserved in fourteen boxes, two feet in length, one to be used for each of the thirteen states and one for the union. An up-to-date index of the whole was planned.[87] It is not known to what extent Coxe carried out this scheme; it was certainly characteristically systematic.

As an assistant Coxe's personal relations with Hamilton seem to have been most cordial. He found his chief, whom

---

[84] Coxe to John Haversham of Georgia, September 14, 1790, MS, Autograph Collection. In so doing he said that he had ceased to act as agent for several holders of the public debt of the United States.

[85] Maclay, p. 252.

[86] Coxe to Rush, June 4, 1790, MS, Rush Correspondence, XXVII; also, Coxe to Rush, May 16, 1790, *ibid.*

[87] Coxe to Rush, June 4, 1790, *ibid.*

he declared to be a man of great virtue, industry and intellect, devoid of show, seeking comfort in simplicity. This, too, he said, was true of Mrs. Hamilton.[88]

The great task of Hamilton, in the accomplishment of which he expected the assistance of Coxe, was that of insuring the solvency of the new government. The latter had been framed in terms of liberal principles of political science; Hamilton hoped to make it function upon the basis of sound economic principles. It was a vast business enterprise; to be successful it had to be solvent; hence the famous " Hamiltonian System."

The concrete nature of the System came to light in his first *Report on the Public Credit,* January 9, 1790.[89] Its purpose was of a dual nature: to drive home the importance of the maintenance of the national credit and to make proposals for securing it. The national credit was important because the United States had little " moneyed capital," and must borrow; to borrow presupposed an ample public credit. There was only one way whereby this could be achieved: make provision for the payment of that which was owed, e. g., state and national debt, which Hamilton aptly termed " the price of liberty." By giving the combined debt of the states and the union an " adequate and stable value," the national union would be cemented; the ship of state would be put on an even keel; progress and greatness would follow. Such are the broad outlines of the famous fiscal program, admitted by Hamilton not to be original.[90] Its soundness was equalled only by its boldness; to secure its acceptance was none the less difficult.

[88] Coxe to Rush, September 10, 1790, *ibid.*

[89] *Report, American State Papers, Finance,* I, 15 ff.

[90] *Ibid.,* p. 23. The sinking fund idea contained in Hamilton's proposals has been declared by Prof. Charles F. Dunbar to be " unmistakably adopted from the English legislation." Charles F. Dunbar, " Some Precedents Followed by Alexander Hamilton," *Quarterly Journal of Economics,* III, 46.

The opposition centered around the assumption of state debts by the national government. In the eyes of Coxe, it was this feature which occasioned the greatest objection in Philadelphia. Slightly two months before becoming the assistant of Hamilton, Coxe wrote him to that effect. Holders of the continental debt opposed the assumption of the state debts because it would draw too heavily upon federal revenues due them; those holding the state debt preferred not to take the chance of being paid by the Federal government.[91] The state debt was small, whereas the amount of continental debt certificates in the hands of Pennsylvanians was large. To these objectors Coxe said he replied that " the revolution of 1789, for as such I view it, was intended to settle a great number of public differences," of which this was one; in all, concessions were to be expected, and here was one which Pennsylvania could be asked to make. By all means, continued Coxe, we should avoid " expensive and uncertain administration of our finances," which " must be the consequence of fourteen systems of revenue. . . ."[92] In two more letters, written in July, 1790, Coxe assured Hamilton that his plan was gaining support in Philadelphia, and added that he believed that the excise would obtain general approval.[93] The latter was a part of the revenue-raising provisions of the scheme, and because of its nature as a direct tax was expected to meet opposition, as indeed it did.[94]

It is to be noticed that the presentation of Hamilton's

[91] Coxe to Hamilton, March 5, 1790, The Works of Hamilton, ed. John C. Hamilton, V, 455-456. An assessment of public opinion in Philadelphia relative to the funding scheme is to be found in Margaret Woodbury, Public Opinion in Philadelphia, 1789-1801 (" Smith College Studies in History,"V, Nos. 1 and 2), pp. 50 ff.

[92] Coxe to Hamilton, March 5, 1790, The Works of Hamilton, V, 455-456.

[93] Coxe to Hamilton, July 9 and 10, 1790, ibid., pp. 457-458.

[94] Edward Channing, A History of the United States (1917), IV, 79.

Report on the Public Credit was not the first occasion of Tench Coxe's adherence to its principles. On the contrary, he had expressed similar views as early as May, 1787, at which time he addressed to the Constitutional Convention his pamphlet, entitled, *An Enquiry into the principles on which a commercial system for the United States of America should be founded; to which are added some political observations connected with the subject.*[95] In it he declared the restoration of public credit to be of prime importance; to accomplish this he recommended an end to the issuance of paper currency, the abolition of legal tender laws ("the engine," he wrote, which "has been employed to give the *coup de grace* to public credit"),—above all, that provision be made for the payment of debts by Congress through taxation and the sale of public lands. Two years later, 1789, Coxe wrote Madison that "this business of the public debt is an immense and most important affair."[96] He warned that consideration must be paid the various state debts; for if they be unwisely handled, our credit would suffer, especially abroad. During his stay in New York he had, he continued, made a study of the country's finances. Massachusetts, he found, owed about $4,000,000; South Carolina, about $3,428,000: "These tho the largest are only a part of the great mass of separate state debts." State debts must be paid off or funded, he concluded.[97]

While Coxe informed Hamilton that Pennsylvania could legitimately be expected to make a concession to the cause of the new Union by supporting the assumption of the state debts, he also thought the demand of a reward for the support not unwarranted. The concession could be made a bargain. In his diary under the date of June 14, 1790, Senator Maclay relates a visit made by him to the

[95] Coxe, *View*, pp. 4-33.
[96] Coxe to Madison, March 18, 1789, MS, Madison Papers, XI.
[97] Coxe to Madison, March 18, 1789, *ibid.*

lodgings of Robert Morris. There he learned from the latter that Tench Coxe had been at the lodgings of Messrs. Clymer and Fitzsimons, and that "their business was to negotiate a bargain: the permanent residence (of the Federal Government) in Pennsylvania for her votes for the assumption, or at least as many votes as would be needful." [98] The plan, however, came to nought. The solution finally settled up, unquestionably marked by intrigue, too, was a compromise: the capital was to remain at Philadelphia for a period of ten years, and thereafter was to be permanently located on the banks of the Potomac. [99] In this manner sufficient voting strength was mustered to carry the plan for assumption of state debts.

Unlike Jefferson, Coxe never had occasion to regret his support of the funding scheme of Hamilton. [100] In his "Reflections on the State of the Union, 1792," [101] he was laudatory in his examination of the operation of the funding scheme. The public credit had been restored; money was to be had readily and cheaply; economic activity had a decided fillip; for all of which the funding scheme stood in a large measure responsible. But he was not blind to the rampant speculation then current. Were the public debt given a stable value, it would be more useful, he declared. Its fluctuating value entailed speculation, attracting thereby funds which could be used to better advantage in the support of land values, manufactures, building, and trade. [102]

[98] Maclay, pp. 284-285.

[99] Channing, IV, 77-79; McMaster, I, 555 ff.; Thomas Jefferson, "The Anas," *The Writings of Thomas Jefferson* (Library ed., 1903), I, 274-276.

[100] Aside from his interest in the funding scheme from the standpoint of American economic advancement, Tench Coxe also appears to have been personally concerned. In a letter to Hamilton, May 6, 1792, he expressed uneasiness over the consequence of the delay being then incurred in the passage of the public debt act: "I, and my family," he feared, "will be left without an establishment. . . ." MS, Hamilton Papers, XVI.

[101] Reprinted in his *View*, pp. 286 ff.   [102] *Ibid.*, pp. 359-371.

Having secured the adoption of his scheme for the restoration of public credit, Hamilton proceeded next to the matter of the establishment of a national bank. The effective use of the restored public credit, and, indeed, its support, called for such an institution, he reasoned. In his *Report on a National Bank* (December 14, 1790) Hamilton listed the advantages to be expected from the establishment of the institution, answered all arguments against it, and called for speedy favorable action. "Everything . . . which tends to lower the rate of interest," he wrote, " is peculiarly worthy of the cares of legislators." [103] The bank would serve to accomplish this end. It must be newly created, since the existing Bank of North America, located in Philadelphia, had had its powers and privileges so limited by the State Legislature as to be wholly unsatisfactory as a basis for a national bank.[104]

In the preparation of this latter phase of his report, which was important as an answer to critics of his proposal on grounds that the government should make use of that which already existed, Hamilton had the assistance of Coxe's pamphlet on the Bank of North America, to which we have above referred.[105] In his letter to Hamilton of March 5, 1790, Coxe enclosed a copy of this pamphlet, stating that he had observed from the *Report on the Public Credit* " some intimations of an intention of establishing a national bank. . . ." Speaking of his pamphlet, Coxe wrote:

[103] *Report, American State Papers, Finance*, I, 76. Compare the thought here expressed with the theory currently expounded by John Maynard Keynes, *A Treatise on Money*, 2 vols. (London, 1930).

[104] *Report, American State Papers, Finance*, I, p. 72. Hamilton did, however, leave the road open for a conversion of the Bank of North America into a national bank such as his proposal called for. But the Bank itself apparently took no steps to realize this proposal. Lewis, pp. 76-79.

[105] See above, pp. 11, 12. Hamilton's plan for a national bank followed the example of the Bank of England, as Professor Dunbar has pointed out. Dunbar, pp. 54-58.

A friend of mine who happened to take a copy of it with him to England informed me that he had conversed upon it with several directors of the Bank of England and with Doctor Price and some other political arithmeticians & Œconomists, whose manner of speaking of it has induced me to think it may be worth your perusal.[106]

The interest of Coxe in the economic advancement of the country naturally led him to support the proposal for a national bank, and, indeed, banking institutions in general. Writing in 1792, he spoke of "these valuable institutions" as having given stability to property.[107] Their establishment had not, he added, garnered too much of the capital of the country. As for the newly established national bank, he found that its usefulness could be increased through the creation of branches. The United States, he pointed out, contained " five or six great local subdivisions of trade, resulting principally from the imperious dictates of *the nature of things."* In each there was a trading town of acknowledged supremacy, which he termed " *commercial metropolies."* They should be guides to Congress in distributing the branches, thus insuring a " reasonable accommodation to the marts of commerce. . . ." [108] The obvious prophesy of what later occurred in the organization of the Federal Reserve System is worthy of note. In conclusion, Coxe expressed the fear that the branches, " like all great objects," would become political instruments; [109] which in fact was Hamilton's reason for

[106] Coxe to Hamilton, March 5, 1790, *The Works of Hamilton,* ed. John C. Hamilton, V, 455-456. In a letter to Hamilton, December 31, 1790, Coxe spoke of sending papers on banking, too. MS, Hamilton Papers, X.

[107] Coxe, "Reflections on the State of the Union, 1792," *View,* pp. 349-352. He put the paid-in capital of all American banks at ten and a half million dollars, three-fourths of which was certificates of public debt. *Ibid.,* pp. 352, 355.

[108] *Ibid.,* p. 353.

[109] *Ibid.,* p. 354.

suggesting in his *Report* that they not be established for the present.[110]

Of all the reports made to Congress by Hamilton that on manufactures most interested Tench Coxe.[111] Unlike the above mentioned reports, this one was prepared at a time when Hamilton enjoyed the services of Coxe as his assistant. The probability is that it was in part a joint-production. For this reason, as well as the important relation of the *Report* to Coxe's conception of a national economy, we shall reserve a detailed consideration of the subject for a later chapter.[112]

Although serving in the Treasury Department as assistant to Hamilton, Tench Coxe by no means confined all of his attention to the economic propositions of his chief. This, as we have seen, was not what Senator Maclay had expected. While serving Hamilton, Coxe was equally assiduous in assisting Thomas Jefferson. Already assured of the good favor of the former, he set himself to the task of gaining the friendship of the latter. This committed Coxe to duplicity. Thereafter his loyalty was always open to question, even indeed among the followers of Jefferson. Had Jefferson been unsuccessful Coxe most certainly would have become a political outcast; for his equivocal attitude toward the Revolution ruled out the possibility of election to any office.

The acquaintance of Coxe with Jefferson began immediately upon the arrival of Coxe in New York to become Hamilton's assistant. The introduction was made

[110] *Report, American State Papers, Finance,* I, p. 73. The Act creating the Bank did, however, provide for the establishment of eight branches. Albert S. Bolles, *The Financial History of the United States, from 1789 to 1860,* p. 129.

[111] Coxe does not appear to have taken much interest in the *Report on the Mint.* In the Hamilton Papers, IX, there is to be found, however, a letter from Coxe to Hamilton, November 15, 1790, on the subject of coins and coinage.

[112] Below, chap. iii.

by Dr. Benjamin Rush, of Philadelphia.[113] In a short while the friendship advanced to the point where Coxe served Jefferson as an unofficial economic adviser. In the preparation of two reports to Congress, the one on the fisheries (February 1, 1791), and the other on the privileges and restrictions of American commerce in foreign countries (December 16, 1793),[114] Jefferson was assisted by Tench Coxe.

The occasion of the first of these was a memorial to Congress from the General Court of Massachusetts, which state had by far the largest interest in the fisheries. Following the Peace, their fisheries had sunk into a ruinous condition, resulting in part from the cessation of the British bounty hitherto enjoyed. A group of Marblehead fishermen took up the matter with the General Court, and it in turn petitioned Congress for relief.[115] To comprehend the situation, the latter body called upon Jefferson, as Secretary of State, to render a report on the fisheries.

In the fulfillment of this task Jefferson had little in the way of past experience to serve him. He was a Virginian and a farmer. In the assistant to Hamilton, however, he soon found a willing helper. Though he, too, had no first-hand knowledge of the subject, Coxe was anxious to assist Jefferson, to whom he wrote:

> I must . . . observe, that though I have been a practical merchant, the fisheries never formed an object in the commerce of Philadelphia. You will consider me therefore as a theorist upon this subject, and will find it best to scrutinize cautiously any novelty I may have suggested.[116]

[113] Rush to Jefferson, May 4, 1790, MS, Papers of Thomas Jefferson (hereinafter referred to as " Jefferson Papers "), LIX.

[114] The report on fisheries may be found in *The Writings of Thomas Jefferson* (Library ed.), III, 120-144; that on commerce, *ibid.*, pp. 261-298.

[115] McMaster, I, 301; Speech of Fisher Ames, *Annals of Congress*, 2d Cong., 1st sess., pp. 367-374.

[116] Coxe to Jefferson, marked by Jefferson as received November 23, [1790], MS, Jefferson Papers, LXIX.

The efforts of Coxe to be of service to Jefferson in the preparation of the report are to be found mainly in an undated manuscript of forty pages entitled, " Miscellaneous Notes on the Fisheries." [117] In addition to this, he submitted at least one other memorandum, consisting of fifteen pages on the Dutch fisheries.[118] In the former he first examined at great length the position of the fisheries in the American economy, following which he suggested numerous improvements that could be made. America, he reasoned, was the best situated nation in the world to carry on the fisheries. Fishing vessels were to be had here at costs much below those obtaining elsewhere. Our seamen were skillful; our ships could be provisioned cheaply. Salt, a requisite in the preparation of the fish for market, was to be had inexpensively, since our ships brought it back from foreign ports as ballast. In short, the fisheries were a vital part of our economy; they were of utmost importance to our naval strength; [119] they must be cared for. His suggested improvements may be listed as follows:[120]

1. The drawback on salt exported in fishing vessels should be advanced so as to provide immediate capital for the poorer fishermen; an impost of twelve cents should be levied on salt.
2. The duty on our fish consumed in the home market should be removed.
3. Fishing vessels should be exempted from six cent tonnage duty.
4. The size of casks used for pickled fish should be made to correspond with that used by foreigners.

[117] MS, Jefferson Papers, LX. It is signed " T. C."
[118] *Ibid.*, LXIX.
[119] Coxe declared that our distance from Europe would render the ocean the scene of the most important action in the event of war. " Miscellaneous Notes on the Fisheries," p. 18.
[120] *Ibid.*, pp. 24 ff.

5. Casks should be inspected before shipment and stamped, " The United States."
6. Knowledge of the best methods to prepare fish for the market should be disseminated.
7. " The introduction of improvements, by invention and importation, in the mode of fishing, and of implements that facilitate and give certainty to the business," should be encouraged.
8. The consumption of the products of the fisheries should be promoted.[121]
9. British piscatory articles, as well as those of all nations having prohibitions on the products of our fisheries, should be excluded.

In conclusion, Coxe declared himself to be against expensive bounties and monopolies. The latter, he thought, accounted for the unprofitableness of the Dutch fisheries.

It is evident from these " notes " that much consideration was given the subject by Coxe. His emphasis upon the creation of greater technical efficiency on the part of the industry itself, rather than reliance solely upon the government for assistance, is to be noted. Here, as elsewhere in his suggestions for the advancement of the national economy, he was against the erection of a paternalistic government.

The report of Jefferson, as finally submitted to Congress, had much in common with the above ideas of Coxe. Jefferson, for his part, was willing to admit the value of the fisheries to this country, particularly as a source of naval strength. They represented an economic activity for which we were fitted by reason of position and resources. As with Coxe, he considered it a proper task of the government to discriminate against those nations which made few concessions to us. Moreover, he argued that it would be advisable to take measures to encourage our carrying

---

[121] In a letter to Jefferson, November 29, 1790, Coxe enclosed a table comparing prices of pickled and dried fish with those of butchers' meat. MS, Jefferson Papers, LVIII.

trade in order that those seamen deprived of a livelihood in the fisheries might have recourse to that branch of commerce. "Admitting their right of keeping their markets to themselves, ours cannot be denied of keeping our carrying trade to ourselves," he wrote.[122] It is to be regretted that Jefferson did not embody in his report the suggestion of Coxe that the fishermen improve their efficiency.[123]

The second report of Jefferson, that on the position of American commerce abroad, was rendered in accordance with a resolution (February 23, 1791) of the lower branch of Congress. As "a practical merchant" Tench Coxe was certainly qualified to assist him in its formulation.[124] In a letter to Jefferson, March 4, 1791, he expressed the desire to do so, enclosing at the same time rough returns of American tonnage.[125] On the following day, in another letter to Jefferson, he enclosed a twenty-five page manuscript entitled, "Thoughts on the Navigation of the United States, and concerning further means of encouraging it." [126]

In this paper Coxe offered for consideration sixteen propositions respecting American navigation. None of

[122] *The Writings of Thomas Jefferson* (Library ed.), III, 143.

[123] Congress did not act upon Jefferson's report until February, 1792. A law was then passed providing that a bounty, based on the ship's tonnage, be granted. See *Annals of Congress*, 2d Cong., 1st sess., p. 1329 ff.

[124] Coxe had earlier begun study of the subject of navigation, and in a letter to Madison, April 6, 1790, spoke of having written a sixty page essay on it. Later, January 13, 1791, he sent Madison a paper on that subject. MS, Madison Papers, XIII.

[125] Coxe to Jefferson, March 4, 1791, MS, Jefferson Papers, LXI. The information on tonnage had been requested earlier by Jefferson in connection with his report on the fisheries. Coxe's estimate for one year was 650,000 tons, which he valued at $5,850,000, conservatively. See Coxe to Jefferson, January 21, 1791, MS, Jefferson Papers, LXI.

[126] Coxe to Jefferson (in third person), March 5, 1791, MS, Jefferson Papers, LXI. The manuscript essay is preserved in this volume. Coxe spoke also of enclosing with this letter copies of his speeches of May 11th and August 9th, 1787, above referred to, pp. 14-15.

them, he advised Jefferson, "should be tenaciously insisted on. . . ." In the first six of them he pointed out the advantages of America in the construction and operation of ships. In the remainder he emphasized the necessity of encouraging our navigation without damaging the agrarian interests. More explicitly, he argued that we should not adopt measures which would produce retaliation on the part of other countries. It would be preferable, he reasoned, to remove existing burdens on our navigation rather than place additional ones on foreign shipping. He was not, of course, blind to the lack of consideration accorded our navigation interests by other nations, and therefore stated in proposition fourteen "That no foreign nation can be reasonably displeased with or consider itself improperly treated by a *general regulation* the tendency of which is to produce the same effect upon their navigation or commerce, which their *general* or *particular* laws produce upon ours." In the margin of the manuscript he drew two lines to stress this point.

Following a statement of his propositions, Coxe made eighteen suggestions as to how our navigation could be promoted. The most important of these related to the adoption by us of a navigation system resembling that of Great Britain. For example, Coxe would have America confine the importation of goods to the ships of nations producing those goods or to our own. Moreover, he suggested that foreigners be excluded from our coastal trade.

In conclusion, Coxe reasserted his belief that the commercial regulations of America should be such as to accord other countries a *quid pro quo*. As a step in this direction he recommended that an additional duty of ten per cent be applied to vessels of those nations not granting us favorable treatment. He was especially anxious that we discriminate against the British, and thought that in this other countries might join us. "Were France, Spain and Portugal to adopt the *confining* regulation," he wrote,

" the carrying trade of the world would sustain a considerable revolution, and consequently considerable effects would be produced upon the balance of naval power." [127]

Following the above memorandum, Coxe continued from time to time to furnish Jefferson with additional facts and figures on the commerce and navigation of the United States.[128] In doing so he must have impressed Jefferson with his knowledge of the subject; for we find that a draft of the intended report was submitted to Coxe for correction. In a letter to Jefferson, Coxe wrote:

Mr. Coxe has the honor to return to Mr. Jefferson the report on which he has taken the liberty to make marks (to connect his notes) with a pencil. These notes apply very unreservedly to questions of fact, and to modes of expression. There are some ideas of importance in relation to the subject in general, and to the present moment on [the] state of things on which Mr. C. will communicate his ideas this afternoon at any hour between 4 & 7, when Mr. J. will be disengaged, being himself particularly engaged till four & at 7.

Mr. Coxe proposes therefore to wait on Mr. Jefferson about 4 o'clock this day. Should he inform Mr. Coxe that he will be unable to see him today, Mr. Coxe will call tomorrow a little before & in the morning.

Tuesday, February 5th.[129]

---

[127] The underscoring in passages quoted occurs in the manuscript.

[128] Coxe to Jefferson, March 14, 1791, MS, Jefferson Papers, LXIX, submitting notes on tonnage entries and distribution by countries of our shipping; Coxe to Jefferson, April 20, 1791, *ibid.*, LXIII, fishing vessel returns; Coxe to Jefferson, April 23, 1791, *ibid.*, "Remarks on the Consular Return," being suggestions for their improvement (manuscript of seven pages); Coxe to Jefferson, June 23, 1791, *ibid.*, LXV, customs returns of Virginia corrected, also table of imports and exports of Cuba; Coxe to Jefferson, June 30, 1791, *ibid.*, LXV, notes on the Portuguese commercial system; Coxe to Jefferson, July 19, 1791, *ibid.*, Dutch commercial regulations; Coxe to Jefferson, December 8, 1791, *ibid.*, LXVII, enclosing a statement of imports of manufactured goods from foreign countries; Coxe to Jefferson, December 15, 1791, *ibid.*, on certain British port charges; Coxe to Jefferson, n. d., *ibid.*, LXIX, information on British and Swedish duties.

[129] Coxe to Jefferson, *ibid.*, LXXXI. The editor of these Papers dates

The manuscript report, upon it the pencil marks of Coxe referring to his accompanying " Notes," appears to have been gone over with care. Here and there corrections made by Jefferson himself show agreement with the suggestions of Coxe. For example, Jefferson wrote of events in this hemisphere as being " as new in the moral as in the physical world," and proceeded to point out that foreign nations in their relations with us ignore the idea of reciprocal rights and duties. They appear to think, declared Jefferson, that we have as the sole purpose of our existence the satisfaction of their happiness. Somehow this passage did not strike Coxe's fancy. He commented:

Do not the laws and practice of the European Kingdoms run in the same line. Will it not be argued that individuals and nations in their political relations are often considered differently from what would prevail in a state of nature—and that the laws of nature cannot apply absolutely either to associated *man* or to associated bodies (or nations) *of men*—yet a modification of this clause may be preferable to striking it out.

As dear as was the idea of a state of nature to Jefferson, he found it none the less desirable to strike out the passage, rather than attempt a modification of it.[130]

As finally submitted to Congress, the report of Jeffer-

---

this letter as of 1793, probably because Tuesday, February fifth, fell in that year. Jefferson, however, in his letter of December 16, 1793, accompanying delivery of the report to Congress, stated that the report was completed during the summer of 1792, and was submitted as it then stood. See *The Writings of Thomas Jefferson* (Library ed.), III, 262. Inasmuch as the published version of the report follows closely the draft which Coxe returned to Jefferson, it may be inferred that Coxe wrongly dated his letter. Coxe's "Notes on the Report of the Secretary of State, made in consequence of the reference of the House of Representatives of the —— day of ————, 1791," is to be found in the Jefferson Papers, LXXXI; the report of Jefferson, with the pencil markings of Coxe, is in volume LXIX.

[130] See draft of the report, Jefferson Papers, LXIX, and Coxe's " Notes," *ibid.*, LXXXI, for this and other corrections made. Jefferson, of course, did not agree with Coxe in every instance.

son embodied a strong plea for the adoption of the principle of reciprocity, wherever possible; failing this, he stood
ready to meet other nations with a *quid pro quo*.[131] He
expressed himself as against unnecessary shackling of commerce and navigation; in this point of view, he had the
full support of Coxe.

The assistance which Coxe rendered in the formulation
of these two reports was the initial step in his change of
political allegiance. Hitherto we have known of him as a
supporter of the new government and the "Hamiltonian
System" instituted under it. As such, we should logically
expect that with the emergence of party government he
would associate himself with the group headed by Hamilton, the Federalists. This he did not do. Though he never
repudiated his support of the Constitution and the Hamiltonian system, Coxe none the less came to reveal a preference for the political views of Jefferson and not those of
Hamilton.[132] The choice, as we shall see, was founded

[131] See *The Writings of Thomas Jefferson* (Library ed.), III, 275-283.
[132] The politics of Jefferson and Hamilton definitely became divergent
during the spring of 1792. See John Spencer Bassett, *The Federalist
System* ("American Nation Series," XI), p. 50; Channing, IV, 160-161.
Channing, p. 151, states that party lines became definable in 1793. It
may be noted here that although Coxe preferred to follow Jefferson, he
yet was shrewd enough to retain an office in the Treasury Department
until as late as 1797. Washington in May, 1792, made him Commissioner of the Revenue. In this way he was called upon to administer
the collection of revenue from the excise on distilled spirits. This particular measure proved anathema to the Jeffersonians, and in 1794 occasioned a revolt in western Pennsylvania. Coxe in reply to a letter from
Hugh Henry Brackenridge, a prominent figure in western Pennsylvania,
heartily disapproved the use of force in obtaining repeal of the excise
law. He at the same time purposely avoided a discussion of the merits
of the law, no doubt for political reasons. See Brackenridge to Coxe,
August 8 and September 15, 1794, in H. M. Brackenridge, *History of
the Western Insurrection in Western Pennsylvania*, pp. 144-147; Coxe
to Brackenridge, August 26, 1794, *Pittsburgh Gazette*, September 20,
1794, with Coxe's name suppressed. Coxe's certificate of appointment to
the commissionership is reproduced in White, p. 182; his state papers
in connection with the office are to be found in *American State Papers,*

upon a non-economic issue—the supposed monarchism of Hamilton and others.

Before, however, recounting Coxe's espousal of this supposition, we may note his anti-Federalist views on the Jay Treaty. These he expressed in the newspapers and in letters to Jefferson. To the latter he wrote on March 20, 1795, that he did not think Britain was very generous to us in the Treaty insofar as he could learn of its contents.[133] In another letter, July 30, 1795, he declared that the Treaty ought to be "further amicably negotiated & amended," adding that as it stood it was as selfish in its nature as was the navigation system of Britain.[134] His newspaper attack consisted of four essays, entitled, "An Examination of the Pending Treaty with Great Britain." [135] It was signed, "Juricola," and addressed to President Washington. In the first of these essays Coxe opposed acceptance of those clauses of the Treaty relating to commerce, arguing that they did not accord us reciprocity. In the remaining three he discussed at length the matter of compensation for slaves carried off by the British during the Revolution, reinforcing his arguments by frequent citations of international law. In a letter to Jefferson, October 30, 1795, he spoke of having written several other essays, too, but, having learned of the President's intention to sanction the Treaty, he thought it proper not

---

Finance, I, 173-175, 191, 199-200, 249-251, 280-281, 386-400, 403, 558-575.

[133] Coxe to Jefferson, March 20, 1795, MS, Jefferson Papers, XCVIII. Following Jefferson's retirement in 1793, Coxe wrote freely to him on foreign affairs. See Coxe to Jefferson, February 22 and 27, March 16, July 7, 1794, MS, Jefferson Papers, XCVII.

[134] Coxe to Jefferson, July 30, 1795, MS, Jefferson Papers, XCVIII. See also, Jefferson to Coxe, September 10, 1795, MS, Jefferson Papers, XCIX, in which Jefferson wrote that the views of Coxe coincided with those of the people at large.

[135] They appeared in the *Philadelphia Gazette*, July 31, August 4, 8, and 12, 1795. For identification, see Coxe to Jefferson, October 30, 1795, MS, Jefferson Papers, XCIX.

to print them lest it be assumed by readers that he was censuring the President. In this letter he also reiterated his belief that the Treaty was too favorable to British interests.[136] While he does not say so in his essays or letters, it is very probable that Coxe was also opposed to the Treaty on the grounds that it forbade export of our cotton for twenty-five years. Coxe, in short, was pro-Jefferson during the struggle for ratification of the Jay Treaty.

Coxe's disapproval of the Treaty was followed by an outright disavowal of Federalism: in 1796 he opposed the election of John Adams to the Presidency. Writing as a "Federalist," he contributed ten articles to the *Gazette of the United States,* in which he sought to reveal John Adams as a friend to monarchism.[137] His positive arguments in favor of Jefferson were few in number, but he left the reader in no doubt as to his preference. Thus was completed a drastic change in the political faith of Coxe. He had managed it while at the same time receiving the favors of those whom he now renounced.

That Coxe could long remain in office after this episode is hardly to be expected. Nor did he. The inauguration of John Adams meant the day of reckoning was near at hand. It occurred in December, 1797, when he was dismissed from office.[138] In an effort to clear his record of

[136] *Ibid.* On April 22, 1796, Coxe wrote Jefferson that he was doubtful whether the House would pass the legislation necessary to carry into effect the Treaty. *Ibid.,* C.

[137] These essays, addressed "To the Electors of the President of the United States," appeared in the issues of November 9, 11, 14, 15, 16, 17, 18, 21, 24, 25, 29, 30, 1796. For identification, see a letter of Coxe published in the *Aurora,* November 1, 1800, at which time he was again opposing Adams.

[138] Gaillard Hunt, "Office Seeking during the Administration of John Adams," *American Historical Review,* II, 256, terms this Adams' "most important removal from office for political reasons. . . ." Coxe, it is interesting to note, forwarded to Adams soon after his inauguration a lengthy memorandum on the subject of American neutrality. In it he

any suspicion, Coxe immediately addressed a letter to the
Speaker of the House of Representatives, requesting an
examination of his official conduct.[139] Nothing, however,
came of this plea. In the eyes of the Federalists he had
received his due reward. As George Cabot expressed it,
Coxe was a traitor and should have been ousted earlier.[140]
In the opposition camp, Jefferson, a master politician,
viewed the misfortune of Coxe calmly. " The dismission
of Tench Coxe from office without any reason assigned,"
he wrote James Monroe, " is considered as one of the bold
acts of the President. *Tant mieux.*" [141] It may be inferred
that Jefferson saw in the outcast Coxe a determined and
well-informed opponent of the Federalists. Such a character could well serve the Republican cause. This, indeed,
was the final outcome.

In the Presidential election of 1800 Coxe did yeoman
service in behalf of Jefferson.[142] His first act was to
furnish the editor of the Philadelphia *Aurora,* a rabid
Republican, with a copy of a letter which John Adams had
sent him in May, 1792. Published on August twenty-

took a somewhat pro-French position. See reprint of it, *Pennsylvania
Magazine of History and Biography,* XXX, 118-121.

[139] Coxe to Speaker of the House, December 27, 1797, *Annals of Congress,* 5th Cong., Special sess., 1797-1798, p. 775. The first public
defence of himself, so far as the writer is aware, was made by Coxe in
an address to the editor of the *Aurora,* November 1, 1800. He here
expressed the view that outside influences brought about his dismissal.
Adams, he said, " was duped." In a letter to Jefferson, written during
the early part of 1801, Coxe declared that his removal was due to Hamilton's dislike for him because of his associations with Jefferson. Hunt,
II, 260-261.

[140] George Cabot to John Adams, January 19, 1798, George Gibbs,
Memoirs of the Administrations of Washington and John Adams, II, 9.
See also, William Smith to John Adams, January 3, 1798, *ibid.,* p. 55.

[141] Jefferson to Monroe, December 27, 1797, *The Writings of Thomas
Jefferson,* ed. Paul Leicester Ford, VII, 184; also, Jefferson to Madison,
January 3, 1798, *ibid.,* p. 189.

[142] In 1799 he had unsuccessfully attempted to establish a Republican
newspaper in Philadelphia. See Jefferson to Coxe, May 21, 1799, *ibid.,*
pp. 378-381, in which Jefferson expresses sorrow over the failure.

eighth, it was an immediate sensation.[143] In the letter
Adams had merely expressed the belief that the development of manufactures required " good government "; he
also voiced the opinion that the Pinckneys, Charles Cotes-
worth and Thomas, had British attachments. Intended as
a personal communication by its author, it was a harmless
document; but put into print in an atmosphere shot
through with suspicion and ill-will, it proved otherwise.
Coxe became the man of the hour, fortunately or unfortunately. Legal action was taken against William Duane,
the editor.[144] In short, a bitter fight was on.

Following publication of Adams' letter Coxe furnished
Duane with several more letters from his own pen. The
burden of these was a defence of his past conduct and a
restatement of his belief that Adams was a monarchist.[145]
He was led to defend himself because of caustic attacks
from Federalist quarters.[146] The monarchist bogey was
good campaign material in behalf of the Republicans.[147]

[143] *Aurora*, August 28, 1800. It was also republished in the issues of
August 30, September 9, October 3, 23, and 30, 1800. Other papers,
especially in the South, reprinted it, too. McMaster, II, 508. Coxe had
already made use of the letter in other connections. *Ibid.*, pp. 496-497.
Its use in the present campaign was expected by certain Federalists.
Gibbs, II, 414.

[144] *The Gazette of the United States*, Federalist paper of Philadelphia,
on October 27, 1800, published Adams' vindication addressed to Thomas
Pinckney, along with the original letter to Coxe.

[145] See *Aurora*, October 2, 6, 9, 15, 18, 25, 30, November 1, 4, 7, 28,
1800. On the subject of Adams' supposed monarchist sympathies, consult
Louise Burnham Dunbar, *A Study of " Monarchical " Tendencies in the
United States, from 1776 to 1801* (" University of Illinois Studies in the
Social Sciences " [1920], X, No. 1), pp. 119, 120 ff.; Abraham Bishop,
Connecticut Republicanism; John Taylor, *Inquiry into the Principles and
Policy of the Government of the United States*, pp. 10 ff.; Adams to
Rush, April 18, 1790, *The Works of John Adams*, ed. Charles F. Adams,
IX, 566; Graydon, p. 392.

[146] *Gazette of the United States*, October 9, 29, November 1, 4, 1800.

[147] For further use of this device, see Coxe's *Strictures upon a letter
imputed to Mr. Jefferson, addressed to Mr. Mazzei*. This was signed
" Greene " and printed in June, 1800. See also an address *To the*

Throughout the campaign Coxe no doubt had upper-most in his mind a reëntry into the government service should Jefferson be successful. He had a large family the support of which was proving difficult at this time.[148] Indeed, for several years back, even while serving in the Treasury, Coxe had been financially pressed.[149] Moreover, his talents and interests were such as to prompt a desire for Federal employment. Put otherwise, Tench Coxe in 1800 was motivated by something more than a mere fond-ness for Jeffersonian democracy, the principles of which certainly did not match his economics. The zeal with which he sought office under the victorious Jefferson supports this belief.

Jefferson had been in office but a few days before Coxe made known to him his ambition. In a letter of March 10, 1801, Coxe emphasized his miserable plight, which he said was brought on by the Federalists; he therewith submitted his application for an office.[150] Thus was begun

Republican Citizens of the State of Pennsylvania, Lancaster, September 17, 1800, signed *inter alios* by Coxe and probably written by him. Copies of each of these pamphlets may be found in the Rare Book Room, Library of Congress.

[148] Coxe to Jefferson, April 18, 1801, quoted in Hunt, p. 260.

[149] Coxe to Hamilton, July 5, 1794, MS, Hamilton Papers, Second Series, III; Coxe to John Nicholson, April 11, 1796, MS, Simon Gratz Collection, Historical Society of Pennsylvania, case 1, box 24; Coxe to Fox, December 26, 1796, February 5, 1797, *ibid.*, case 1, box 4; Coxe to the President and Directors of the Bank of Pennsylvania, February 3, 6, 11, 12, 1797, *ibid.*; Coxe to Robert Morris and John Nicholson, February 23, 1797, MS, Dreer Collection, Historical Society of Pennsylvania; Coxe to Robert Morris and John Nicholson, December 28, 1798, MS, Personal Papers, Miscellaneous, Library of Congress. All of these letters reveal the financial plight of Coxe. By the will of his father, who died October 11, 1801, Coxe appears to have received some property but no ready cash. Nelson, p. 87. It is to be noted that following loss of the Commissioner-ship Coxe had been made Secretary of the Pennsylvania State Land Office. A portion of his official correspondence in this office, occupied until 1802, is to be found in the *Pennsylvania Archives,* Second Series, XVIII, 389-430.

[150] Coxe to Jefferson, March 10, 1801, quoted in Hunt, pp. 258-259.

what proved to be a lengthy and despairing quest for recognition. It is a pathetic story.

Although Coxe wrote repeatedly to Jefferson and Madison of his sacrifices in behalf of the public cause, in particular, the Republican party, he went without reward until 1803.[151] On June twenty-first of that year, Albert Gallatin, a major voice in the giving of patronage in Pennsylvania, addressed a letter to Jefferson in which he admitted that justice demanded that something be done for Coxe, for whom he had no " personal predilection." [152] He suggested that Coxe be made Purveyor of Public Supplies. Shortly afterwards, Jefferson acted accordingly.

This appointment could hardly have been pleasing to Coxe. The salary was small, being but two thousand dollars *per annum*.[153] Furthermore, the office entailed a tremendous amount of work. Coxe was called upon to make purchases of supplies, mostly for the army, and to settle the bills for these. In addition, he had to employ and supervise the work of many women engaged in the making of articles of clothing for the army. The work of the office became especially laborious in the years immediately preceding the War of 1812.[154]

---

[151] See Coxe to Jefferson, marked by Jefferson as received April 18, 1801, quoted in Gaillard Hunt, "Office-Seeking during Jefferson's Administration," *American Historical Review*, III, 259; Coxe to Madison, April 3, 1801, MS, Madison Papers, XXII; Coxe to Madison, June 11, 1801, *ibid*.

[152] Gallatin to Jefferson, June 21, 1803, *The Writings of Gallatin*, ed. Henry Adams, I, 123-124. In the Jefferson Papers, CXIV, there is an undated note by Gallatin in which he writes of " the seven offices applied for by T. Coxe," including that of the Secretaryship of the Navy. Gallatin here concluded that Coxe should receive the combined offices of inspector and collector of the internal revenue at Philadelphia.

[153] Gallatin to Jefferson, June 21, 1803, *The Writings of Gallatin*, I, 123-124.

[154] For Coxe's duties, see Washington's message to Congress, January 7, 1794, *A Compilation of the Messages and Papers of the Presidents*, ed. James D. Richardson, I, 149; *Annals of Congress*, 3rd Cong., 2nd sess., pp. 801, 803-804. What remains of the official papers of Coxe as

Exacting as were the duties of the office upon the time and energy of Coxe he was yet forced to contemplate, if not attempt, outside work to increase his income. On December 8, 1803, he wrote the Attorney-General in quest of a ruling upon the legality of such a procedure. Dejectedly, he declared that, "I am not certain that I can find time, but as I mean to apply to such private business large portions of my nights & times of relaxation, which I used to apply in promoting the cause of public liberty & the general prosperity of the country, I trust that I have yet enough of health & strength to go thro the duties of the Purveyorship & to execute the business I have in mind. . . ."[155] What became of this proposition is not known.

During his occupancy of the office of Purveyor, Coxe maintained his interest in public affairs. Somehow, he could never divorce himself from such matters. In 1804 we find him, for example, an active participant in the local and congressional elections. In a factional struggle which then occurred within the local Jeffersonian party Coxe sided with Governor McKean; thereafter he was constantly attacked by Duane, who spared no effort to revive the accusations made by the Federalists in 1800.[156] Also, Coxe throughout this period continued his active interest in the economic welfare of America. The impact of the

Purveyor is to be found at the Schuylkill Arsenal, Quartermaster Depot, U. S. Army, Philadelphia.

[155] Coxe to Levi Lincoln, December 8, 1803, MS, in Letter Book, pp. 243-244, box 4, of the official papers of the Purveyor's office, U. S. Arsenal, Philadelphia. Coxe revealed the proposed business as "that of an agency, for the sale of unimproved lands and other real estate."

[156] *Aurora*, August 17 to October 10, 1804. In reply to an assertion that he had used his office to influence the elections, Coxe wrote "An Exposition of some Facts Relative to the Personal Conduct, and Business of the Office of Tench Coxe, December 10, 1805." He here expressed willingness to face the charges "without the aid of counsel or the support of a single friend." During the fight the newly established paper, *The Freeman's Journal*, supported Coxe. See, for example, issues of July 10 and 12, 1804.

Napoleonic struggle upon our economy induced him to reassert his faith in the principles of a national economy. This he did in several publications, an examination of which we shall reserve for later chapters.[157]

In 1810 it seemed that Coxe would again be without an office. On April twenty-fifth of that year Joel Barlow wrote to President Madison in behalf of Coxe, informing the President that it was his understanding that the Purveyorship was to be abolished by a bill providing for a quartermaster's department. Assuring Madison that he had personal knowledge of the domestic affairs of Coxe, whose " family is large and now at the most expensive time of life," Barlow suggested that he be given the proposed new office.[158] The Purveyorship, however, was not abolished until 1812.

Loss of this office once again occasioned a lengthy correspondence in search of a new one. In successive letters to Madison, Coxe requested appointment as Superintendent of Military Stores, Deputy in charge of the Commissary, and again, Superintendent of Military Stores.[159] Though Coxe with justice pointed out in these letters that he had sacrificed his family interests in the public service, he received neither of the offices. Instead, he was given the office of Collector and Supervisor of the Revenue at Philadelphia, the pay of which he soon found to be insufficient for his needs.[160] Accordingly he once more wrote Madison in quest of a re-examination of his case; this time he expressed preference for an appointment as Collector of the Revenue for Pennsylvania. He further informed Madison that " considerations of necessity and public good had in-

[157] See below, chaps. iv and v.

[158] Barlow to Madison, April 25, 1810, MS, Madison Papers, XL.

[159] Coxe to Madison, August 13, 31, September 1, 1812, respectively, MSS, Madison Papers, XLIX. See also, Mathew Carey to Madison, January 25, 1813, ibid., LI. Carey, in strong terms, supported Coxe's plea for an office.

[160] Coxe to Madison, July 16, 1813, ibid., LII.

duced me to attempt, in the face of great obstacles, the establishment of a liberal and free press." Competition of eight existing papers, however, necessitated more capital than he himself was then able to supply. If he were granted the Collectorship, he would be able to continue with the project.[161] But this office was not given him. On November 15, 1813, he wrote Madison to thank him for an appointment as Collector of the direct taxes and internal revenue at Philadelphia.[162] Not only was the salary small, but duration of the office was uncertain. Coxe, therefore, was again forced to take up his plight with Madison. In a letter to the latter, January 3, 1814, he sought the office of Postmaster of Philadelphia, left open by the death of its occupant.[163] What became of this request is not known. Coxe during the following month wrote Madison an expression of appreciation for an honor conferred upon him;[164] but this could hardly have been the postmastership. It appears that instead Coxe continued in the revenue service, reverting to his old office of supervisor.[165] A little later, he also accepted appointment by the State of Pennsylvania as Clerk of the Quarter Sessions Court.[166] Doubting the legality of this combination he

[161] Coxe to Madison, July 16 and 22, 1813, *ibid.* See also, Coxe to Madison, September 2, 1813, *ibid.*, LIII.

[162] Coxe to Madison, November 15, 1813, *ibid.* As an alternative office, he was offered that of naval officer of Philadelphia, which he rejected. He had applied for the latter office, November 6, 1813, when he feared that nothing else could be had. Coxe to Madison, November 6, 1813, *ibid.*

[163] Coxe to Madison, January 3, 1814, *ibid.*, LIV.

[164] Coxe to Madison, February 27, 1814, *ibid.*

[165] See a circular letter, March 15, 1814, to Dr. Joseph Shippen, MS, Papers of the Shippen Family, Historical Society of Pennsylvania, VIII; also, Coxe to Madison, January 18, 20, 1815, MSS, Madison Papers, LVIII.

[166] Probably at the beginning of 1815. On February 21 of that year he wrote George Bryan, Auditor General, for information upon reports which he was required to render as Clerk. Coxe to Bryan, February 21, 1815, MS, Gratz Collection, case 1, box 4.

gave up the revenue office.[167] The clerkship he retained
until about 1818.[168] After 1815 there is no indication that
Coxe ever again held a federal office. That he did not do
so was through no lack of effort on his part.

In a letter to Jefferson, November 11, 1820, Coxe wrote
of his financial distress, declaring that his family consisted then of eight unmarried children, all over twenty
years of age. His pen was of no use in obtaining support
for them, since it had always been his habit to write for the
public interest and not personal profit. His only hope was
a public office. Would Jefferson assist him? [169] This same
plea was put before Madison on the next day. In a letter
to him Coxe recounted his record of public service: " *the
national economy* . . . domestic manufactures, especially,"
had always engaged his attention. Such work, he wrote,
" would give me a pension or an office in many
countries." [170]

The reply of Madison was that, aware of the valuable
services of Coxe, he would write President Monroe in his
behalf.[171] This he did, November 19, 1820, declaring that
he had " ever considered him [Coxe] among the most
strenuous & faithful laborers for the good of his country."[172] Further to assist Coxe, Madison invoked the aid

[167] Coxe to Madison, January 18 and 20, 1815, MSS, Madison Papers,
LVIII. Coxe, it may be noted here, was also at this time corresponding
with Madison *in re* the appointment of two of his sons as Midshipmen in
the Navy. Coxe to Madison, January 4, 25, 1815, *ibid.* He had earlier
offered to serve with his six sons in defence of the country. Coxe to
Madison, August 30, 1814, *ibid.*, LVI.

[168] See Coxe to George Bryan, May 4, 1818 (photostat), American
Letters and Documents, 1652-1845, U. S. Miscellany, Library of Congress.

[169] Coxe to Jefferson, November 11, 1820, MS, Jefferson Papers,
CCXVIII; see also, Jefferson to Coxe, October 13, 1820, *ibid.*

[170] Coxe to Madison, November 12, 1820, MS, Madison Papers,
LXVIII. (Underscoring in original.)

[171] Madison to Coxe, November 14, 1820, MS, Madison Papers,
LXVIII.

[172] Madison to Monroe, November 19, 1820, *The Writings of James
Madison*, ed. Gaillard Hunt, IX, 32-33.

of Senator Barbour of Virginia. In a letter to him, November 25, 1820, Madison praised the services of Coxe, adding that he considered him " as a sound politician, as particularly enlightened on the subject of commerce, and as a man of literary accomplishments." [173] Informing Jefferson of these efforts, Madison wrote that he sincerely wished " something proper in itself could be done for him [Coxe]. He needs it and deserves it." [174] Finally, Madison wrote again to Monroe: " Your dispositions to-wards Mr. T. Coxe are such as I had counted. I shall regret, if it so happens, that nothing can properly be done for him." [175] The latter, in fact, appears to have been the outcome. That Coxe should have gone unprovided for was no doubt due to his desire to remain in Philadelphia, rather than go to Washington, where more offices were available.[176]

Although the Republican party refused to recognize his services, Coxe nevertheless had no desire to bolt it. On the contrary, during the Presidential campaign of 1823-1824 he was as ready as ever to use his pen in its defence. At the beginning of that year he wrote Jefferson and Madison jointly of his intention to reveal in the public prints threats to our governmental institutions.[177] If we take the series of articles which he published in *The Democratic Press* as characteristic of his line of thought,

---

[173] Madison to Barbour, November 25, 1820, MS, Madison Papers, LXVIII. Barbour replied that he had spoken to Monroe in behalf of Coxe, and expected favorable results. Barbour to Madison, December 12, 1820, *ibid*.

[174] Madison to Jefferson, December 10, 1820, *ibid*.

[175] Madison to Monroe, December 28, 1820, *ibid*.

[176] In a letter to Madison, July 22, 1813, Coxe declared that he could not stand the climate of Washington during the summer months. *Ibid.*, LII. See also, Gallatin to Jefferson, June 21, 1803, *The Writings of Gallatin*, I, 123, wherein Gallatin wrote of Coxe's disinclination to serve in Washington.

[177] Coxe to Madison and Jefferson, January 31, 1823, MS, Madison Papers, LXX.

it proved an old one.[178] He there attacked the Adamses,
father and son, for declaring the British constitution to
be superior to our own; he read into their words the implication that they were for the destruction of our government. This was an argument he had used in supporting
the candidacy of Jefferson. He now hoped that its repeti-
tion would turn the tables on John Quincy Adams.[179]

On October 3, 1823, Coxe wrote what was perhaps his
last letter to Madison. In it he asserted that he had no
fear of any harm ever being done the memory of Washington or the Republican cause. Too many persons were
alive who knew the truth, including himself, to permit
that.[180] But Tench Coxe was not long to be among this
group. He died on July sixteenth of the following year.[181]

[178] Coxe, as "Sidney," eight letters addressed "To the Friends of the
Principles of the Constitution of the United States," *The Democratic
Press*, January 6, 11, 16, 23, 28, 31, and February 11 and 18, 1823. In
the last letter Coxe wrote that "the country must be saved in 1823-1824
as in 1800."

[179] John Quincy Adams was no admirer of Tench Coxe. In his diary,
May 24, 1819, he wrote of the "wily, winding, subtle and insidious
character" of Coxe. *Memoirs of John Quincy Adams*, ed. Charles F.
Adams, IV, 370.

[180] Coxe to Madison, October 3, 1823, MS, Madison Papers, LXXII.

[181] See Obituary notice, *The National Gazette*, July 16, 1824, and
Poulson's American Daily Advertiser, July 17, 1824, both of Philadel-
phia. Coxe was buried in Christ Church cemetery, near the grave of
Benjamin Franklin.

CHAPTER II

Coxe and the Federal Constitution

Although the inadequacy of the Articles of Confederation was manifest from the outset,[1] Tench Coxe does not appear to have showed interest in a reform until 1785. In that year the trade of the country was in a deplorable condition,[2] in the face of which Congress was, as it had always been, impotent. Convinced that such a situation could not continue without dire results, Tench Coxe and other Philadelphia merchants on April 6th forwarded a memorial to the State Assembly.[3] They deplored the absence of a national commercial policy. So circumstanced, the country could not, they asserted, take effective steps to meet European restrictions upon our trade. They therefore besought the Assembly to secure from Congress a recommendation that it alone be vested with power to control the commerce of the country. At another meeting on the twentieth of the same month they pursued the matter, declaring that "nothing but a full power in Congress, over the commerce of the United States, can relieve it from its present oppressions."[4] For the present they suggested that local manufactures be fostered in every possible way—a suggestion in accordance with a bill read in the Pennsylvania Assembly, March 22, 1785.[5]

[1] John Fiske, *The Critical Period of American History, 1783-1789*, pp. 56, 95-96; Francis A. Walker, *The Making of the Nation, 1783-1817*, pp. 5-8; Pelatiah Webster, "A Dissertation on the Political Union and Constitution of the Thirteen United States of America" (1783), *Political Essays*, p. 199; cf., however, Henry B. Dawson, "The Motley Letter," *Historical Magazine*, Second Series, IX, 157-201.

[2] See circular letter addressed by firm of Coxe & Frazier to European merchants, Library of Congress Broadsides, No. 146; also *Pennsylvania Packet*, June 3, 4, and 20, 1785.

[3] *Pennsylvania Packet*, June 2, 1785.

[4] *Ibid.*, June 21, 1785.

[5] George Bancroft, *History of the Formation of the Constitution of the United States of America*, I, 187.

Unhappily, however, the Pennsylvania Assembly did not avail itself of the opportunity presented by the merchants to institute the desired commercial reform. Instead, it responded to the memorial by enacting a tariff designed expressly to foster local manufactures.[6] Almost immediately, New Jersey and Delaware created free ports through which goods passed into Pennsylvania.[7] Other states followed the example of Pennsylvania, each of them with a view to its own particular interests.[8] The uselessness of a Congress devoid of control over commerce could hardly have been more clearly demonstrated. We may be sure that Coxe viewed the development with dismay. During the following year he readily accepted an invitation of the Pennsylvania Assembly to serve as a delegate to the Annapolis Convention. In that capacity his contacts with Hamilton, Madison, and others gave him additional knowledge of the plight of America; with them he joined in the movement of constitutional reform shortly afterwards instituted. "The picture of our country, drawn at the Annapolis Convention," Coxe wrote later, "alarmed me; . . . public life became my principal engagement." [9]

It was not until the following year, however, that Coxe publicly expressed his views on the need of reform. On May 11, 1787, shortly before the Constitutional Convention had fully assembled, he read before the Philadelphia Society for Political Enquiries, convened at the home of Benjamin Franklin, a paper entitled: "An Enquiry into

[6] *Pennsylvania Packet*, September 22, 1785; Malcolm R. Eiselen, *The Rise of Pennsylvania Protectionism*, pp. 11-13. A twelve and one-half per cent duty was levied on iron manufactures, leather goods, paper, and clothing. *Ibid.*, p. 13.

[7] *Ibid.*, pp. 14-15.

[8] Nevins, p. 558; William B. Weeden, *Economic and Social History of New England, 1620-1789*, II, 819; Samuel Flagg Bemis, *Jay's Treaty*, pp. 24-25; Albert A. Giesecke, *American Commercial Legislation before 1789*, pp. 134-135, 140-142; Bancroft, I, 191.

[9] Coxe to Madison, June 11, 1801, MS, Madison Papers, XXII.

the principles, on which a commercial system for the United States of America should be founded; to which are added some political observations connected with the subject." [10] Our condition was precarious, he declared—

Our money absorbed by a wanton consumption of imported luxuries, a fluctuating paper medium substituting in its stead, foreign commerce extremely circumscribed and a federal government not only ineffective but disjointed, tell us indeed too plainly, that further negligence may ruin us forever.[11]

More specifically, Coxe noted the muddled state of our public finance, state and national. The issuance of paper money must cease; acts for its enforced circulation must be annulled. Moreover, the desultory commercial acts of the several states, contradicting one another and in general upsetting the very bases of future development—certainty and confidence—must go. These acts were, he added, more detrimental to our welfare than " the restrictions of any one power in Europe." [12] Some of the states which bitterly complained of the latter were themselves guilty of applying similar treatment to sister states.[13]   In short, *"A system which will promote the general interest with the smallest injury to particular ones has become indispensably necessary."* [14]

Details of the " system " which Coxe here calls for were given by him at length during the course of his address. They constitute a classical statement of his idea of a national economy for America. Because of their impor-

----

[10] Published in Philadelphia by Robert Aitkin, May, 1787.   Copy in Library of Congress, Miscellaneous Pamphlets, vol. 1092.   Mathew Carey published the essay in *The American Museum* (June, 1787), I, 432-444.   It was also incorporated by Coxe in his *View*, pp. 4-33, to which reference is hereinafter made as, Coxe, " Enquiry," *View*.

[11] Coxe, " Enquiry," *View*, p. 5; see also, *ibid.*, p. 29.

[12] *Ibid.*

[13] *Ibid.*, p. 20.

[14] *Ibid.*, p. 29.   (Italics in original.)

tance viewed in terms of his later economic opinion, we shall postpone a consideration of them until the next chapter. It may be noted, however, that Coxe, as the context of his paper shows, thought the Philadelphia Convention would do little more than was contemplated when the Annapolis Convention assembled, namely, standardize the commercial and currency practices of the several states. The promulgation of an entirely new Constitution was perhaps more than he thought possible at the time, though, as we have just seen, he acknowledged the Confederation to be futile. Coxe accordingly incorporated in his proposal for a national economy several suggestions of practical reform in the existing commercial system. These he wished the Convention to act upon.

Stated briefly, the suggestions of Coxe were as follows: Firstly, he would have the coastal trade restricted to Americans. This was the policy of most nations; we could do no better than follow their example.[15] He did not think that such a measure would curtail the transportation facilities available to our farmers in the disposal of their produce. Knowing the dominant importance of agriculture in our economy he had, of course, to recognize this possibility. It plagued the minds of many Southerners when they came to pass on the Constitution. Secondly, Coxe thought it " safe and expedient " for the Convention to levy a duty or enact a prohibition on the foreign competitors of our fisheries.[16] Thirdly, he found the British regulation requiring that imports shall be transported in vessels belonging to the country producing them or else in British bottoms to be worthy of adoption by us. We could thereby curb our competitors in the carrying trade and avoid to a certain extent the costly entrepôt business. The fact that this might entail a loss of credit facilities should not deter us from adopting it; for " we

[15] *Ibid.*, pp. 9-10.   [16] *Ibid.*, p. 11.

should first lay out, to the best advantage, our funds in hand." [17] Concluding this phase of his discussion, Coxe cautioned against recourse to temporary expedients, lest more harm than good be done.[18]

The practical reforms here suggested by Coxe were, needless to say, inappropriate to the work of the Convention. That body had assembled, it turned out, not for the purpose of effecting a particular set of changes in our commercial system, but on the contrary to draft a complete, new framework of government, truly national in scope and power. The particular reforms mentioned by Coxe were to come later. And as he was then to admit, the idea of the Convention was a sound one.[19]

The drafting of the new Constitution to serve as " a depository of the national interests " [20] meant that the halfway stage had been reached in the great movement of reform. Leaders had appeared; followers must now be found. In short, the task of obtaining adoption of the new instrument remained. Amongst a people the majority of whom had not yet grasped the idea of a national government, whose existence, indeed, was characterized by " Community Isolation," [21] the prospects of success were not bright. Conscious of this fact, Coxe lost no time in participating in the struggle for ratification.

As we shall see, Coxe supported the movement for ratification by publishing essays designed to meet particular instances of opposition. His first contribution was a series of essays setting forth what he declared to be the democratic character of the proposed government. Growth of the opposition movement in the western counties of

[17] *Ibid.*, p. 12.
[18] *Ibid.*
[19] *Ibid.*, pp. 11, 14, footnotes appended to the essay in 1794.
[20] Alexander Hamilton, *The Federalist*, No. xxiii, ed. Bourne, I, 156.
[21] Albert J. Beveridge, *The Life of Marshall*, I, chap. viii. A vivid description of the condition and ideas of the people at this time is here presented by Beveridge.

Pennsylvania was in a large measure responsible for these, though he also intended that they be of use in other sections of the country. These essays appeared in September, 1787. His next published defence of the Constitution was in December of the same year. Here his purpose was to explode the fears of Richard Henry Lee concerning the commercial powers to be granted Congress by the Constitution. In January of the following year (1788), Coxe reverted to the Pennsylvania scene, publishing an address to the minority of that state. It is likely that he also circulated in the western counties essays defending the Constitution; of these, however, we have no record. The desire to discount the importance of the Pennsylvania opposition led Coxe in February to address the people of the United States. Local politics, rather than the character of the proposed government, motivated the dissenters in Pennsylvania, he argued. Following this address, Coxe appears to have allowed several months to elapse before again using his pen in defence of the Constitution. In May, 1788, however, he returned to the task, this time addressing the Virginia Convention, which was about to assemble. His purpose was to show why Virginia should ratify and to answer objections which he suspected would be raised in the Convention. In June this procedure was repeated in an address to the New York Convention. During July and September, 1788, Coxe wrote essays in which he pleaded with the opposition groups to abide by the decision of the majority and to support the Constitution. His desire was to obtain the election of a Congress favorable to the new Constitution. Finally, in March, 1790 Coxe pleaded with the Rhode Islanders to accept the new government. In what follows, attention has been paid not only to the content of Coxe's essays but also to the nature of the particular occasions which prompted him to write. Only those essays for which positive identification can be had are used.

In Coxe's native state leaders of the movement for adoption (e. g. the Federalists) were so determined to get a favorable consideration that even before Congress submitted the proposed Constitution to the states they had introduced in the Assembly a resolution providing for a convention to consider it. Fearful of an attempt to rush through ratification, members from the western counties remained away when the time came to fix the day of election and manner of choosing delegates, thus preventing a necessary quorum. Not to be outdone, the Federalists had the recalcitrants brought in by force, their "clothes torn and faces white with rage." [22] The necessary business was then transacted. Commenting upon this incident, Coxe wrote Madison as follows: " I am sorry for anything that appears irregular, or looks like an interruption of peace, but I have no doubt of a large majority of the Convention adopting the new frame of government in toto." [23]

The optimistic outlook here entertained by Coxe was, however, soon tempered. The dissenters in the Assembly, who were for the most part from the western counties of the state, took their case to the people with a determination that the membership of the Convention should not have a majority in favor of the new Constitution. In an "Address" to their constituents, September 29, 1787, they explained that the Federal Convention had exceeded its powers in discarding the Articles of Confederation; that the landed interest was not represented in the Pennsylvania delegation to the Convention; and that those delegates who were chosen to represent the state were from the party in opposition to the State Constitution.[24] Examining the proposed Federal government, they found

[22] *Pennsylvania and the Federal Constitution, 1787-1788*, eds. John Bach McMaster and Frederick D. Stone, pp. 3-5.

[23] Coxe to Madison, September 28, 1787, MS, Madison Papers, VIII.

[24] See "Address" of the sixteen seceding members of the Pennsylvania Assembly, McMaster and Stone, pp. 73-79; also, *ibid.*, p. 21.

that it would be costly to maintain. Moreover, compared to their own state government, it was undemocratic. What was worse, by its extensive taxing powers and judiciary, it could and no doubt would destroy the severalty of the states. The fact was, they reasoned, that a veiled attempt was being made to restore the old Charter government of Pennsylvania; to return political power to the conservative classes of the eastern part of the state.

To appreciate these criticisms, it is necessary to bear in mind the fact that the people in the western counties were, generally speaking, Scotch-Irish frontiersmen. Ancestral background and environment made them individualistic in habit and thought. Fervently democratic, they viewed external authority as anathema. An attempt by the old Charter government to enforce the state excise law among them failed; after the Revolution they even resorted to violence to avoid paying the duty.[25] And when the Federal government, the creation of which they were now to oppose, enacted a national excise, their fury waxed into open rebellion. The spirit of the French Revolution had in the meanwhile influenced them.[26]

To the potency of this western opposition, Coxe was not blind; nor were other supporters of the movement for ratification. A feeling of uneasiness over the outcome developed. Prompted by James Wilson, Dr. Benjamin Rush, and others,[27] Coxe made use of his pen for the first time to defend the Constitution. During September, 1787, he wrote four essays collectively entitled, " An Examination of the Constitution of the United States," and signed, " An American Citizen." [28] These essays were

[25] Sydney G. Fisher, *Pennsylvania, Colony and Commonwealth*, pp. 394-395.

[26] *Ibid.*, p. 396.

[27] Coxe to Madison, October 21, 1787, MS, Madison Papers, VIII.

[28] They were printed in the *Pennsylvania Gazette*, October 24, 1787, and in *The American Museum* (September and October, 1787), I, 300-306 and 387-391, respectively, under the title, " On the American Gov-

published in several newspapers, and were among the first to appear in favor of ratification.[29] Explaining his purpose in writing them, Coxe wrote Madison that:

My anxiety in favor of the new federal Constitution had induced me to attempt some comments on it, that might render it more clear and agreeable to the people at large, than the concise manner in which it was necessarily drawn up, would admit of. A friend, with whom I ventured to converse on the subject, has pressed me to pass them thro the papers of Virginia and New York. This will apologize to you for the trouble I give you in enclosing to you copies of the first and second numbers. I beg the favor of your perusing them with Colonel Hamilton, to whom make my apology also for the liberty, and, if you and he think they will be of any service be pleased to have them reprinted in the papers of those States. I would beg leave to suggest, that if they appear worthy of this, it would be most useful to have them inserted in such. Virginia papers as circulate most in your western counties. By the next post I will forward the third number, which treats of the house of representatives. The good effects of the government I have not spoken of. My object has been to remove apprehensions & to obviate popular reasonings drawn from the public feelings. In doing this in a public newspaper more attention to those feelings, in the language I have used, was necessary, than if I had addressed a philosophic mind.[30]

In the first number of his " Examination " Coxe pointed

---

ernment." In 1788 they were published in pamphlet form in Philadelphia. A copy of the latter, in the Library of Congress, Duane Pamphlets, vol. 96, is hereinafter referred to as Coxe, " Examination."

[29] *Pamphlets on the Constitution of the United States, published during its discussion by the people 1787-1788*, ed. Paul Leicester Ford, p. 133. Pelatiah Webster, of Philadelphia, addressed at this time an essay to the western opposition, a copy of which Coxe sent to Madison and Hamilton. Coxe to Madison, October 21, 1787, MS, Madison Papers, VIII. Webster's essay, " Remarks on the Address of the Sixteen Members of the Assembly of Pennsylvania to their Constituents dated September 29, 1787," is to be found in his *Political Essays*, pp. 403 ff. Webster had already gained a reputation for his essays on money and finance under the Confederation; he expected the new Constitution to make possible many improvements in the American economy.

[30] Coxe to Madison, September 27, 1787, MS, Madison Papers, VIII.

to the necessity of a national government, declaring that
the people had failed to erect one in 1776. The Confederation, created during the confusion of the Revolution,
was a Federal government; it was "*now universally admitted to be inadequate to the preservation of liberty,
property, and the union.*"[81] He next compared the proposed Constitution with the British form of government.
In Great Britain the King was "the great bishop" with
church patronage, holding office for life. Under our Constitution the President would not have any such patronage.
He was to be elected for four years, and could be maintained in office cheaply. Membership in our Senate was to
be by election, and not by appointment, as was true of the
British House of Lords. Those and many other compari-
sons were made by Coxe. All of them were, of course,
favorable to the American project. The cleverness of Coxe
in using this strategy is obvious when one considers that
in the mind of the average American in 1787 there was no
worse form of government than that from which the
country had so recently loosed itself. Hamilton the following year, 1788, also employed this device.[32] In the second
number, Coxe discussed the structure and functions of the
Senate. The safety of the people was, he assured his
readers, secured by the restraints imposed on that body.
Membership in it was open to all on an elective basis;
ability and not property would determine the success of
those who aspired to become Senators. No revenue measures could be initiated in that body. In the third number,
the House of Representatives was considered. Its membership was to be chosen directly by the people, both poor
and rich. Consequently, there would be no rotten boroughs
or votes for sale as in Great Britain. A representative must
be a native of his state. He would thus be acquainted

[81] Coxe, "Examination," p. 5. (Italics in original.)
[32] Hamilton, *The Federalist*, No. lxix, ed. Bourne, II, 47.

with its problems at first hand. In the House, voting of members and proceedings would be public. In the fourth and final number Coxe pointed to " The security for national safety and happiness, resulting from other parts of the federal government." Again, he stressed the democratic character of the government, declaring that all its offices were open to the people without religious or property tests. Furthermore, no standing army was provided for or intended by the Constitution. Army appropriations could only be for two years duration; they would be made by the representatives chosen directly by the people. In reply to those who decried the absence of a Bill of Rights, he asserted that the Articles of Confederation did not contain such; that they were properly contained rather in the respective state Constitutions: " relating only to *personal* rights, they could not be mentioned *in a contract among sovereign States.*" [33] From this last assertion he would have the reader infer that the new government was not one of consolidation in the sense that the state governments would be entirely destroyed. The latter was thought by many people to be the case, as we shall see hereafter. Concluding, Coxe pleaded for adoption of the Constitution, altering it later by amendments, if necessary. In general, the essays were cleverly conceived and executed. The sentiments expressed, judged in the light of his subsequent writings, were sincere.

During October, 1787, Coxe continued to be uncertain of the prospects of success. Opposition in the western counties of Pennsylvania, he found, was growing.[34] For the present, however, he appears to have been content to let matters stand as they were and direct his attention to the movement for ratification in other states, particularly Virginia.[35] It may have been that he was acquainted with

[33] Coxe, " Examination," p. 19. (Italics in original.)
[34] Coxe to Madison, October 21, 1787, MS, Madison Papers, VIII.
[35] Coxe probably wrote an address " To the Freeman of Pennsylvania,"

the fact that the opposition group in Pennsylvania was acting in concert with opponents in the last mentioned state.[36]

In Virginia, as in Pennsylvania, the opposition group contended that the proposed government was one of consolidation; that it did not expressly provide a Bill of Rights. Furthermore, much was made of the economic implications of the new Constitution insofar as southern interests were concerned. In particular, the prospect of a Navigation Act under the commerce clause by a majority vote proved a strong objection. Earlier, in the Constitutional Convention, George Mason and Edmund Randolph of Virginia had insisted that a two-thirds vote of those present in both branches of Congress should be required to enact such a measure.[37] Otherwise, they reasoned, southern farmers might find themselves forced to rely upon an inadequate American merchant marine with consequent high rates for services rendered. The admission of slaves freely until the year 1807 as a compromise settled the dispute for the time being.[38] When, however, the Constitution was submitted to the states for consideration, the controversy arose again, with George Mason and Richard Henry Lee playing an important part in opposition to adoption. Fearful lest defeat of adoption might ensue, Coxe directed his attention toward the Virginia

signed, "By one of the People," and printed in the *Pennsylvania Gazette*, October 17, 1787. At any rate, its style and arguments, which emphasized the importance of the Constitution as the basis for our future economic development, suggest the work of Coxe. It is not, however, mentioned in any of his available correspondence.

[36] See William Wirt Henry, *Patrick Henry*, II, 335, where he calls attention to this concert; also McMaster and Stone, p. 23.

[37] Chas. Pinckney of South Carolina and James McHenry of Maryland took a similar position. William M. Meigs, *The Growth of the Constitution in the Federal Convention of 1787*, pp. 127-129, 135-136, 163-164, 166-168; Bernard C. Steiner, *The Life and Correspondence of James McHenry*, p. 101.

[38] Andrew Cunningham McLaughlin, *The Confederation and Constitution, 1783-1789* ("American Nation Series," X), p. 265; Meigs, p. 166.

battle, especially to the opposition of Lee. He knew that the decision of Virginia would be influential elsewhere in the movement for adoption.

Insofar as the opponents of the new government could be said to have possessed a national leader, surely Richard Henry Lee deserves recognition as such.[39] During the week of October 8th, 1787, he wrote and published five " Letters from the Federal Farmer to the Republican." [40] In these, though he acknowledged the existing government to be useless, he at the same time declared the proposed substitute to be shameless consolidation, which should be prevented so far as possible. For his part, Lee appears to have favored a semi-consolidation of governmental powers, with the authority of levying and collecting taxes in the hands of the separate states. The proposed change he found to be one of a transfer of power from the many to the few. In regard to the polemical question of the regulation of commerce, he pointed out that the eastern states would profit by such national control. On this score he did not write at length here, but in a letter to Governor Edmund Randolph, October 16, 1787, he expressed the belief that a majority control over commerce would permit seven northern states to ruin the southern ones.[41] This particular letter found its way into several newspapers, including two published in Philadelphia.[42] Lee became an opponent with whom someone had to reckon.

This Tench Coxe did in " A Letter to the honourable

[39] Ford, p. 277, states that Lee was "foremost in opposition to the Constitution." See also, Bancroft, II, 230, 241, 266, 339, Appendix, p. 451.

[40] Ford, pp. 277-325. Four editions of these " Letters " in pamphlet form appeared in rapid succession, and were circulated in several states.

[41] Lee to Randolph, October 16, 1787, *The Letters of Richard Henry Lee*, ed. James C. Ballagh, II, 454.

[42] *Pennsylvania Packet*, December 20, 1787; *Pennsylvania Herald*, December 29, 1787.

Richard Henry Lee, Esq.," which he signed, " An American." [43] Accounting for his action, Coxe wrote Madison
on December 28, 1787, as follows:

> Finding from a conversation with Mr. Wilson and Dr. Rush,
> that the idea of Mr. R. H. Lee's letter to your Governor concern-
> ing the commercial powers of Congress was doing mischief in
> Virginia I devoted last Sunday to an investigation of it. I take
> the liberty of enclosing a couple of copies of it, under the signa-
> ture *An American*. I shall take some pains to have it republished
> to the *Southward*, and wish it could be inserted in some of the
> country newspapers of New York and New England, or that it
> might be in the hands of some proper person in the Connecticut
> Convention to be made use of, if *occasion* should appear.[44]

In his letter to Lee, Coxe spared no effort to justify the
constitutional provision for a majority vote on acts of commerce. In such a regulation he saw no danger to the
agrarian interests. All of the delegates from the commercial states were not devoid of agrarian connections. The
fact was, Coxe averred, that four out of five representatives from Pennsylvania " have not the slighest interest in
trade." In so writing he had reference to the old Congress.
But the work of that ineffectual assembly was not taken
seriously, and Coxe's assertion therefore had little force
in it. Perhaps aware of this fact, he proceeded to point
out that New Jersey and Delaware were to be put in a
class with the southern states; furthermore, the admission
of Kentucky and Vermont as states would add to the
preponderance of the landed interest in the new Con-

[43] Published in the *Pennsylvania Herald*, December 29, 1787; *Pennsylvania Packet*, January 2, 1788; *Pennsylvania Gazette*, January 16, 1788;
and in *The American Museum* (January, 1788), III, 78-83, to which
reference is hereinafter made.

[44] Coxe to Madison, December 28, 1787, MS, Madison Papers, VIII.
(Underscoring in original.) The work of James Wilson in behalf of
the Constitution is well known: for that of Dr. Rush, foremost medical
man of his time in this country, see Nathan G. Goodman, *Benjamin
Rush*, pp. 74-75.

gress.[45] In short, the landed interest was an "irresistible power"; "the importance of our commerce is well understood," he wrote, "but its most sincere and powerful friends admit, and even assert the superior importance of agriculture."[46] To attest this, Coxe quoted at length from his "Enquiry," referring to it as from the pen of "a merchant (not a landholder) of Philadelphia."[47] In this essay, as will be noted in the next chapter, he emphasized the dominance of agriculture in the American economy. Finally, perhaps as a touch of sarcasm, Coxe wrote that Virginians, if need be, could build ships as cheaply as New Englanders and attract seamen by high wages and certainty of employment.[48] In any event, he could not conceive of any "interference of the commercial with the agricultural interests of the United States. . . ."[49] In this view, Coxe was supported by at least three contemporary southern writers.[50]

The reply of Coxe to Lee pleased Madison. "Your arguments," he wrote, "appear to me to place the subject to which they relate in its true light, and must be satisfactory to the writer himself whom they oppose, if he can

[45] Coxe, "Letter," *The American Museum* (January, 1788), III, 79. Hamilton in *The Federalist*, No. xl, ed. Bourne, I, 412, also stated that the landed interest would always control Congress.

[46] Coxe, "Letter," *The American Museum* (January, 1788), III, 80.

[47] *Ibid.*, pp. 80-81.

[48] *Ibid.*, p. 82.

[49] *Ibid.*, p. 83.

[50] See "Answers to Mr. Mason's objections to the New Constitution, recommended by the late Convention," January, 1788, by "Marcus" (James Iredell of North Carolina), Ford, *Pamphlets on the Constitution*, pp. 333-370; "Remarks on the New Plan of Government by Hugh Williamson, Printed in the State Gazette of North Carolina, 1788," *Essays on the Constitution of the United States, published during its discussion by the people 1787-1788*, ed. Paul Leicester Ford, pp. 397-406; and "Observations on the Proposed Plan of Federal Government. With an Attempt to answer some of the Principal Objections that have been made to it. By a Native of Virginia. Petersburg, 1788," in Madison Papers, Printed Material, LXXVII.

suspend for a moment his preconceived opinions . . .
they will unquestionably be of service in Virginia, and
probably in other southern states." Hamilton, Madison
added, had read the letter "with equal pleasure and
approbation." [51]

Pending the assembling of the Virginia Convention in
June, 1788, Coxe interested himself in developments elsewhere. On January 16, 1788, he sent to Madison a bundle
of sixty copies of the debates in the Pennsylvania Convention, requesting that they be forwarded to Rufus King
for use in the Massachusetts Convention, if needed.[52]
There, as in Virginia, the opposition attacked the majority
vote on acts of commerce. In the "Letters of Agrippa,"
which Coxe did not mention, it was asserted pointedly
that "the right to regulate trade without any limitations,
will, as certainly as it is granted, transfer the trade of
this state to Pennsylvania." [53] In a letter to Madison,
written on January 23rd, Coxe spoke of the prospects of
success in Massachusetts as not being hopeful.[54] In Vir-

[51] Madison to Coxe, January 3, 1788, MS, Madison Papers, VIII.
Madison in this letter informed Coxe of circulation of the latter's "Ex-
amination" in Virginia. He intended, he said, to send a copy of the
"Letter" to South Carolina and Georgia.

[52] Coxe to Madison, January 16, 1788, MS, Madison Papers, VIII.
The debates of the Pennsylvania Convention, it is to be noted, were not
printed in toto. When the Convention assembled, Thomas Lloyd, a short-
hand writer, sought permission to take down and publish all that was
said; he, however, was bought up by the Federalists. His published
account of the proceedings was a thin volume, containing only the
speeches of the two leading Federalists, James Wilson and Thomas
M'Kean. See McMaster and Stone, pp. 14-15. Coxe, therefore, was not
giving any assistance to the opposition in Massachusetts. A. J. Dallas
reported the Pennsylvania debates as of November 30 in the *Pennsylvania
Herald*; further publication was prevented by the Federalists who with-
drew their subscriptions to the newspaper. *Ibid.*, p. 15.

[53] See Letter No. XIII, January 14, 1788, Ford, *Essays on the Constitution*, pp. 97-98. These letters are accredited to James Winthrop.

[54] Coxe to Madison, January 23, 1788, MS, Madison Papers, VIII.
See also, Coxe to Madison, January 27, 1788, *ibid.*, enclosing more
copies of the Pennsylvania debates for use in Massachusetts.

ginia, however, he had learned that " a real change " was taking place, and that Lee might be expected to alter his conduct but not his ideas. In Connecticut, he continued, a favorable reception would be of assistance in securing adoption by New York and Massachusetts. In these and other states it was the fear of consolidation that was retarding progress: " It does all the mischief in Pennsylvania," he wrote; " I have therefore thought a few well-tempered papers on this point might be useful and have commenced them under the signature of the freeman in this day's Gazette, of wch I send you a copy." [55] Republication in Massachusetts and New York was suggested.

In an immediate reply to this letter Madison wrote that Coxe's appraisal of the opposition was a sound one: " What goes by the name of consolidation in Pen^a is I suspect at the bottom of the opposition to the new Gov^t almost everywhere; and I am glad to find you engaged in developing the subject." [56] To assist him, Madison sent along some papers relating to the matter. Commenting upon the situation in Virginia, Madison agreed with Coxe that " there is certainly a favorable change taking place. . . ." Lee, he thought, was relaxing in his opposition. In Massachusetts, the prospects were also more favorable to adoption.[57]

The minority group of Pennsylvania, to whom Coxe addressed his essays, had doggedly opposed ratification of the Constitution by the State Convention. But they were defeated by a vote of 46 to 23.[58] On December 12, 1787,

[55] Coxe to Madison, January 23, 1788, *ibid.* Coxe's essays, three in number, were entitled, " Address to the Minority of the Convention of Pennsylvania." They were published in the *Pennsylvania Gazette*, No. 1, January 23, 1788, No. 2, January 30, 1788, and No. 3, February 6, 1788; they also appeared in the *Pennsylvania Packet*, January 25, January 31, and February 7, 1788, respectively; and in *The American Museum* (February, March and April, 1788), III, 158-161, 242-245, and 365-367, respectively, to which reference is hereinafter made.

[56] Madison to Coxe, January 27, 1788, MS, Madison Papers, VIII.

[57] *Ibid.*   [58] McMaster and Stone, p. 20.

three days before the Convention adjourned, they again
addressed to their constituents an explanation of their opposition to the Constitution.[59] The Pennsylvania delegates
to the Federal Convention, they repeated, were chosen
from those who opposed the State Constitution. The
Federal government now offered to the people was one
intended to consolidate the states under a national Congress that would become " an iron handed despotism." [60]
How could it be otherwise, they inquired, when the
Federal government was to be given full power over the
purse and sword? The Federal laws were to be supreme.
The two governments—state and national—must therefore come to grips, with the state losing. " In short, consolidation pervades the whole constitution." [61] A direct
taxing power in the hands of Congress, they continued,
would be hideous: " This tax is so congenial to the nature
of despotism, that it has ever been a favorite under such
governments." [62] By presenting arguments such as these,
the minority undoubtedly had in view a strengthening of
the opposition in other states. In fact, associations, societies, and corresponding committees were created in the
western counties to cooperate with the opposition groups
in other states.[63]

In his reply to the dissenters, Coxe emphasized the
inadequacy of the Articles of Confederation, which, he
said, contained at least an element of consolidation. The
latter he saw in the fact that the " free inhabitants of each
state were rendered, to all intents and purposes, free
citizens of all the rest." [64] The expression, " We, the

[59] See "The Address and Reasons of Dissent of the Minority of the
Convention of the State of Pennsylvania to their Constituents " (December 12, 1787), McMaster and Stone, pp. 454-483.
[60] Ibid., p. 465.
[61] Ibid., p. 470.
[62] Ibid., pp. 477-478.
[63] McMaster and Stone, p. 24.
[64] Coxe, " Address to the Minority of the Convention of Pennsylvania,"
p. 159.

people," in the proposed Constitution was not indicative of consolidation, as they thought; it was only "a mere form of words." Were the severalty of the states to be destroyed, the Constitution would have read, "We, the people of America," reasoned Coxe.[65] In the remainder of his essays, he entered into a detailed examination of what Congress could not do and what the states could and must do. This he did with a view to supporting his denial of the presence of consolidation. Finally, touching upon the Federal power of taxation, Coxe asserted that it would always be used with discretion. Congress under the Confederation, he admitted, could not force the states to pay the requisitions levied upon them to support the general government. Had such power been granted, however, Congress would have been fully justified in using it.

In thus answering the opposition, Coxe, it must be said, took a too feeble stand. That more power had to be lodged in Congress than was accorded by the Articles, he knew; but in driving home this truth he was unnecessarily cautious. James Wilson, on the other hand, openly declared that the states had no sovereignty in the first instance; that they were mere creatures of delegated powers. Sovereignty, he averred, was lodged in the people. Power, where transferred to the national government under the Constitution, had hitherto been abused by the states, as in the wholesale emission of paper money, tender acts, and the like. The people now wanted a national government with power, and this they were to get.[66]

Desirous of discrediting the Pennsylvania minority in other sections of the country, Coxe during February, 1788 addressed four essays "To the People of the United

[65] *Ibid.*, p. 160.
[66] See speeches of Wilson before the Pennsylvania Convention, December 1 and 4, 1788, McMaster and Stone, pp. 301-310 and 315-323, respectively.

States." [67] In the first of these he explained the political situation in Pennsylvania with a view to showing that the opposition to the Federal Constitution there was more a matter of local political discontent than a question of the merits of the proposed Constitution. Pennsylvania, Coxe wrote, was distracted by "unhappy and baneful party contentions. . . ." The measures and addresses of the minority involved "deep rooted personal enmities, [and] considerations surely foreign" to the Federal Constitution.[68] In a word, the opposition group was fearful that adoption of the new government would result in a new State Constitution, too. But what merits were to be attached to the State Constitution, which these people cherished so highly? This question Coxe answered in his second essay. An independent judiciary, Coxe wrote, was the bulwark of a republican government; but the State Constitution did not provide for such. On the contrary, the judges held office for seven years and were subject to removal at any time for misbehavior by the State Assembly. Moreover, the Supreme Executive of the state was also head of the superior Court, thus joining the executive and judiciary branches of the government.

Again, the electoral provisions of the Constitution were not democratic. Each county elected one member to the Supreme Executive Council. There were nineteen counties, ten of which had but 24,000 electors out of a total of 69,000 for the whole state. Representation upon the Council of Censors, which met every seven years to revise or amend the Constitution, was also without regard to the distribution of the population of the state. The legislature was unicameral. Only "the deluded followers of

[67] These essays, signed, "A Pennsylvanian," appeared in the *Pennsylvania Gazette*, February 6, 13, 20, and 27, 1788. Identification is to be had from a letter of Coxe to Madison, February 15, 1788, MS, Madison Papers, VIII. In this letter Coxe also wrote that he had sent a package of pamphlets to Contee of Maryland.

[68] Coxe, Essay No. 1 (February 6, 1788).

Daniel Shays " were in favor of this, Coxe wrote. Government under the Pennsylvania Constitution was, he concluded, a " tyrannical oligarchy." [69] What of the proposed Federal Constitution? In his third essay Coxe defended it against the arguments of the minority. There would be no consolidation—annihilation of state powers—as maintained by them. Congress, it was true, would control the purse, but not in an autocratic fashion. Each state legislature was to choose two Senators who could throw out any undesirable revenue measure. Ample sources of revenue would remain to the states, since the latter could levy " any internal tax, excise or duty whatsoever." The people would elect the House of Representatives; hence they could prevent the levying of a direct tax, so detestable to the minority. As to the power of the sword, it was in the hands of the people. They formed the militia.[70] In the fourth and final essay, Coxe gave a precise definition of the relation of the state governments to the national government:

> The fœderal government and the state governments are neither co-ordinate, co-equal, nor even similar. They are of *different natures*. The general government is fœderal, or an union of *sovereignties*, for *special* purposes. The state governments are *social*, or an association of *individuals*, for *all* the purposes of society and government.[71]

The Federal government, he continued, could not swallow up the state governments, for the powers of the latter were not derived from the Federal Constitution. Avoiding notice of the fact that the proposed Constitution did, however, destroy certain powers of the states, as, for example, the emission of paper money, Coxe proceeded to inquire, derisively: " Does not this tenaciousness of some

[69] *Ibid.*, Essay No. 2 (February 13, 1788).
[70] *Ibid.*, Essay No. 3 (February 20, 1788).
[71] *Ibid.*, Essay No. 4 (February 27, 1788). (The italics are Coxe's.)

of the state legislators about the powers of the bodies to which they belong evince a greater attachment to their own seats, than to the interests of their constituents?" The fact was, Coxe wrote, that even if "considerable powers" were to be granted Congress by the Constitution, it was yet true that the people themselves chose one branch of that body, and the state legislatures the other. In truth, a comparison of the Federal Constitution with that of the states would show the former to be more truly republican; it made no provision for property qualifications for electors or those elected.[72]

From February, 1788, when the above mentioned essays were published, until the following May, we have no record of Coxe's participation in the movement for adoption of the Constitution. That he ceased his literary activities during this interim is, however, improbable. At any rate, on May 19, 1788 he wrote Madison that "the fate of the Constitution is now hastening to a crisis." Were Virginia to reject it, success in New York, New Hampshire, and North Carolina would be rendered more uncertain. He therefore had written some observations on the relation of the Constitution "to the prosperity of Virginia and the United States." These he hoped would be useful.[73] In addition thereto, but not mentioned in this letter, Coxe also prepared an "Address to the honourable the members of the convention of Virginia."[74]

In the last mentioned essay Coxe employed a style more vigorous than any he had hitherto used. It smacks of impatience. That Virginia should oppose ratification because

[72] *Ibid.*

[73] Coxe to Madison, May 19, 1788, MS, Madison Papers, VIII. The writer has been unable to find any copies of these essays.

[74] Signed, "An American," it appeared in the *Pennsylvania Gazette,* May 21 and 28, 1788. It was reprinted by the *Virginia Gazette and Weekly Advertiser,* June 5, 1788. It is also to be found in *The American Museum* (May and June, 1788), III, 426-433 and 544-548, respectively. It is here ascribed to Coxe by the editor, Mathew Carey.

the Constitution provided for a majority vote on acts of commerce, he could not understand. Any other provision would be " establishing tyranny by law." Repeating what he had earlier written Richard Henry Lee, Coxe averred that " The landed interest must ever possess a commanding majority in the state and federal legislatures." As to the objection that Virginia would not have a Congressional representation commensurate with her importance, he replied in a vehement tone that she would get what she was entitled to and no more. " You (suffer me respectfully to say so)," Coxe wrote, " have least cause of complaint." In support of this contention he cleverly pointed out that there were property qualifications for voting in Virginia, but none in the Constitution. Furthermore, he continued, Virginia must not forget that the different sections of the country were interdependent. In the event of European wars, would not southern agriculture have to depend on New England navigation? Rejection of the Constitution by Virginia would be no gain on her part, nor on that of any of the other states. Instead, " thirteen jarring sovereignties—two or three contending confederacies—or a feeble union," would be the only courses open to the people. " Ye friends of religion and morality! ye lovers of liberty and mankind! will ye not seize this opportunity proffered you by the bounty of heaven, and save your country from contempt and wretchedness? " inquired Coxe.[75]

The procedure of the opposing parties in the Virginia Convention was followed attentively by Coxe. The decision of the Convention, at the instance of George Mason, to debate the Constitution clause by clause pleased him,[76] and rightly so, since it enabled the proponents to offer a

[75] See Coxe, " Address," *The American Museum*, ibid., pp. 426-433, 544-548. The quotations and analysis above made are from this source.

[76] Coxe to Madison, June 11, 1788, MS, Madison Papers, IX; see also, Madison to Coxe, June 11, 1788, *ibid*.

ready defence: they could talk in generalities.[77] But at
that, victory was not easily achieved. Ratification was
had by a majority of only ten votes.[78] The anxiety of Coxe
over the outcome in other states must thereby have been
allayed.

On June 11, 1788, two weeks before ratification by Virginia, Coxe issued an address " To the Honorable the
Convention of the State of New York." [79] In that body
the followers of Governor Clinton were stubborn in their
opposition.[80] The powerful arguments contained in *The
Federalist* proved fruitless.[81] The work of Hamilton,
Madison, and Jay, these essays were more of the nature of
a scholarly commentary upon the Federal Constitution
than campaign material. Unlike the essays of Coxe, they
were characterized by a remarkable grasp of the science
of government.[82] Moreover, they contained a much more
detailed defence of the Constitution than was ever undertaken by Coxe. His address to the New York Convention
therefore is hardly deserving of comparison with *The
Federalist*. In a simple manner Coxe emphasized the
democratic character of the proposed Federal government.
" Corrupt boroughs," he assured the Convention, could not
appear in America. Nor was our Senate to be hereditary.
The State Legislatures would choose its membership.

[77] Hugh Blair Grigsby, *The History of the Virginia Federal Convention of 1788* (" Collections of the Virginia Historical Society," New
Series, IX and X), I, 70-72; Beveridge, I, chap. x.

[78] Grigsby, I, 345.

[79] Signed, " A Pennsylvanian," this address was printed in the *Pennsylvania Gazette*, June 11, 1788. For identification, see Coxe to Madison, June 11, 1788, MS, Madison Papers, IX.

[80] McMaster, I, 496-500.

[81] *Ibid.*, p. 484.

[82] Coxe suspected that Madison was one of the authors, and wrote him
for verification. Coxe to Madison, September 10, 1788, MS, Madison
Papers, X. Madison apparently did not approve of Coxe's curiosity.
In a letter to Madison, September 26, 1788, *ibid.*, Coxe apologized for
the request.

Failure to adopt the Constitution could only mean a continuance of commercial wars among the states, he wrote. Economic conditions were in need of improvement. Congress had even to borrow funds to pay interest: " The canker worm of *interest upon interest* is eating up the produce of our fields, and even the lands we cultivate," Coxe warned.[83] New Jersey and Connecticut already had adopted the Constitution; New York must not expect the trade of these states, if she failed to accept the new government. She must follow the other states, Coxe concluded, if she wished to avoid economic ruin.

During July, 1788, Coxe again focussed his attention upon the dissenting group in Pennsylvania. The dissenters there, as well as elsewhere, he wrote Madison, were calling for a larger House of Representatives; they were also complaining bitterly of the prospect of Congress levying a direct tax.[84] If such ideas continued, they might work harm. An answer to them was needed. Coxe believed he had one. These people, for the most part inhabitants of the western counties, thought very highly of their State Constitution, he continued. How excellent was it in comparison with the new Federal Constitution? Not as much so as they were prone to think, he answered. The new national government was more representative of the people than the existing state governments, the only exception being that in the slave states three-fifths of the slaves were to be counted in determining representation in the lower branch of Congress. Furthermore, Coxe wrote, in some states small counties or election districts had a representation in the legislature equal to that of other counties or districts twice as large. Surely, it would be preferable to have the power of direct taxation exercised by the Federal government with its ideal representation.[85]

[83] Coxe, " To the Honorable the Convention of the State of New York," *Pennsylvania Gazette*, June 11, 1788. (Italics his.)
[84] Coxe to Madison, July 23, 1788, MS, Madison Papers, IX.
[85] *Ibid.*

Signing himself " A friend of Society and Liberty,"
Coxe incorporated this reasoning in an address " To the
Inhabitants of the Western Counties of Pennsylvania." [86]
In deliberating upon the Constitution, the people should
use their courthouses as gathering places, he advised, since
in taverns spirituous liquors were served. Strong drink
and hasty conclusions were handmaids, he thought.[87]
Under the Federal government, Coxe carefully noted,
offices were open to either rich or poor. Furthermore,
there was no occasion for the westerners to fear the imposition of a direct tax by the Federal government. The latter
would derive its revenue from a five per cent impost; this,
in turn, would lessen the land tax. Indeed, by use of homespun the burden of taxation could be thrown upon the
rich, who used imported fineries. The minority faction in
other states had agreed to support the Constitution now
that it was adopted, he concluded.[88] Commenting upon
this essay, Madison assured Coxe that its arguments were
" as well timed as they are judicious." [89]

[86] *Pennsylvania Gazette*, July 23, 1788. For identification, see Coxe to
Madison, July 23, 1788, MS, Madison Papers, IX. During September,
1788, the anti-Federalists of Pennsylvania sent delegates to a meeting in
Harrisburg to propose amendments to the Constitution. A circular letter
sent out by Governor Clinton of New York, advising such action,
prompted them. See McMaster, I, 500 n. This assembly occasioned an
address " To the People of the United States, and particularly to the
Independent Electors of Pennsylvania " by Coxe. It was signed, " A
Federal Centinel," and appeared in the *Pennsylvania Gazette*, September
10, 1788. For identification, see Coxe to Madison, September 10, 1788,
MS, Madison Papers, X. In this essay Coxe deplored the furtive manner in which the Harrisburg Convention had been arranged. He warned
the people against deception. These " conspirators," he wrote, should
not be permitted to influence the state elections. The Convention, it
may be noted, sent a memorial to the State Legislature beseeching that
body to take steps toward having the Constitution amended and revised.
See *Pennsylvania Gazette*, September 10, 1788; McMaster and Stone,
pp. 557-564.
[87] Coxe, " To the Inhabitants of the Western Counties of Pennsylvania."
[88] *Ibid.*
[89] Madison to Coxe, July 30, 1788, MS, Madison Papers, IX.

In subsequent correspondence with Madison, Coxe was able to write of the favorable support accorded federalism in nearly every state, the notable exception being Rhode Island.[90] North Carolina, it is true, hesitated in accepting the Constitution, even after eleven states had led the way. North Carolinians, according to Coxe, feared " the honest payment of debts that would be produced by disuse of a paper medium." [91] Opposition to the Constitution in that state, however, does not seem to have particularly interested him. Its Convention agreed to ratification on November 21, 1789.[92] In Rhode Island, on the other hand, the case of federalism was well-nigh hopeless. Determined to make his fight one to a finish, Coxe attacked the opposition in that quarter. In a letter to Madison, March 31, 1790, he spoke of having written on the Sunday morning past an essay which he hoped would assist the Rhode Islanders in coming to their senses. It was, he assured Madison, " a pious work"; that state was in need of a " reformation." [93]

With this assault of Coxe upon the last oppositional stronghold, our story of his participation in the movement of constitutional reform is ended. In summary of it, we may quote the following from a letter which he wrote to Madison, September 9, 1789:

> Since my journey to Annapolis, when I hazarded a vote *unsupported,* and unauthorized by my powers, I have deemed capital alterations in our general government indispensibly necessary. . . .

[90] Coxe to Madison, September 25, 1788, October 22, 1788, January 22, 1789, January 29, 1789, MSS, Madison Papers, X; Coxe to Madison, September 20, 1789, *ibid.*, XII. See also, Madison to Coxe, February 16, 1789, *ibid.*, X.

[91] Coxe to Madison, June 11, 1788, MS, Madison Papers, IX.

[92] McMaster, I, 501.

[93] Coxe to Madison, March 31, 1790, MS, Madison Papers, XII. See also, Coxe to Madison, March 21, 1790, *ibid.*, in which he requested information and advice on the situation in Rhode Island. The writer could not find a copy of Coxe's essay.

The first thing I ever committed to paper was the little enquiry into our commerce, wch was printed at the meeting of the convention. Occupied by a profession that is very disagreeable to me and unused to any kind of composition—especially upon subjects of so great moment, you may judge of my anxiety upon the subject of the Constitution when I assure you that I got thro near thirty lengthy publications before the expiration of a year from its formation. My profession was too often postponed—and I am now suffering very seriously for it, and my health was nearly sacrificed by the sedentary habits I was led into.[94]

In the chapter which follows we shall examine Coxe's idea of a national economy. Throughout the whole of the movement for adoption of the Constitution he was motivated by the desire to bring about the basis for national economic development and stability.

[94] Coxe to Madison, September 9, 1789, *ibid.* Later, 1808, when seeking an appointment to office, Coxe wrote Madison as follows: " When I examine the labors of my commercial brethren to improve the trade of our country I find none, who have expended on that subject more pains, time or money than myself. If our present Constitution is a blessing, at least as to industry, no one did more to obtain it than I." Coxe to Madison, August 5, 1808, *ibid.*, XXXIV.

CHAPTER III

THE PLEA FOR A BALANCED NATIONAL ECONOMY

While in itself not a solution to the economic problems of the time, the new government none the less was, as subsequent developments were to show, a valuable instrument to that end. And it was well that it proved to be such; for during the hard fought struggle that brought it into being, conflicting economic interests became more real than ever before. Debtors had been pitted against creditors, the inland against the lowland counties, and the commercial interests against the agrarian. Public spirited men realized that unless these conflicts were in a measure lessened, the confusion and spirit of hopelessness which hitherto characterized the people would continue and, perhaps, be accentuated.

These domestic problems also presented foreign implications. More particularly, the unsettled nature of our commercial relations with Great Britain needed correction. Misconceptions founded upon a distortion of facts continued rife in that country. These, coupled with the sectional conflicts within America, rendered a satisfactory settlement of difficulties trying to both parties.

This, in short, was the situation which faced the first Congress under the new government. Its work of reform was in a large measure the product of the statesmanship of Alexander Hamilton. In accordance with his idea that the national government should be made the " depository of the national interests," [1] he furnished Congress with a series of reports having that object in view. The " Hamiltonian System," a masterful and timely answer to those who demanded constructive action, neatly coincided with the wishes of Tench Coxe, expressed somewhat earlier.

[1] Hamilton, *The Federalist*, No. xxiii, ed. Bourne, I, 156.

In the essay read before the Philadelphia Society for Political Enquiries, May 11, 1787,[2] Coxe enunciated with vigor his conviction that the American economy was in need of reform, and that the latter must be with a view to the creation of a national economy. The people, he reasoned, must consider not only the perplexities of the present but also the possibilities of the future. In more specific language he adduced strong arguments in favor of the introduction of manufacturing enterprise on our part.[3] Our economy could thereby be balanced in its own parts, and the ideal of a nation-state in the economic sense achieved. Aware of the far-reaching implications of such a program, Coxe knew that it could not be readily put into practice. This he showed in his analysis of the economic situation in America.

Agriculture he found, of course, to be foremost in importance.[4] Commerce, while important, was much less so than commonly assumed, even in New England. " Calculations carefully made," Coxe wrote, " do not raise the proportion of property, or the number of men employed in manufactures, fisheries, navigation and trade, to one-eighth of the property and people occupied by agriculture, even in that commercial quarter of the Union." [5] In the

[2] Coxe, " An Enquiry into the principles on which a commercial system for the United States of America should be founded . . . ," in his *View*, pp. 4-33.

[3] The first known indication of Coxe's interest in manufactures is his membership in the United Company of Philadelphia for Promoting American Manufactures, 1775. See above, chap. i, p. 4; below, chap. v. In a letter to Benjamin Franklin, however, undated as to the year, Coxe wrote that " It is almost a year since accident suddenly turned my attention to the subject of American manufactures." Study and observation had convinced him, he added, " that we may derive considerable *immediate* and immense *future* advantages from them." Of the nature of the " accident," Coxe gave no details. Coxe to Franklin, June 22 (?), MS, Franklin Collection, XLVIII, Part I. (Underscoring in original.)

[4] Coxe, " Enquiry," *View*, pp. 6-7.

[5] *Ibid.*, p. 7. Coxe was careful to point out that, in arriving at this estimate, he had " deducted something from the value and population of

country as a whole the proportion was even smaller—
nine out of ten people being engaged in agriculture.[6] On
this score, however, he saw no need for alarm: the future
of the country as founded upon agriculture was a hopeful
one, and nothing should endanger it. But, continued Coxe,
"While we feel an absolute conviction, that our true
interests should refrain us from burdening or impeding
agriculture in any way whatever, we must be ready to
admit, that sound policy requires our giving every encouragement to commerce and its connexions [the fisheries
and manufactures—footnote], which may be found consistent with a due regard to agriculture."[7] In more
concrete terms, he wrote that manufactures should not be
attempted in those states "where the people are fewer,
tillage much more profitable, and provisions dearer than
in several others. . . ."[8] By way of example, South Carolina was described as a farming area; Massachusetts, on
the other hand, should foster manufactures. The two
sections represented by these states should develop in
time a mutual exchange of their products. In this wise
a harmony of interests would be established.[9]

Having declared that manufactures should be developed
in America, and at the same time having pointed to the
dominance of agriculture in the existing economy, it remained for Coxe to show wherein the situation was
favorable to manufacturing enterprise. This he had little
trouble in doing. America, he wrote, had numerous mill
seats that could be used to save manual labor; otherwise,
they "would be given by Providence in vain."[10] Our
climate was ideal for manufactures.[11] The practice of

---

the large towns for the idle and dissipated, for those who live upon
their incomes, and for the supernumerary domestic servants." *Ibid.*, p. 7.
  [6] *Ibid.*, p. 6.   [9] *Ibid.*, pp. 13-14.
  [7] *Ibid.*, p. 9 and footnote.   [10] *Ibid.*, p. 14.
  [8] *Ibid.*, p. 13.
  [11] *Ibid.*, pp. 18-19. He pointed to our "clean air and powerful sun"
as of great value in the process of bleaching cloth. In Europe, "drugs

cash sales obtaining locally would require less capital.[12]
Of raw materials we had many. More would be obtained
by discoveries and improvements in our agriculture, cotton being a notable example.[13] In regard to the controversial question of necessary protection, Coxe found that
a tariff for revenue would suffice. Owing to numerous
charges encountered in the purchase and shipment to this
country of European goods, our manufacturers already
possessed a differential advantage of at least twenty-five
per cent on the least bulky goods. " Here is," Coxe wrote,
" a solid premium, operating like a bounty, while it happily costs the consumer nothing but what he would otherwise be obliged to pay; for the charges of importation
are unavoidable, and the duty being *merely for the purpose of revenue,* is applied to pay the public debts and
expenses of which he owes his proportion." [14] Further
assistance, he added, might be had by permitting the free
importation of raw materials. From the standpoint of the
agricultural interests this, he thought, would be " safe
and expedient." [15] In a final effort to prove his point that
manufacturing enterprise could be profitably pursued by
America and without damage to agriculture, Coxe gave a
long list of articles the manufacture of which " may be
considered as established." [16]

Concluding, Coxe depicted the American economy as
it would be if the measures he suggested were adopted:

In *the foreground* we should find the mass of our citizens—the

---

and machines " were used; these, he thought, impaired the quality of the
cloth.

[12] *Ibid.*, p. 19.

[13] *Ibid.*, p. 20.

[14] *Ibid.*, pp. 16-17. (Italics his.) In a lengthy footnote, *ibid.*, Coxe
explained in detail his calculation of the twenty-five per cent bounty.
He assumed a five per cent revenue tariff.

[15] *Ibid.*, pp. 17-18. Pelatiah Webster in his revenue program, published in 1783, also suggested the free importation of raw materials,
Political Essays, p. 245.

[16] Coxe, " Enquiry," *View*, p. 25.

cultivators (and what is happily for us in most instances the same thing) the independent proprietors of the soil. Every wheel would appear in motion that could carry forward the interests of this great body of our people, and bring into action the inherent powers of the country. A portion of the produce of our lands would be consumed in the families or employed in the business of our manufactures—a further portion would be applied in the sustenance of our merchants and fishermen and their numerous assistants, and the remainder would be transported by those that could carry it at the lowest freight (that is with the smallest deduction from the aggregate profits of the business of the country) to the best foreign markets. *On one side* we should see our manufacturers encouraging the tillers of the earth by the consumption and employment of the fruits of their labours, and supplying them and the rest of their fellow citizens with the instruments of their occupations, and the necessaries and conveniencies of life, in every instance wherein it could be done without unnecessarily distressing commerce and increasing the labours of the husbandmen, and the difficulties of changing our remaining wilds into scenes of cultivation and plenty. Commerce, *on the other hand*, attentive to the general interests, would come foward with offers to range through foreign climates in search of those supplies, which the manufacturers could not furnish but at too high a price, or which nature has not given us at home, in return for the surplus of those stores, that had been drawn from the ocean or produced by the earth.[17]

This is the plea of Coxe for a balanced national economy—for a " system." Only in this manner could we harmonize the diverse economic interests, fully utilize what Nature had endowed us with, and achieve national greatness. In the version here given, one is impressed with the appreciation which Coxe had of the reality of things. He never tired of stressing the dominating importance of agriculture in our economy. Yet he was convinced that the possibilities of manufacturing in this country were great, and should be attended to. Coxe may

[17] *Ibid.*, pp. 23-24. (Italics his.)

be said to have abided by his own precept, namely, "*The circumstances of the country, as they relate to this business* [manufacturing], *should be dispassionately and thoroughly examined.*" [18]

During the summer following his appearance before the Society for Political Enquiries, Coxe was again requested to give a statement of his views upon the subject of manufactures. This particular occasion was an assembly of Philadelphians at the University of Pennsylvania, August 9, 1787, for the purpose of organizing a society for the encouragement of manufactures and the useful arts.[19] In his address to them, Coxe pursued further, but with greater attention to details, the arguments previously given in his " Enquiry."

Manufactures, he asserted, had during colonial times received no assistance whatever. On the contrary, many obstacles were placed in the way of their development. Among these were bounties on the export of British manufactures to us; the " preference for those goods, which habit carried much beyond what their excellence would justify "; and lastly, bounties inducing the exportation to England of semi-manufactures of the colonies.[20] Under such circumstances it was to be expected that agriculture should surpass manufactures in our economy. But now that we were independent of Britain, the situation had measurably changed. Work for those rendered unemployed by the late decline of our navigation; the necessity of a market for the increasing produce of our lands and fisheries; and " *the certainty of supplies in the time of*

[18] *Ibid.,* p. 13. (Italics his.)

[19] Coxe, " An Address to an assembly of friends of American manufactures, convened for the purpose of establishing a society for the encouragement of manufactures and the useful arts, in the University of Pennsylvania, on Thursday, the ninth of August, 1787," in his *View,* pp. 35-54. Hereinafter referred to as Coxe, " Address," *View.*

[20] *Ibid.,* p. 37.

war,"—these factors, he submitted, rendered imperative the establishment of local manufactures.[21]

It had been objected, however, continued Coxe, that " *the high rate of labour,* which involves the price of provisions—*the want of a sufficient number of hands* on any terms, *the scarcity and dearness of raw materials—want of skill* in the business itself and *its unfavorable effects on the health of the people,"* would prevent our developing manufactures.[22] Upon due consideration he found these arguments were not valid.

The scarcity and high price of labor Coxe could not deny; but, as he argued, this difficulty could be overcome by the use of " water-mills, wind-mills, fire, horses, and machines ingeniously contrived. . . ." By these devices labor costs could be reduced; furthermore, the necessity of drawing laborers from agriculture would be avoided. Pointing to the example of Britain, he declared that " Strange as it may appear, they also card, spin and even weave, it is said, by water. . . ." [23] We could do likewise. As for fire (steam power), there was ample opportunity for its use in our industry. This was especially true of those locations where water power was not to be had. Horses could be used for relief from temporary difficulties. But of all these, machines offered the brightest prospect. Use of them directly reduced the demand for human labor. In Europe, " Several instances have been ascertained, in which a few hundreds of women and children performed the work of thousands of carders, spinners, and winders," [24] when machinery is employed. " Perhaps I may be too sanguine," continued Coxe, " but they

[21] *Ibid.* (Italics his.)
[22] *Ibid.*, p. 38. (Italics his.) A good statement of the stock arguments advanced against the development of American manufactures at this time is to be found in Brissot de Warville, *New Travels in the United States of America performed in 1788,* II, 66 ff.
[23] Coxe, " Address," *View,* pp. 38-39.
[24] *Ibid.*, p. 40.

[machines] appear to me fraught with immense advantages to us, and not a little dangerous to the manufacturing nations of Europe. . . ." [25] Improvements in machinery in England, he thought, might throw many workers out of employment there; these people in turn would settle among us.[26] But how were we to obtain machinery? Answering this query, Coxe suggested that we could borrow the inventions of other nations, as well as develop some of our own. The inventive genius of David Rittenhouse, who " epitomized the motions of the spheres, that roll throughout the universe," attested our ability along these lines.[27] If need be, we could stimulate our inventors by offering premiums to be paid in land.[28]

Finally, and of equal importance to Coxe, our labor supply might be increased by foreigners, who, growing tired of the disordered state of affairs in their native lands, unemployment and unnecessary restrictions upon their personal liberty, would come to us in search of freedom and a livelihood.[29] The proposed Society, Coxe advised, should have a committee meet each incoming vessel to inquire as to whether there were aboard any persons " capable of constructing useful machines, qualified to carry on manufactures, or coming to us with a view to that kind of employment." [30] The emphasis here placed upon the use of foreign laborers was not without favorable results. As we shall see later, the Philadelphia Society prompted the migration to our shores of one Samuel Slater—" the father of the American cotton industry." [31]

[25] *Ibid.*
[26] *Ibid.*
[27] *Ibid.*, p. 41.
[28] *Ibid.*, p. 48.
[29] *Ibid.*, p. 42.
[30] *Ibid.*, p. 48. The immigrant laborer, Coxe pointed out, was the mainstay of the handicrafts in Pennsylvania. *Ibid.*, p. 38, footnote. " Agrippa" (James Winthrop), writing in opposition to the adoption of the Constitution by Massachusetts, asserted that Pennsylvania had permitted its morals and intellect to be wrecked by the admission of foreigners! See " Letters of Agrippa," No. ix, December 28, 1787, Ford, *Essays on the Constitution*, p. 79.
[31] See below, chap. v.

Considering next the matter of raw materials, Coxe reiterated what he had said in his " Enquiry." Flax and hemp could be easily supplied domestically in accordance with the demand, he thought.[32] So, too, for wool: the western counties could raise sheep and drive them to market, however bad their road systems.[33] Cotton, the manufacture of which offered great possibilities, could be grown with profit in the southern states.[34] Other raw materials, such for example as silk, iron, lead, copper, madder and other dye stuffs, were to be had readily, though in some cases at high costs, he admitted.[35]

As to the health of the people, it could not be adversely affected by the introduction of manufactures. There were agrarian activities which damaged the health of the people, examples being the reclaiming of marshes, and the cultivation of rice and indigo. But, continued Coxe, " this objection is urged principally against carding, spinning and weaving, which *formerly* were entirely manual and sedentary occupations." In the future, when, as he suggested, " *Horses, and the potent elements of fire and water, aided by the faculties of the human mind, are to be in many instances, our daily laborers,*" [36] this reasoning would lose some of its force. Furthermore, it was to be noted that manufactures would palliate crime by giving

---

[32] Coxe, " Address," *View*, p. 43.

[33] *Ibid.,* pp. 43-44. In a letter to Madison, March 31, 1790, MS, Madison Papers, XII, Coxe attached a memorandum on Spanish wool. In this he said that there was a great deficiency of wool in this country, and advised that we should encourage its importation from Spain in such manner that that country would not become wise to our intentions to develop the woolen industry locally. The development of the woolen industry in this country, Coxe continued, would enable us to frighten the British. This was, as he himself admitted, a " fine-spinning " of the future; cotton supplanted wool in importance soon after the turn of the nineteenth century.

[34] Coxe, " Address," *View*, p. 44. See also, below, chap. v.

[35] *Ibid.,* p. 45.

[36] *Ibid.,* p. 42. (Italics his.)

employment to " such of our poor, as cannot find other honest means of subsistence. . . ." [37]

These were the principal reasons why Coxe believed America could profitably undertake the manufacture of its raw produce. So far as they go, it must be admitted that they were clever and, though not in every respect original, at least economically sound, certainly from a long-time point of view. Coxe was well aware of the extent to which agriculture engaged at a profit most of the people, and that laborers for the development of manufactures were few in number and expensive. By pointing to the use of power-driven machinery and foreign immigrants, however, he possessed a good rebuttal on that score. Few, if any, writers at the time equalled his presentation of the case for the use of machinery and power in the development of American manufactures.[38] William Barton, for example, in an " Essay on the Promotion of American Manufactures," published in *The American Museum,* September, 1787—the month following Coxe's address—dismissed the labor supply question by pointing to the prospect of an increase in the country's population and the settling in our midst of foreign workers.[39] He made no mention of the possible use of machinery.

[37] *Ibid.,* p. 49.

[38] An exception should, however, be made in favor of Silas Deane. In his travels in England Deane used every opportunity to observe English machinery and manufacturing techniques. Writing to Samuel B. Webb from London, July 16, 1785, Deane complained that Americans visited England to purchase goods but never " to learn how they are made, or to inquire into the construction of those ingenious machines by which they are afforded at so low a rate." He lauded the use of steam engines, and added that had he " the means of doing it, and could have an exclusive privilege for a certain number of years," he would introduce them into America. Deane to Webb, July 16, 1785, *New York Historical Society Collections,* XXIII, 460-461.

[39] *The American Museum* (1787), II, 258. Barton was made Secretary of the Philadelphia Society for the Encouragement of Manufactures and the Useful Arts, formed in 1787. See below, chap. v.

But a supply of labor was not all that was needed to establish manufactures in America; the important factors of capital and skill remained. With respect to these, Coxe had nothing to say other than to mention in a footnote the possibility that European workers would bring to us " their capital and skill." [40] Two years later, as will be seen, he was still unable or unwilling to discuss these obstacles. Insofar as the question of capital was concerned, it remained for Hamilton to propound a solution. As regards skill in the practice of manufacturing, the assertion of Coxe proved a valid one in time, as witness Samuel Slater.

Concluding his address, Coxe once again examined the moot question of the relation of manufactures to agriculture. Manufactures he believed to be " *indispensibly necessary to the prosperity of* [the] landed interest." [41] Already, agriculture was " encreasing to super-abundance." [42] The situation therefore demanded a diversification of crops with a view to cultivating that raw produce which could be manufactured locally. By way of example, he cited the fall in the price of wheat, suggesting that more barley should be cultivated in its stead. A market for the barley could be had in the development of the manufacture of malt liquors. [43] In the rich stretches of land along the Ohio, Potomac, and Susquehanna Rivers, wrote Coxe, the time had long since arrived when manufactures were a necessity. Evincing a remarkable prescience, he declared that this particular region would become " the greatest factory of American raw materials for the United States," when these rivers could be freely navigated and the value of their water-power understood. [44]

[40] Coxe, " Address," *View*, p. 53, footnote.
[41] *Ibid.*, p. 55. (Italics his.)
[42] *Ibid.*, p. 53.
[43] *Ibid.*, pp. 43, 51. See also, " Enquiry," *View*, p. 15, where the same idea is stated.
[44] Coxe, " Address," *View*, p. 53.

The ideas expressed by Coxe in this address, as well as those given earlier in his " Enquiry," constitute his conception of the need for and the method by which we could consolidate our economic interests. That this should come about he had not the slightest doubt. His work in behalf of the adoption of the Constitution had that end in view. " A weak and relaxed civil authority and a very sparse and extending population," he wrote Madison, September 20, 1789, " presented to my mind no prospect of the restoration of order among ourselves, or of confidence among our foreign friends." [45] Given a strong national government, the country was in need of manufactures to " cement " the people together. The south would be agricultural; the north would annually increase its manufactures. An exchange of goods would follow.[46] As between the upland and lowland counties, there was likewise a need for greater economic contacts. Our rivers, Coxe wrote Madison earlier in the same year, should be cleared to their headwaters; canal and road systems should be constructed.[47] An exchange of goods could thereby be fostered between the two regions, while at the same time excluding the British and Spanish from this lucrative trade. A further reason for such a program he found in the necessity of maintaining contacts with large numbers of our people who were then migrating westward.[48]

[45] Coxe to Madison, September 20, 1789, MS, Madison Papers, XII.

[46] Ibid. See also, Coxe, " Thoughts on the Present Situation of the United States," dated October, 1788, and printed in The American Museum (1788), IV, 401-404. He here called attention to the progress of American manufactures. A copy of this essay appears to have been sent by Coxe to Madison, with the suggestion that it be re-printed in Virginia. Coxe to Madison, October 22, 1788, MS, Madison Papers, X.

[47] Coxe to Madison, April 21, 1789, ibid., XI. Virginia in particular was confronted with this problem; her western delegates had opposed ratification of the Constitution in the State Convention on the grounds that were they to do so, the Mississippi River would be closed to them. See Grigsby, I, 232-247.

[48] Coxe to R. R. Livingston, February 15, 1789, MS, Roberts Collection, Haverford College Library.

In order to bring his view of American economic potentialities before the first Congress, Coxe wrote and published his *Observations on the Agriculture, Manufactures
and Commerce of the United States. In a letter to a
Member of Congress. By a Citizen of the United States.*[49]
The member of Congress referred to was Peter Muhlenberg, of Pennsylvania. He, before departing for New
York, had requested Coxe to write out anew his views on
the subject of manufactures.[50] In addition to his *Observations,* Coxe also prepared at this time some notes
on a proposed revenue system for the United States. These
he forwarded to Madison.[51]

From the standpoint of systematic approach and cogency
of argument, the *Observations* are somewhat superior
to the earlier attempts of Coxe to investigate the subject
of manufactures. His task in this essay was to examine
the agriculture, commerce, and manufactures of the United
States so as to reveal their present status, the influence of
one upon the other, and to suggest a general plan of
action with respect to them.[52] In some preliminary remarks, he appropriately observed that in any particular
measure of the government the interest of any individual
could not be singled out; the promotion of the general
interests must be its object, despite slight harm to particular groups. Our commercial policies, moreover, should

[49] Published in New York, 1789. Hereinafter referred to as Coxe,
Observations.

[50] See Coxe to Madison, April 21, 1789, MS, Madison Papers, XI.
Coxe here suggested that Madison get hold of the *Observations,* presumably then in manuscript. In a letter to Dr. Benjamin Rush, January
13, 1788, Coxe wrote that manufactures "will require a delicate hand
to manage them with the union at large." MS, Correspondence of Dr.
Benjamin Rush, XXVII.

[51] Coxe to Madison, March 24, 1789, MS, Madison Papers, XI. Coxe
recommended that Madison make these notes available to Messrs. Maclay,
Fitzsimons, Morris, and Clymer, all of whom were members of Congress
from Pennsylvania. (The notes are not preserved in the Papers.)

[52] Coxe, *Observations,* pp. 8-9.

always be such that differences between states would be eliminated as far as possible. In other words, the government must seek a consolidation of diverse economic interests. Having made these general observations, Coxe proceeded to an examination of agriculture.

Agriculture, he asserted, was the foundation of a nation's wealth;[53] it was the most useful, honorable, and important pursuit of this country. Where we could produce enough of a given commodity for our own needs, there should be an exclusion of foreign products of a similar nature. As examples, he cited beef, butter, cheese, indigo, and iron.[54] Iron was included under the heading of agriculture, since he took the latter to include all extractive industries. Where products could be had here in sufficient quantities but were not, he believed that provision should be made for duties and bounties upon them in order that we might become self-sustaining. Examples falling in this class were silk, hemp, and wine. A further reason why we should promote the cultivation of these lay in the fact that other branches of our agriculture were already amply developed. Duties alone he did not think were sufficient to bring about diversification; hence the provision for bounties (premiums).[55] Furthermore, Coxe declared that we should attempt to enlarge our foreign markets through the negotiation of commercial treaties.[56]

But the most profitable method to advance the agricultural interest was, Coxe wrote, the development of manufactures in this country. "The various articles of manufacture made use of by a people," he observed, " amount to a much greater sum than those of subsistence,

---

[53] *Ibid.*, p. 13. On page 84, however, Coxe wrote: " Agriculture and manufactures, I consider as the sources and foundation of national wealth. Commerce the handmaid, or medium, by which the surplus productions of agriculture and manufactures are turned to the best account. . . ." This statement more accurately defines his theory which, it may be said, was not always consistently adhered to.

[54] *Ibid.*, pp. 13-14.   [55] *Ibid.*, pp. 15-17.   [56] *Ibid.*, p. 18.

including every luxury; consequently were a nation so circumstanced as to be obliged to make a choice, it would be found more advantageous to attend to its manufactures, and depend on other nations for its means of subsistence, than to supply itself with these and depend on other nations for its manufactures." [57] Moreover, " An agricultural nation which exports its raw materials, and imports its manufactures, never can be opulent, because every profitable advantage which can be derived from its productions is given into the hands of the manufacturing nation." [58] The difference he estimated (presumably in terms of profit) to be about three hundred per cent in favor of the manufacturing nation. A people devoted exclusively to agriculture could therefore never become powerful.[59] To substantiate this argument, Coxe cited Connecticut as a state which had reached its *ne plus ultra.* If manufactures were introduced there, support could be had for 800,000 people and not just its present 200,000, he declared.[60] In other words, a balanced economy would make for a greater production of wealth. Viewing the nation as a whole, the degree to which its wealth might rise was determined, according to Coxe, by its export surplus.[61] Put otherwise, a nation would become wealthy

[57] *Ibid.*, p. 19.

[58] *Ibid.*, pp. 18-19.

[59] *Ibid.*, p. 19.

[60] *Ibid.* That Coxe was correct in his view here is attested by the fact that by 1818 Connecticut had deveolped such a surplus population as to cause heavy emigration to other sections; its manufactures had not been sufficiently advanced. See Grace Pierpont Fuller, *An Introduction to the History of Connecticut as a Manufacturing State* (" Smith College Studies in History," I, No. 1), p. 26.

[61] Coxe, *Observations*, p. 20. Coxe never defined his use of the expression, " wealth of a nation." It appears that he thought of a wealthy nation as one whose inhabitants were flourishing because they engaged jointly in manufactures and agriculture. Writing of Adam Smith, Professor Cannan notes that " A rich or wealthy ' country,' no doubt, suggested to him, as it does to us, not flourishing inhabitants so much as a large produce from a given area of land." Edwin Cannan, *A History of the Theories of Production and Distribution . . .* , p. 12.

in proportion as it relied less and less upon other nations for its manufactures.

Examining next the benefits which this country could expect to derive from manufactures, Coxe listed these: our national strength would be increased; "circulating property," by which he meant the precious metals, would be retained; the greatest possible value would be given to agricultural produce; a more profitable commerce would ensue; and lastly, our imports would consist of those goods that would add eventually to our wealth.[62]

It had been objected, however, that we could buy goods abroad cheaper than we could produce them ourselves. Answering this objection, Coxe took labor expended as " the original standard " by which the value of goods must be assessed. On this nebulous basis he believed that we paid more for our imports than it would cost us to manufacture them ourselves.[63] Precisely what Coxe had in mind when he wrote this is not clear from the text, especially since he went on to point out that less labor was applied in foreign manufactures than in our own.[64] It would therefore follow from his analysis that Britain could undersell us. Here as elsewhere in his analysis, Coxe was prone to be careless and superficial. In expressing the belief that increased local production would bring lower prices, he was taking a more secure position.[65] In reply to the assertion that the cheapness of land would always attract the people, Coxe wrote that foreigners would come to us who either did not know how to farm or care to learn. They would find employment in our manufactures. Again, it was to be noted that agriculture was a much more laborious pursuit than manufactures; many would therefore prefer the latter.[66] Finally, Coxe answered those who argued that manufactures would

[62] Coxe, *Observations*, p. 22.
[63] *Ibid.*, p. 23.
[64] *Ibid.*, p. 24.
[65] *Ibid.*
[66] *Ibid.*, pp. 25-26.

harm our agriculture and commerce by curtailing our foreign markets. The home market would be expanded by manufactures, he wrote. In addition, commerce would eventually be supplied with manufactured goods to carry abroad.[67] Concluding this phase of his discussion, Coxe declared that Great Britain labored under greater difficulties than those facing us in establishing her manufacturing enterprise.[68]

Satisfied that he had dispelled the arguments of those who thought we could not manufacture, Coxe proceeded to a consideration of what was needed to develop local manufactures. First, of course, was a sufficient capital. Following the Peace we had, he wrote, the necessary capital, but this we squandered in the needless importation of foreign luxuries. Looking to the future, he asserted that protective measures by the government would offer assistance in obtaining capital.[69] How this was to come about, Coxe was unwilling or unable to explain. As with many other points made by him, he left too much to be taken for granted. Continuing his exposition of the advantages possessed by America, Coxe emphasized the abundance of raw materials. Our cultivators and planters, he wrote, should raise their crops with the demands of manufacturers in view; in short, they should develop the home market.[70] Finally, he considered a protective tariff, then a pressing problem before Congress. On this score he advised that where goods were already produced domestically in sufficient quantities, their importation should be prohibited; where there was the likelihood that an industry would be able to supply the home demand, it should be accorded " a small preference " by a tariff.[71] In the first group he listed over seventy-five articles, among which were anchors, axes, sheet iron, boots and shoes,

[67] *Ibid.*, pp. 26-27.   [70] *Ibid.*, p. 29.
[68] *Ibid.*, p. 27.   [71] *Ibid.*, p. 30.
[69] *Ibid.*, pp. 28-29.

coaches and carriages, fire engines, backgammon tables, clocks, gold and silver plate, wool and cotton cards, musical instruments, and hats.[72]   In reply to the assertion that prohibitions would enable the domestic manufacturers to charge high prices, Coxe answered that without such a measure we shall never get manufactures; that granted prices did rise, it would only be for a short time, since competition would operate to bring them down. In any event, he added, the general interest would have been advanced.[73] " A premature monopoly of the markets," which Hamilton advised against in *The Federalist*,[74] did not enter the mind of Coxe. In the second group, where moderate protection was needed, Coxe included all kinds of cloth, whether made of hemp, cotton, wool, or linen, hosiery, iron shovels and spades, fire arms, gunpowder, paper, and other items.[75]

In concluding his examination of manufactures, Coxe suggested other methods whereby they might be advanced: prohibition of exports of raw materials that could be made up here, citing furs; free importation of such commodities needed in the development of our manufactures but not yet produced in sufficient quantities locally, citing cotton, wool, machines, instruments, fancy woods and several others; special encouragements for the introduction of new manufacturing arts; and lastly, some exemptions from taxation. " The very idea of patronage gives life and vigor to industry and arts." [76]

The final section of the *Observations* was devoted to commerce. The function of commerce, Coxe wrote, was primarily the disposition of surpluses; " and so long

[72] *Ibid.*, pp. 30-31.

[73] *Ibid.*, pp. 30-32. Coxe at this point digressed to point out that the publication of the Scriptures should be regulated; he had seen, he said, some American editions which were faulty. *Ibid.*, p. 32.

[74] Hamilton, *The Federalist*, No. xxxv, ed. Bourne, I, 223.

[75] Coxe, *Observations*, pp. 32-33.

[76] *Ibid.*, pp. 33-34.

as the commerce of two nations or countries is carried on with this in view, and confined within the limits of this rule, it answers its original and essential purpose." [77] Insofar as the prices of merchandise in a given market were concerned, commerce was, he admitted, self-regulatory; but not otherwise. The government, therefore, must intervene, finding justification in the fact that, " The chain of a free and universal commercial intercourse being once broken, by any one nation, every other nation included in the circle of correspondence, is laid under an obligation thereby to secure their own interests, and retain their just share of advantages." [78] In a word, free trade must be universal to be practicable. More specifically, Coxe wrote that America in her foreign trade should import, first, those commodities which could not be supplied domestically; second, any further balance in her favor should be had in " circulating medium." [79] Under no circumstances should luxuries be imported.[80] The prevailing unfavorable balance of trade he found to be not only undesirable but also unnecessary.[81] Accounting for our indebtedness abroad, he pointed to British monopolistic practices in their trade with us, to " the mercenary views " of our merchants, and to liberal credit accorded us abroad. The last-mentioned was especially unfavorable to our best interests, he continued, since it made for higher prices to cover risks and encouraged the importation of luxuries. To avoid this difficulty, he accordingly suggested that a law be passed whereby, from and after five years, no debt

[77] *Ibid.*, p. 43.

[78] *Ibid.*, p. 35.

[79] *Ibid.*, pp. 43, 57.

[80] *Ibid.*, pp. 44-45. See also, pp. 48-49, wherein he deplored the importation by Connecticut of West Indian rum in exchange for horses. The former was of no sound use to us, he advised.

[81] *Ibid.*, p. 57. Coxe opposed our trade with Asia, asserting that it amounted to an extraction of specie. *Ibid.*, p. 41. See also, p. 75, where, for the same reason, our trade with Nova Scotia is objected to.

contracted in Europe could be recoverable in American courts. Stimulation of our manufactures and caution in the creation of debt would follow, he concluded.[82] In any event, the government should take steps to turn the balance of trade in our favor.[83]

In conclusion, Coxe stressed the fact that regulation of commerce could be made a good source of revenue. Property taxes, he wrote in this connection, were grossly unequal in their incidence, aside from other disadvantages. If import duties were employed, they could be levied upon luxuries, thereby placing the burden of taxation where it belonged, namely, upon the rich. Federal regulation of commerce, then, would have three objectives: to derive as much revenue as possible from the rich; to curb the importation of luxuries; and to foster local manufactures.[84] Since Coxe would have the importation of more than seventy-five articles prohibited, including luxuries, it is hardly probable that his revenue scheme could have been a very productive one. In addition to being inconsistent with respect to the matter of luxuries, Coxe also overlooked the truth that a revenue tariff to be productive must have moderate duties and few prohibitions. However, he did recommend internal taxes on carriages, race horses, and packs of hounds; also an excise on rum, brandy, whiskey, tobacco, loaf sugar, gold and silver plate, jewelry, playing cards, hair powder, and other items entering the budgets of the rich.[85] Thus the tax system could be made flexible.

In ascribing a threefold purpose to the regulation of commerce, Coxe was not original. Pelatiah Webster had advanced a similar program in his " Sixth Essay on Free Trade and Finance," published in March, 1783.[86] During the preceding year, Hamilton, in the report on Rhode

---

[82] *Ibid.*, pp. 58-63.
[83] *Ibid.*, p. 57.
[84] *Ibid.*, p. 83.

[85] *Ibid.*, pp. 79-83, 88.
[86] Webster, *Political Essays*, pp. 239-245.

Island's objections to a federal impost, wrote in like terms, though he did not then consider protection to local manufactures.[87]   Later, in *The Federalist*, he developed the subject in its entirety; [88] his analysis of the problem there is much superior to that of Coxe, who apparently wrote out this phase of his *Observations* in great haste.

The question of an appropriate tariff was, as Coxe knew, one which the first Congress had to face at the outset.   Debates upon the subject began, in fact, on April 8, 1789, when James Madison submittted for consideration the impost which Congress had advocated without success since 1783.[89]   On the next day, Fitzsimons of Pennsylvania came forward with a plea for a permanent system of duties, " adequate to our present situation, as it respects our agriculture, our manufactures, and our commerce." [90]   After much debate, the members agreed to this proposition, rather than that of Madison.[91]   As stated in its preamble, the tariff was " necessary for the support of government, for the discharge of the debts of the United States, and the encouragement and protection of manufactures." [92]   It included none of the prohibitions

[87] William Hill, " The First Stages of the Tariff Policy of the United States," *Publications of the American Economic Association*, VIII, No. 6, 105, Appendix No. xiii.

[88] Hamilton, *The Federalist*, No. xxi, ed. Bourne, I, 139; see also, *ibid.*, Nos. xxx-xxxvi.

[89] *Annals of Congress*, 1st Cong., 1st sess., pp. 106-107.

[90] *Ibid.*, p. 110.

[91] *Ibid.*, pp. 106 ff.; Hill, pp. 109-129, gives a careful analysis of the debates.

[92] Tariff Act of July 4, 1789, *Tariff Acts Passed by the Congress of the United States from 1789 to 1909*, 61st Cong., 2d sess., H. Doc. No. 671, p. 13.   The extent to which the framers of this tariff had in mind protection for American manufactures has been questioned.   Hill has given strong arguments in support of the contention that protection was as much its purpose as revenue.   Consult also, Frank W. Taussig, *The Tariff History of the United States*, pp. 14-15; Henry Carter Adams, *Taxation in the United States, 1789-1816* (" Johns Hopkins University Studies in Historical and Political Science," 2d Series, V-VI), pp. 25-26;

which Coxe had suggested; instead, it properly levied moderate duties, both specific and *ad valorem*. Writing in 1794 Coxe referred to it as a "revenue tariff," and stated that it had been of great benefit to our manufactures.[93] A duty of three cents per lb. on cotton, to be effective from and after December 1, 1790, was, however, especially obnoxious to him, as we shall see later.[94]

Although the Tariff of 1789 did not provide as much protection to American manufactures as Coxe at the time seemed to desire, the debates occasioned by it none the less served to impress upon the public mind the importance of the subject. Congress, the following January, thought it expedient that a study of our manufacturing enterprise be made, and accordingly requested the Secretary of the Treasury to undertake the task. This step must have been gratifying to Coxe; it offered the prospect of securing a greater attention to the subject than had his own essays.

Shortly after Hamilton had been called upon to make the report, he needed a new assistant owing to the retirement from the Treasury of William Duer. Learning of this opening, Coxe on April 6th and 27th wrote Hamilton to offer his services.[95] Hamilton, who had already received from Coxe "much useful information and many valuable observations,"[96] readily accepted the offer. This

Ugo Rabbeno, *The American Commercial Policy*, pp. 119 ff., 309; O. L. Elliott, *The Tariff Controversy, 1789-1833*, p. 73. Taussig agrees with Hill. Adams and Rabbeno interpret the purpose of the tariff of 1789 as one of retaliation to the British restrictive commercial policy. Elliott states that its purpose was primarily to bring in revenue.

[93] Coxe, "Summary Statement of Facts which characterize American People and their Country," *View*, p. 429.

[94] Below, chap. v.

[95] See Hamilton to Coxe, May 1, 1790, quoted in White, pp. 180-181.

[96] Hamilton to Coxe, December 24, 1789, quoted in White, p. 180. Coxe on November 30 and December 16, 1789, forwarded to Hamilton at the latter's request one paper on navigation, two the subjects of which were not mentioned, and two on foreign affairs. These letters are reprinted in White, pp. 178-179 and 179-180, respectively.

he did in a letter to Coxe, May 1st, 1790, adding that
" The state of public business under my care, is such as
to make me desire to see you as soon as may consist with
the dispositions which your change of situation will render
necessary." [97]

As the assistant to Hamilton, there can be little doubt
that Coxe played an important rôle in the preparation of
the famous *Report on Manufactures*. Hamilton, busy at
the time with the administration of the public debt, in all
probability relied heavily upon Coxe in the gathering of
material for the report, which he submitted to Congress in
December, 1791.[98] On March 10, 1791, for example, we
find Coxe addressing a circular letter to William Webb,
Collector for Bath, Massachusetts, in which he requested
that information on the manufactures, commerce, fisheries, and navigation of that state be forwarded to the
Treasury Department. " These things frequently offer
Gentlemen in public stations valuable assistance," he
wrote, " and will be of the greatest importance to this
country, which 'till the last two years has had few national officers." [99] The material so gathered and which

[97] Hamilton to Coxe, May 1, 1790, *ibid.*, pp. 180-181. See also,
Hamilton to Pickering, May 13, 1790, *The Works of Alexander Hamilton*, ed. Henry Cabot Lodge, IX, 468.

[98] *Report, American State Papers, Finance*, I, 123-144.

[99] See circular letter, dated March 10, 1791, and signed by Tench
Coxe, in U. S. Treasury Department Circulars, September 24, 1789—July
31, 1802, Library of Congress; also letter of George Cabot, January 24,
1791, probably addressed to Coxe. Hamilton Manuscripts, X. Dr.
Arthur H. Cole, in his *Industrial and Commercial Correspondence of
Alexander Hamilton anticipating his Report on Manufactures*, Introduction, p. xviii, states that the original circular letter was dated June 22,
1791. This could hardly be in light of the letter of Coxe, above cited.
" A Mechanic," writing in the *Independent Gazetteer* of Philadelphia in
criticism of the S. U. M. (see below), declared that William Duer, who
preceded Coxe as Hamilton's assistant, had written in quest of facts on
manufactures for Hamilton's use in the report. Davis, I, 436. See also,
White, pp. 49-50, who wrote that " there can be no doubt that Washington's first secretary of the treasury is indebted for those valuable sta-

has been preserved to the present time is, as has been pointed out, conspicuously devoid of reports from the middle states.[100] It is probable that, aside from his own knowledge of this region, Hamilton saw fit to rely upon Coxe who was, as his essays show, well versed in developments there.[101]

The extent to which Hamilton made use of the ideas of Coxe in drafting his report is impossible to determine exactly upon the basis of available material. A comparison of the report with the three essays of Coxe, in particular his *Observations*, does not reveal any striking similarities which would warrant the belief that Hamilton made extensive use of Coxe's ideas.[102] Many ideas are, of course, common to both. For example, both writers stressed the advantageous use to which labor-saving machinery could be put in this country; also the employment of immigrants so as to avoid a drain on agricultural

tistics, which enabled him to draw up his report on manufactures, to the important assistance of Tench Coxe."

[100] Cole, pp. xxiv-xxv, who adds that he does not think the material could have been lost.

[101] Cole, *ibid.*, points out that Hamilton was obviously familiar with the middle states; furthermore, that he made use of an essay on American manufactures by William Barton of Philadelphia. Dr. Cole overlooks the important fact that Hamilton had Tench Coxe assisting him at this time, and that Coxe was especially equipped with a knowledge of this and other sections of the country. See, for example, Coxe's "A Summary View of the State of Pennsylvania," written during the middle of 1790, *View*, pp. 57 ff.; also, the account which he gives in his "A Brief Examination of Lord Sheffield's Observations on the Commerce of the United States," *ibid.*, pp. 157-158, of the hat industry in the western counties of Pennsylvania.

[102] See, however, above, Preface, p. viii. The interesting manner in which Hamilton made use of Adam Smith has been discussed at length by Rabbeno, pp. 313 ff.; and Edward G. Bourne, "Alexander Hamilton and Adam Smith," *Quarterly Journal of Economics,* VIII, 328-344. It was noted earlier by Charles F. Dunbar, "Economic Science in America, 1776-1876," *North American Review,* CXXII, 131; and by Adams, *Taxation in the United States, 1789-1816,* p. 21. William Graham Sumner, *Alexander Hamilton,* p. 108, erroneously denied Hamilton's use of Smith in the report.

labor.[103]   Bounties and premiums, protecting duties and prohibitions, were recommended by each.[104]   Above all, the idea that a secure home market is preferable to an uncertain foreign one was emphasized by the two; both believed that a nation which does not combine manufactures with agriculture cannot achieve the highest degree of national opulence.[105]

In short, it may be said that the circumstances prevailing at the time—a deranged and choked foreign commerce, a farm produce approaching superabundance, and absence of a sense of mutual dependence of the economic interests within the country—gave rise to the promulgation of an identical economic program on the part of Hamilton and Coxe.   That program was, as we have seen, one of economic consolidation; it was an economic answer to a problem that was in a large measure political. Such a conception of the national interest could not have been otherwise if it were to answer the needs of the time.[106]

[103] See Hamilton, *Report, American State Papers, Finance*, I, 126-127; Coxe, above, pp. 83-84, 86, and 92.

[104] Hamilton, *Report, American State Papers, Finance*, I, 135-136; Coxe, above, pp. 80, 84, 90, and 93 ff.; also, Coxe to Madison, March 21, 1790, MS, Madison Papers, XII, in which he suggested that Congress lay off a million acres of choice western land as the basis of a fund to reward inventors, native and foreign.   Ten days later, Coxe wrote Madison again upon this subject, stating that the idea was an old one with him.   Coxe to Madison, March 31, 1790, *ibid*. Hamilton's references to a price differential of from 15 to 30 per cent existing in the American markets, our goods as compared with foreign, and operating as a natural bounty in favor of the development of American manufactures, may have been at the instance of Coxe.   Coxe, as we have seen, had written at length upon this point.   See Hamilton, *Report, American State Papers, Finance*, I, pp. 130, 136; Coxe, above, p. 80.

[105] Hamilton, *Report, American State Papers, Finance*, I, 127-128, 133-134; Coxe, above, pp. 87, 90-92.

[106] See Charles A. Beard, *The Idea of National Interest*, pp. 48-49; Frederick Scott Oliver, *Alexander Hamilton: An Essay on the American Union*, pp. 466-467; Cole, pp. 231-243; Rabbeno, p. 309.   Cf., however, Sumner, pp. 172-173, wherein he deems the program of Hamilton to be little more than a resurrection of mercantilism.

In addition to the *Report on Manufactures,* there was
another important matter which engaged the attention
of Hamilton when he made Coxe his assistant, or soon
thereafter. Desirous of creating a concrete example of
what might follow were the theory of the report accepted,
Hamilton had interested himself financially and pro-
motionally in the formation of a manufacturing concern.[107]
Known as the New Jersey Society for Establishing Useful
Manufactures (S. U. M.), this enterprise was incorporated
by the Legislature of that state on November 22, 1791—
two weeks before the report was submitted to Congress.[108]
To Coxe it was a pleasing proposition, and one in which
he doubtless had an active hand.

The first suggestion in the newspapers of the idea of
such a manufacturing concern was made by Coxe in the
third of a series of six essays which he wrote in the early
part of 1791 under the general title, *A Brief Examination of Lord Sheffield's Observations on the Commerce of
the United States.*[109] Lord Sheffield was the most prominent exponent in Great Britain of the view that Americans
in achieving independence had committed political and
economic suicide. These sentiments he voiced in his *Observations on the Commerce of the American States with
Europe and the West Indies,* first published in 1783.[110]

---

[107] Davis, I, 349, 366.

[108] *Ibid.,* pp. 349, 352. Dr. Davis has written at length on the
S. U. M., *ibid.,* I, 349-518; liberal use of his account is made in what
follows.

[109] First printed in *The American Museum,* the third number appearing in April, 1791. In the same year it was enlarged and published
separately in Philadelphia by Carey, Stewart & Co. (copy in the Library
of Congress, Miscellaneous Pamphlets, Vol. 1092). In 1794 Coxe incorporated the essays in his *View,* pp. 111-279. Davis, I, 350, credits Coxe
with having first publicly suggested the idea.

[110] The work by the following year had gone through six enlarged editions. George Chalmers wrote in a similar vein in his *Opinions on
Interesting Subjects of Public Law and Commercial Policy. . . .* For
an account of Sheffield, see *Dictionary of National Biography* (British),

The work was widely read in this country, and several writers here undertook to answer it.[111] In brief, Sheffield asserted that the independence of America should in no wise occasion an alteration in the Navigation System, which he dubbed "the guardian of the prosperity of Britain." [112] The British empire could and should be self-sufficing; trade relations with America must be reduced to a minimum.[113] The economic future of America he characterized as hopeless. In particular, he saw no prospects of our ever manufacturing to any great extent.[114]

That Coxe should have answered Sheffield's work in 1791 can be explained by the fact that, first, it carried weight in British circles, governmental and private, and hence was a target worth shooting at; second, in 1791 he had at his command a complete collection of data relating to the American economy, details of which he could in this manner put before the public, American and British; and third, it would make an excellent background for his

XXVII, 201; *Palgrave's Dictionary of Political Economy*, III, 390-391. Coxe, writing in 1807, referred to Sheffield as Britain's "most distinguished commercial writer, member of the Irish lords and British commons." See Coxe, *An Examination of the Conduct of Great Britain respecting Neutrals*, p. 69.

[111] James McHenry, "Observations relative to a commercial treaty with Great Britain, &c. written in 1784," *The American Museum* (1789), V, 317-319, 464-467, 550-554; "Essay on the advantages of trade and commerce," by "American," dated 1786, Charleston, *ibid.* (1787), II, 328-332; "Reflexions on the policy and necessity of encouraging the commerce of the citizens of the United States of America, and of granting them exclusive privileges in trade—written by St. George Tucker, Esq. of Petersburg," *ibid.* (1787), II, 263-276; Wm. Bingham, *A Letter from an American containing strictures on Sheffield's Observations* . . . , Duane Pamphlets, Library of Congress, Vol. 86, No. 1; Wm. Bingham to Thos. Fitzsimons, London, November 29, 1783, MS, Gratz Collection, case 1, box 3.

[112] Sheffield, *Observations*, 6th ed., p. 1. Coxe made use of this edition in his attack.

[113] *Ibid.*, pp. 223, 226, for example.

[114] *Ibid.*, pp. 239-240.

plea for manufacturing establishments in this country, of which the S. U. M. was to be an example.[115]

In his "Brief Examination" Coxe did not follow any definite plan, and his work accordingly suffers.[116] In answering the sweeping assertions of Lord Sheffield as regards the future of American manufactures, however, Coxe drew heavily upon the returns of the United States marshals.[117] He was thus able to show that America already possessed numerous manufactures.[118] Our country, he would have the reader understand, was an economic power with which Britain must reckon. "Should impediments be thrown in the way of our fisheries, shipping and foreign commerce, there can be no doubt that policy, interest and feeling will prompt us to pursue with decision and ardour the object of *manufactures,* which will give employment to our own capital, and that which we may derive from foreigners," Coxe wrote.[119] To facilitate the growth of our manufactures, the government need not rashly impose "*generally* heavy duties, burdensome to the nation. . . ." Instead, it may accord "effectual encouragement *to one branch of manufactures at a time.*" [120] The re-

[115] See Coxe's Introduction to his "Brief Examination," *View,* pp. 111-112; also, Coxe to Jefferson, March 20, 1791, MS, Jefferson Papers, LXII.

[116] As Coxe put it, "any important object, which presents itself, will be concisely noticed." "Brief Examination," *View,* p. 114.

[117] See for example, the two tables depicting the status of household manufactures in Virginia, "Brief Examination," *View,* pp. 260-261, obviously from the Virginia returns for 1791. The last mentioned are reproduced in Cole, pp. 93 ff.

[118] See, for example, shoes, "Brief Examination," *View,* p. 122; linseed oil, *ibid.,* pp. 140-141; coaches and carriages, *ibid.,* pp. 141-142; iron and steel, *ibid.,* pp. 144-146; books, *ibid.,* pp. 160-162. An English reviewer of Coxe's essays admitted that the predictions of Sheffield were disapproved by Coxe. See *The Monthly Review* (London, 1792), IX, 220.

[119] "Brief examination," *View,* p. 221. (Italics in original.) In a footnote, p. 223, Coxe gave a long list of goods already being manufactured in America. The value of these, he pointed out, exceeded that of the exports of Great Britain to all countries other than America.

[120] *Ibid.,* p. 222. (Italics in original.)

finement of the position taken with respect to protection in his *Observations* is worthy of note. There, as has been pointed out, Coxe advised numerous prohibitions. Continuing, Coxe wrote:

If it be selected with judgment—if the use of manual labour be confined within as narrow limits as possible—if labour-saving machines be used—if the raw articles it works on, be made free of impost duty—if the growth of them be encouraged at home— if a convenient progressive duty be imposed, there can be little doubt of success. The example of a well-arranged and fortunate attempt once set, others will naturally follow; and nations, some of whose politicians now grudgingly perceive them to take from us food they are unable to raise, and who treat as a favour the reception of our precious raw materials, may discover, when it will be too late, the evils induced by an over-driven spirit of monopoly.[121]

"The example of a well-arranged and fortunate attempt," to which Coxe here referred, was unquestionably the S. U. M. The details of such a project he gave the reader in the third essay as follows:

The first judicious European capitalists, who shall take good situations in the United States, and establish manufactories, by labour-saving machines, must rapidly and certainly make fortunes. They cannot, it is presumed, be long insensible to this; but if they should continue so, the appreciation of our public stocks will probably bring some of our own capitalists into the business. The public creditors, the owners of perhaps fifteen millions sterling of now inactive wealth, might at this moment do much towards the introduction of the cotton mills, wool-mills, flax and hemp-mills, and other valuable branches of machine manufacturing. It is past doubt, that were a company of persons of character and judgment to subscribe a stock for this purpose of 500,000 dollars in the public paper, they might obtain upon a deposit of it, a loan of as much coin from some foreign nation, at an interest less than six per cent. Were such a company to be

[121] *Ibid.*, pp. 222-223.

incorporated, to have its stock transferable as in a bank, to receive subscriptions from 400 dollars upwards, to purchase 500 or 1000 acres of land well situated for receiving imported materials and exporting their fabrics—were they to erect works in the centre of such a body of land, to lay out their grounds in a convenient town-plat, and to proceed with judgment and system in their plan, they would be sure of success in their manufactories; they would raise a valuable town upon their land, and would help to support the value of the public debt.

Were a few establishments, like that described, to take place (and there are room and funds for many of them) even the manufactories of *piece goods,* of every kind in which machinery could be applied, would soon be introduced with profit into the United States. It cannot, on cool reflection, be expected, that a country remote from all the manufacturing nations, able to produce the requisite raw materials and provisions, and subject to many interruptions in their exportation to foreign markets, will continue to depend on distant transmarine sources, for the mass of her necessary supplies. The wonderful progress of other nations, which have commenced manufactures under disadvantages much greater than any we have to contend with, will powerfully incite us to exertion. . . .[122]

This account of the proposed manufactory appeared, to repeat, in the April, 1791 issue of *The American Museum.* On the fifteenth of the same month Coxe forwarded to Jefferson a more detailed outline of it, entitled, " A Plan for a Manufacturing establishment in the United States." In the letter accompanying the " Plan," Coxe wrote:

I have taken the liberty to enclose to you a plan of a manufacturing establishment which it is possible may apply happily in the federal district. I am not certain that any but the fine arts are desirable in a great degree at the actual seat of Congress, but in a tract of 64,000 acres there may be a scene, wherein a great power of water may be found, and in which this scheme might be carried into execution. It is a favorite idea of mine on the subject of manufactures, that this country should endeavor to employ

[122] *Ibid.*, pp. 165-167.   (Italics in original.)

in them, as much as possible, the great labor saving machines. Agriculture being the most natural employment & manufacturers being often an intemperate and disorderly class of people, modes of manufacture which do not require them, and which indeed in a certain degree supercede the occasion for them, appear to be very desirable. This sketch is meant to be disposed of as you may think proper. I have retained a copy of it, if I should have occasion for it. I would just observe that the mode of raising *the fund* was obtained from the Secretary of the Treasury, who has every reason to believe that an establishment embracing the principal ideas in the plan will be very soon attempted in New Jersey upon subscriptions from New York, New Jersey & Pennsylvania. It may be worth considering whether the Potomack Navigation Company might not find it their interest to admit of sales of shares for 6% stock estimated at par, and when they shall have sold the whole a loan at $5\frac{1}{4}$% might be effected. The public paper would yield an interest more than equal to what they would have to pay and when our funds rise to par the paper might be sold, & the debt in specie discharged.[123]

What Jefferson thought of this scheme is not known. We may infer, in the light of his known views on the subject of manufactures,[124] that he did not find it attractive. At any rate, there is no evidence that Jefferson gave much attention to the " Plan." [125] That Coxe should have written Jefferson concerning the proposition is doubtless to be explained by the fact that Coxe had always praised the agricultural interests, and was accordingly a fit person to broach the matter to Jefferson, a stanch agrarian.[126]

[123] Coxe to Jefferson, April 15, 1791, MS, Jefferson Papers, LXIII. (Italics in original.) The " Plan " is to be found in *ibid.*, LXXX; it is also reproduced in full in Davis, I, 351, and in White, p. 283. For an account of the Potomac Navigation Company, to which Coxe referred, see Davis, II, 121-136.

[124] Jefferson, " Notes on Virginia " (1781), *The Writings of Thomas Jefferson*, II, 229-230. Coxe was familiar with Jefferson's " Notes," referring to them in his " Summary View of the State of Pennsylvania," written in 1790. See Coxe, *View*, p. 59.

[125] Davis, I, 356.

[126] The acquaintance of Coxe with Jefferson was not at this time of

At any rate, the letter in question throws some light on
the part played by Coxe in the formulation of the scheme.
It seems to justify the conclusion of Dr. Davis that, " At
all events the plan sprang from the Treasury Department, and it is probably accurate to say that the idea
developed out of the intercourse there between the two
men, Coxe supplying the suggestions from the side of
manufactures and Hamilton elaborating the details and
furnishing the connection with his funded debt." [127]

In August, 1791 the project was put before the public
through the press of Philadelphia and other cities.[128] The
initial capital was to be not less than $500,000, in $100
shares. Subscriptions were to be made in the public debt
certificates of the United States, or in specie.[129] Use of the
public debt as capital was, it may be noted, a favorite

---

long standing. See above, chap. i, pp. 28-29. Jefferson for his part, however, was familiar with at least one of Coxe's essays, namely, the
" Enquiry " of 1787. His papers, XXXVI, contain some notations which
he made relative to the contents of this essay, in particular its emphasis
upon the dominance of agriculture in our economy.

[127] Davis, I, 356. This important phase of the matter is so clouded
in uncertainty that even such a careful student as Dr. Davis is not able
to be consistent about it. For example, on p. 355, *ibid.*, he admits that
it is not impossible that Coxe conceived of the idea. Again, he points
out that in later documents, Hamilton is credited with the project
" almost invariably " ; he cites a letter of Coxe to Hamilton, MS, Hamilton Papers, XIII, " probably written in July, 1792," in which Coxe himself acknowledged that Hamilton was the author of the scheme. White,
p. 177, wrote that " I have no doubt but that the chartered company of
Paterson, New Jersey, though the plan is generally attributed to Hamilton,
originated with the assistant secretary of the treasury [Coxe] ; this is
proved by the letter of Fisher Ames." White, however, does not give
an exact reference to Ames' letter. He probably had reference to one
which he had earlier quoted from, namely, Ames to Coxe, July 11, 1793,
wherein Ames merely acknowledged receipt of a copy of Coxe's *Plan*,
and praised his ability as a writer on the subject of manufactures. The
plan here referred to is one which Coxe wrote out in 1793. See below,
chap. iv. The claim of White is therefore not securely founded.

[128] Davis, I, 356-358.

[129] *Ibid.*, pp. 381, 473-474. Stock of the Bank of the United States was
later added.

idea of Hamilton. The stock so obtained, it was reasoned, could be used as collateral to obtain loans at lower interest than that derived from the securities (e. g. collateral).[130] Happily, the public response was favorable; by December, 1791 upwards of $625,000 had been subscribed.[131] Many of the subscriptions, however, were never paid up.[132] In 1792 there was a collapse of a speculative boom, principally in government securities. The undertaking, as a consequence, was nearly wrecked. William Duer, formerly Hamilton's assistant and an important figure in the operations of the S. U. M., failed miserably.[133]

Thereafter many people bitterly attacked the project, associating it with Hamilton's funding system and national bank.[134] One opponent, signing himself as " A Farmer," declared that the S. U. M. would foster an inequality of fortune; the government, he thought, should give it no encouragement. Citing the authority of Adam Smith, he praised a policy of *laissez faire*.[135] In reply, " A Freeman "—probably Tench Coxe [136]—wrote and published an elaborate defence. The government, he said, was not interested in the S. U. M. There was no reason why the people should fear it. The yeomanry of Pennsylvania might erect, with the assistance of their State Legislature,

---

[130] *Ibid.*, pp. 359-360, 473-474.

[131] *Ibid.*, p. 389. Coxe had no active interest in this phase of the scheme, though in 1792 he made known to Hamilton his willingness to serve as a Director. *Ibid.*, 445 n. Coxe did, however, assist the officers in selecting a mill site. See his letters to Thomas Marshall, September 18, 27, October 10, 1791, and an undated letter, all in Cole, pp. 208-214, 217-218.

[132] Davis, I, 405. He estimates that all told, between $240,000 and $300,000 was received from stockholders, p. 475.

[133] *Ibid.*, p. 410.

[134] *Ibid.*, pp. 427-453; Woodbury, p. 49.

[135] " Five letters addressed to the yeomanry of the United States . . . ," *The American Museum* (1792), XII, 159-167, 213-217.

[136] The style and ideas suggest the name of Coxe. See also, Davis, I, 448 n.

such an establishment on the Susquehanna.[137]   In short, the S. U. M. was an example which they could follow with profit. Though this defence of the S. U. M. was ably conceived and written, the fact remained that inefficient management, the lack of experience, as well as other deficiencies, operated to make a continuance of the undertaking increasingly difficult. During the early part of 1796 its operations came to an end.[138]

The economic recession of 1792, involving as it did a stunning blow to the S. U. M., did not in the least, however, undermine the faith of Coxe in the principles upon which he and Hamilton would have the country create a national economy.   On the contrary, Coxe believed the adoption of them more necessary than ever before.   This was the point he sought to establish in his " Reflections on the state of the American Union in the year M, DCC, XCII." [139]

Therein Coxe examined anew the case for manufactures, seeking especially to dispel the idea that they could damage the agrarian interests.   " An opinion has prevailed," he wrote, " that the southern states will be sacrificed to the eastern, and in some degree to the middle states, by the plan of manufactures." [140]   The answer of Coxe to this was that which he in his earlier essays and Hamilton in his report had sought earnestly to make, namely, that the people of this country were interdependent in their economic pursuits. They must become increasingly so. The soil of the eastern states, Coxe argued,

---

[137] Coxe had suggested this as early as 1787. See his *View*, p. 52.

[138] Davis, I, 497-501.   A contemporary made the interesting observation that the extra charges which imported goods had to bear were not sufficient protection to local manufactures. *Ibid.*, pp. 497-498.   This, as before noted, was not Coxe's conclusion.

[139] Printed in his *View*, pp. 286-378, to which reference is here made. It was also published in *The American Museum* (1792) ; and separately in pamphlet form, 1792, by Mathew Carey.

[140] Coxe, " Reflections," *View*, p. 294.

was not such as to produce a sufficient supply of provisions and raw materials for their needs; hence these states furnished a market for southern produce, and to some degree, for that of the middle states. As concrete examples, Coxe pointed to hemp, the price of which (five cents) was maintained by rope and twine manufactories of the middle and eastern states.[141] Again, the brewers of Philadelphia obtained as much of their barley from the Chesapeake region as they did from their native state.[142]

Pursuing his argument further, Coxe emphasized the need for the development of manufactures, even in the southern states. The latter he found to "abound with iron, and have much more fuel of all kinds than the northern states, and they have streams for the most powerful water works."[143] These the South should utilize. He continued:

> In short, the all-important landed interest would languish, and its progress in prosperity would be retarded in the counties of the southern states, even near the sea, if our present manufactures were to be abolished, and all future establishments of that kind were to be given up. *But their inland and western counties cannot flourish unless manufactures shall be promoted and introduced among them.*[144]

To give a practical turn to this thesis, Coxe pointed out that the inland towns could make their hemp into sail-

[141] *Ibid.*, pp. 294-295.
[142] *Ibid.*, p. 295.
[143] *Ibid.*, p. 296; see also *ibid.*, pp. 303-310.
[144] *Ibid.*, p. 286. (Italics in original.)   Mathew Carey and his son, Henry Charles, wrote similarly.   See Kenneth Rowe, *Mathew Carey* ("Johns Hopkins University Studies in Historical and Political Science," Series LI, No. 4), p. 57; A. D. H. Kaplan, *Henry Charles Carey* ("Johns Hopkins University Studies in Historical and Political Science," Series XLIX, No. 4), p. 53. In the South, William Gregg grasped the importance of manufactures, publishing in 1844 his "Essays on Domestic Industry." For an excellent account of this prophet of industrialism in the South, see Broadus Mitchell, *William Gregg*, especially chap. ii.

cloth, sending the finished product to the coastal cities. As it was, the raw product brought only four or five cents per pound; when manufactured it would be worth thirty cents and could be transported more cheaply.[145] In any event, the folly of transporting foreign goods inland at great cost should cease. The inland counties could and should manufacture; and " 'Til that shall be the case, we shall continue to drag those raw materials through the same bad roads, and ship them under charges of carting and freight equal to a third, an half, and two-thirds of their whole value, according to the distance." [146]

The "Reflections" of Coxe, it is evident, reveal an undiminished faith in the future greatness of America were she to take to manufacturing. In this manner all sections of the country, whatever their particular economic pursuits, could be brought into a joint movement in which the national interest would be advanced. Thereby America would derive the economic foundations of a true national political state. "The political concord and attachments, which grow out of mutual benefits are," Coxe wrote, " the most rational and permanent. To encourage these is *the piety* of American patriotism. In this view, the cement, which will be given the national union, by the interchanges of raw materials, provisions, fuel, and manufactures among the several states, is of inestimable value." [147]

Here, indeed, is a bold mind at work. In the next chapter we shall examine the circumstances under which the ideas of Coxe became applicable.

[145] Coxe, " Reflections," *View*, p. 297.
[146] *Ibid.*
[147] *Ibid.*, p. 326. (Italics in original.) Fisher Ames wrote Coxe that " The principles and facts," which his essay contained, " are valuable as an acquisition to our political literature." Ames to Coxe, June 14, 1792, quoted in White, p. 51.

CHAPTER IV

The Economic Impact of the Napoleonic Struggle Upon America

The unsettled nature of American commerce, due in large measure to the absence of an agreement with Great Britain, was one reason why Coxe and Hamilton formulated a program of economic consolidation. This we have seen in the preceding chapter. At the time there were many who doubted its applicability. Our country, the dissenters reasoned, was devoted almost entirely to agriculture, the surplus of which could and should be sent abroad in exchange for manufactures. Thus our interests would most properly be furthered. But, obviously, this argument presupposed the existence of an unfettered commerce. That did not obtain at the time; nor did the future then offer such prospects. Conscious of this fact, Congress in February, 1791, requested the Secretary of State to render a report upon our commerce, with suggestions as to means whereby it could be improved.[1] Submitted to Congress in December, 1793, the report was used as the foundation of a series of resolutions introduced by Madison. Their object was to have America practice reciprocation where possible; otherwise there was to be retaliation. In short, it was asserted that the time had come for America to take a definite stand in her commercial relationships.[2]

While Congress was debating the propositions of Madison, the whole question was given an entirely different turn through the outbreak of war between France and Britain. This occurred in February, 1793. Hostilities then

---

[1] See above, chap. i.

[2] The debates in Congress on Madison's resolutions revealed the presence of two factions, the one pro-British (Federalist), the other pro-French (Republicans). McMaster, II, 179-182, 186-188.

begun were not to cease until all Europe and ourselves were engulfed. Insofar as the American economy was concerned, the struggle was one of far-reaching consequences.

Situated as we were, far from the actual scene of hostilities and possessed of ample supplies of raw materials and foodstuffs, the most logical course for America to have followed was that of strict neutrality. This was the one which Washington marked out for us in his Proclamation of April 22, 1793.[3] It was naturally expected that America would glean the profits of a lucrative neutral trade in the goods of our own and other countries. Of such a result Coxe had written in 1787: " Our ships would carry for them, or instead of theirs, and our lands and manufactories would furnish the supplies of their fleets and islands in the West-Indies." [4] It was soon learned, however, that the exact nature of what constituted neutral commerce was open to many interpretations; that these latter were more often made to coincide with the military interests of the parties at war.

At the outset of the struggle, the French National Convention by a decree of February, 1793, threw open to Americans the French West Indian trade, with privileges equal to those accorded their own vessels. But the British for their part lost no time in prohibiting such profitable intercourse on the ground that it was not in accord with the so-called " Rule of 1756." By the latter it was held that trade forbidden to a neutral in time of peace could not be permitted in time of war; to do so was *ipso facto* a war measure and to be met as such.[5] In addition to this attack upon our trade, Great Britain in March, 1793, also

---

[3] *Ibid.*, p. 98.
[4] Coxe, " An Enquiry into the principles on which a commercial system for the United States of America should be founded. . . ." (1787), *View*, pp. 21-22.
[5] A. T. Mahan, *Sea Power in its Relations to the War of 1812*, I, 90.

concluded a treaty with Russia whereby each party bound itself to forbid all neutral trade with France. Before the year was out, similar agreements were made with Spain, Prussia, and Austria.[6] Thereafter numerous measures of retaliation and counter-retaliation were adopted by France and Britain.[7]

In spite of these restrictions, changes in which American merchants were often unable to know of in time to protect themselves, our foreign commerce reached large proportions. This was particularly true of the indirect trade. It consisted of the importation of sugar, coffee, cocoa, spices and other articles in ready demand abroad, only to re-export them, large profits resulting. In 1797, for example, we exported twenty million dollars worth of foreign goods; in 1806 the amount was sixty millions.[8] In carrying on this indirect trade, American merchants maintained that goods once landed in this country were rendered American even though they might have come from an enemy country in the first instance. The British High Court of Admiralty in 1800-1801 sustained them in this view.[9] As the trade grew larger and larger, however, it became manifest that the measures of the British government to weaken the economic strength of France and her allies were being evaded. So reasoned James Stephen in his *War in Disguise*, published in London, 1805.[10] Neutral commerce, he wrote, should be totally abolished.

[6] See *American State Papers, Foreign Relations*, III, 263, for relevant extracts from these treaties, all of which sought to " annoy the commerce of France." Anne C. Clauder, *American Commerce as affected by the Wars of the French Revolution and Napoleon, 1793-1812*, p. 30, states that the British had in mind the conclusion of a similar treaty with America.

[7] *American State Papers, Foreign Relations*, III, 262-294; Clauder, pp. 9-14.

[8] *Ibid.*, pp. 67 ff.; in particular, her charts on pp. 73-74; also, Timothy Pitkin, *Statistical View*, p. 146.

[9] Clauder, p. 81; McMaster, III, 222-225.

[10] Clauder, pp. 79-80.

A step in this direction was taken by the High Court of Admiralty, July, 1805, in the famous *Essex* case. Therein the Court reversed its previous decisions by declaring that a broken voyage did not constitute neutral commerce.[11]

The following year brought even more disturbing elements into the course of our neutral trade. On May 16, 1806, the British ordered a blockade of the coast of the continent from the Elbe River to Brest. For several months Napoleon took no positive action in retaliation; but having annihilated the Austrian army, he made it the occasion for the promulgation of his famous Berlin Decree, November 21, 1806. Therein he declared that the British Orders of May sixteenth had violated the law of nations; that until those orders were revoked the British Isles were to be in a state of blockade, and all trade with them interdicted.[12] On November 11, 1807, the British again made an assault upon neutral commerce. Orders in Council issued on that date forbade all trade with any continental port from which British vessels were excluded. There was an exception in the case of vessels calling first at a British port, paying duties on its cargo and obtaining a new clearance.[13] An Act of Parliament, March 28, 1808, set down a schedule of these duties, whereby cotton was to be taxed nine pence per pound and tobacco three half-pence. Thus two important exports of America were virtually denied a European market.[14] Again Napoleon hit back, this time with his Milan Decree of December 17, 1807. By its terms any vessel which called at a British port, paid custom duty, or submitted to an examination by British authorities, became denationalized and subject to confiscation as a

[11] *Ibid.*, p. 81; McMaster, III, 226-227.
[12] *American State Papers, Foreign Relations*, III, 289-290; Clauder, pp. 99 ff., traces the effect of the Berlin decree upon American commerce.
[13] *American State Papers, Foreign Relations*, III, 269-270; Clauder, pp. 118 ff.
[14] *American State Papers, Foreign Relations*, III, 274-281; Mahan, I, 177-178.

lawful prize.[15] Neutral commerce became more and more insecure.

Aside from these depredations upon our neutral commerce, there was also the important matter of impressment of our sailors by the British. John Jay had failed to obtain from Britain any satisfactory agreement upon that subject in 1794. As the struggle between Napoleon and Britain grew in intensity, efforts on the part of Congress to secure protection for American seamen likewise proved fruitless.[16] How best to meet the situation was a problem which tried the minds of many.

The adverse decision in the *Essex* case had occasioned several resolutions in Congress for non-intercourse with Great Britain. This was an expedient with which the country was familiar, it having been used during the Revolution. After protracted debate Congress in April, 1805, enacted into law principles to that effect contained in a resolution of Nicholson. It was provided that most of our imports from Great Britain, directly and indirectly, were to cease after November 15, 1806.[17] At about the time of the passage of this law, James Monroe and William Pinkney were made joint commissioners to Britain, to explain its purpose and to assure that country that we would not rescind it until the impressment of our sailors ceased and a broken voyage was acknowledged to be neutral commerce.[18] In short, all matters of difference between ourselves and Britain were to be settled; the newly enacted measure prohibiting trade with her was a lever to be used in our favor. Pending the negotiations of Monroe and Pinkney, the American public was deluged with

[15] *American State Papers, Foreign Relations*, III, 290-291; Eli Heckscher, *The Continental System*, p. 124.

[16] McMaster, III, 242-247.

[17] *Ibid.*, pp. 228-236.

[18] See letter of instructions to Monroe and Pinkney, May 17, 1806, *American State Papers, Foreign Relations*, III, 119-124.

pamphlets on our commercial difficulties.[19] Among those
participating in the discussion was Tench Coxe.

The effects of the European debacle on American
economy early attracted the attention of Coxe. At the
beginning of the war he was prompted to assert anew his
plea for manufactures in this country, declaring that the
distance from our foreign markets as well as the general
war prevailing in Europe rendered their development imperative. This is the keynote of his paper, "Some Ideas
concerning the creation of manufacturing towns and villages in the United States, applied, by way of example, to
a position on the river Susquehannah," written in the
spring of 1793.[20] The war demand abroad had increased
the prices we must pay for manufactures; furthermore,
freight rates had risen because of war-risks. Under the
circumstances, we must look to the development of local
manufactures as a solution to our difficulties: "It will be
wise then," Coxe wrote, "to devise new methods of increasing our manufactures, in order *to cheapen and multi-
ply supplies, and to extend the home market for our agricultural productions.*"[21]

The plan of Coxe to achieve this end was very similar
to that of the New Jersey Society for establishing useful
Manufactures.[22] It is probable that he used as a model
that undertaking, then (1793) facing grave difficulties.
A capital of $500,000 was proposed, to be raised in one of
three ways: first, 5,000 subscriptions of one hundred dollars each; second, a lottery of 100,000 tickets of five
dollars each, or one of 50,000 at ten dollars each; and
third, by the support of the State of Pennsylvania. Profits

[19] A list of the more important pamphlets is given by McMaster, III,
235-236, footnote.
[20] See Coxe, *View*, pp. 380-404. Hereinafter referred to as, Coxe,
"Some Ideas," *View*. Fisher Ames had a copy of the plan inserted in
the *Boston Centinel*. See Ames to Coxe, July 11, 1793, White, pp. 51-52.
[21] Coxe, "Some Ideas," *View*, p. 382. (Italics in original.)
[22] See above, chap. iii.

of the project arising from an increase in land values, he put at one hundred per cent.[23] In the remainder of the plan a detailed account was given of the way in which the capital so obtained was to be spent. Two thousand acres of land on the western bank of the Susquehanna " at some proper place between the confluence of its eastern and western branches, and the lower end of its present navigation," [24] would be purchased, and there a town laid out. Exact details as to streets, houses, alleys, and the like followed. The industrial make-up of the town would include: two mills for preparing hemp; one for preparing flax; a mill of about 800 spindles for spinning flax, hemp, and combed wool; three rope walks; four tan yards; a paper mill; one oil mill (for processing flax, hemp, and rape seed); a grist mill; two bake houses; two slitting and rolling mills; a steel furnace; a soap boiler's and tallow chandler's shop; a malt house; a brewery; ten grain and fruit distilleries; two printers' offices, one for English, the other for German; six blacksmiths' shops; two coopers' shops; one cedar cooper's shop; four hatters' shops; a bleach yard and house; and about 162 other buildings of various descriptions, including a church and library. All told there would be about one thousand houses in the project. For power the river would be diverted from its natural channel (presumably by a dam and race). Thus, he thought, no labor need be drawn from agriculture. So constituted, the project might be compared, he wrote, to " the bottom of a great bag or sack, into the upper parts of which natural and agricultural produce is poured from the north-east, from the north, and from the west." [25]

[23] Coxe, " Some Ideas," *View*, pp. 398-400, where he gives detailed calculations.

[24] *Ibid.*, p. 385.

[25] *Ibid.*, p. 395. For details of the plan, see *ibid.*, pp. 386-393. Thomas Lowry in a letter to Hamilton, October 14, 1791, had called attention to

In presenting his plan, Coxe did so only "*to exemplify what might be done with a given capital.*" [26] But, as he himself was soon to learn, the prospects of its adoption were rendered hopeless by the great expansion of our foreign commerce, occasioned by the war in Europe. In a letter to Thomas Jefferson, June 7, 1797, he spoke of the growing importance of our commerce, and pointed to the necessity of a study of it.[27] Nothing, he informed Jefferson, was more necessary than such a study, unless it be a work on representative government. Commerce, he concluded, was no more than an auxiliary and at that, quite susceptible of producing an expensive war.[28] This view, which Jefferson shared with him,[29] was adhered to by Coxe without further qualifications. It constitutes the clue to

the use of coal to be found in the mountains along the Susquehanna River in establishing manufactures. MS, Hamilton Papers, XII. It is worthy of note that Coxe in writing the above once more assumed the rôle of a prophet. His project to use the Susquehanna River to derive power for industry is today realized in the Conowingo hydro-electric power plant, located on the Susquehanna just above tidewater in Maryland. Begun in March, 1926, and completed by the summer of 1928, Conowingo supplies electrical energy to Coxe's native city of Philadelphia as well as to other great industrial centers. In size, it is second only to the power plant at Niagara. See *Conowingo*, a brochure issued by the firm of Stone & Webster, who engineered the development.

[26] Coxe, "Some Ideas," *View*, p. 383. (Italics in original.)

[27] Coxe to Jefferson, June 7, 1797, MS, Jefferson Papers, CI. Whether Coxe ever undertook such a study himself is not known. In a letter to Madison, January 4, 1802, he spoke of sending Madison a book of tables, statements, and representations concerning our commerce, earlier written. MS, Madison Papers, XXIV. No copy of this is to be found in the Papers.

[28] Coxe wrote similarly in his *Observations on the Agriculture, Manufactures and Commerce of the United States* (1789), p. 92.

[29] Jefferson in a letter to John Jay, August 23, 1785, wrote that commerce would carry as its price frequent wars. We would thus need a navy, which Jefferson did not think we could support: "If a war with England should take place, it seems to me," he wrote, "that the first thing necessary would be a resolution to abandon the carrying trade, because we cannot protect it." See Jefferson to Jay, August 23, 1785, *Memoir, Correspondence and Miscellanies from the papers of Thomas Jefferson*, ed. T. J. Randolph, I, 291-292.

his thoughts concerning the commercial crisis of 1805-1806.

Writing to President Jefferson, May 22, 1806, Coxe pointed out that the establishment of a strong navy was being agitated in seaport towns by editors who " lived by the patronage of persons interested in trade." [30] With such a solution, he could not agree: " It will pay us to devise other defences for trade than an expensive navy." [31] Insofar as we were to arm, we should do so, he thought, solely for defensive purposes by providing ten million dollars for a military establishment. These remarks of Coxe were by way of an introduction to his *Thoughts on the Subject of Naval Power in the United States of America,* a copy of which he enclosed to Jefferson.[32]

This essay was Coxe's contribution to the public discussion of the commercial crisis of 1806. He began it by asserting a

thorough conviction, that no branch of commerce, nor even trade in general, should be so pursued, permitted, encouraged, or defended by the United States, as to hazard the public liberty at home, the principles of freedom abroad, or taxes the whole nation, nearly as great as, equal, or superior to the exclusive profits of the mercantile body. We have rejected the example of Europe as to standing armies, political churches, the penal code, and other dangerous errors and aberrations from right; and the splendours and temptations of naval power and external commerce, as established and extended in Europe, have their full share of influence over many persons of great worth and judgment in the United States.[33]

[30] Coxe to Jefferson, May 22, 1806, MS, Jefferson Papers, CLIX.
[31] *Ibid.*
[32] *Ibid.* The full title of Coxe's essay was, *Thoughts on the Subject of Naval Power in the United States of America; and on certain means of encouraging and protecting their commerce and manufactures.* Two copies are preserved in the Madison Papers, Printed Material, LXXIX. They were probably sent to Madison by Coxe.
[33] Coxe, *Thoughts on the Subject of Naval Power,* p. 3.

To reinforce this argument, Coxe proceeded to show that the British navy was and had been an instrument of oppression, both to the British people and others. It had been used against us in the Revolution and all along against the Irish. " It is in evidence," therefore, " that *a great navy may destroy liberty, at home and abroad, by force.* . . ." [34] In this respect it might be likened to a great standing army. Commerce, he continued, required the protection of a navy; to protect ours, some people desired that the United States provide and permanently maintain " *a considerable naval power.*" [35] Answering this contention, Coxe declared that the British spent annually seventy to eighty-five millions of dollars on their navy. We could not, accordingly, begin to match them in naval power: a navy one-tenth the size of theirs would cost us more than the whole profits of our foreign trade during the best year; and at that, it would be insignificant in the face of Britain's. [36] The truth of the matter was, Coxe declared, the United States did not need a large navy. She was not an island, and her trade was too valuable to other nations who relied upon her for foodstuffs, raw materials, and a market for their manufactures to permit it to be jeopardized. At the most, all we could be said to need in the way of a navy was a few ships to be used against

[34] *Ibid.*, p. 7. (Italics in original.)

[35] *Ibid.*, p. 8. (Italics in original.) Fisher Ames was notable among those who pled for the development of a great navy by America: " Let every real American patriot insist," he wrote in 1806, " that our government should place the nation on its proper footing, as a naval power." See Ames, " Dangerous Power of France," *The Works of Fisher Ames,* p. 342. Ames seemed possessed of the idea that the French would capture the British fleet and then sally forth to conquer us! See *ibid.*, p. 374.

[36] Coxe, *Thoughts on the Subject of Naval Power*, pp. 8-9. In his " Brief Examination of Lord Sheffield's Observations on the Commerce of the United States," *View*, p. 195, Coxe had written that Britain's rule of the seas must be broken and that other nations should assist the United States in the task. He called for a " balance of naval power." This he wrote in 1791.

small powers with whom we did not have a large commerce upon which to retaliate, if need be. The Barbary States he cited as an example.[37]

Passing next to the question of what should constitute our commercial pursuits, Coxe ruled out that trade " internal or external *which injures agriculture, or benefits the merchants only, at a great expence to the rest of the community. . . .*"[38] The commerce which we *should* foster was the importation of those things alone which facilitated the development of our manufactures; above all, we should promote internal commerce " of which manufactures are a most valuable part." In a word, violation of our commercial rights abroad should be met, not by the creation of a great navy and war, but by the development of a self-sufficing economy.[39] Towards this end, consumption by Americans of foreign goods into which our raw produce had not gone should be forbidden. Exclusion of British linen, woolen, and silk cloth, not made of American raw material, would force the manufacturers of that country to make substitutes for them out of our cotton, thus expanding the market for the latter, he thought.[40] Again, such a measure would promote our own manufactures. Nicholson's resolution and the Act of Congress founded upon it had these objects in view and were therefore to be praised.[41] Furthermore, Coxe continued, we could match foreign duties on our trade by a *quid pro quo.*[42] Should our merchants sustain losses because of such

[37] Coxe, *Thoughts on the Subject of Naval Power*, p. 11.
[38] *Ibid.*, pp. 11-12. (Italics in original.)
[39] *Ibid.*, p. 12.
[40] *Ibid.*, p. 14.
[41] See letter of Madison to Monroe and Pinkney, May 17, 1806, explaining the use to which the Non-Importation Act should be put by them in their negotiations with the British. This Act, Madison wrote them, was designed, *inter alia*, to foster our manufactures. *American State Papers, Foreign Relations*, III, 119.
[42] Coxe, *Thoughts on the Subject of Naval Power*, pp. 14-17.

a policy, then Coxe had a novel scheme whereby they could be recompensed. He would have the damages assessed by a standing board of commissioners and charged with interest against the American government. The government in turn would demand payment from the country inflicting the injury, granting that nation a year in which to settle. Were a settlement not made then, our government would place special duties on imports from the country in question, thus obtaining funds to pay our injured citizens.[43] Recourse to statutes with a view to retaliation was to be preferred to a big and costly navy, he reiterated. That our commerce had been unjustly treated and our nation insulted, he could not deny. Yet America, he thought, must not be so foolhardy as to wage war; this would be a cure worse than the disease: let us seek " *the peaceful maintenance of the rights and interests of the United States, and the exemption of human nature from the evils of discord and the crimes and miseries of war.*" [44]

This plea of Coxe for a peaceful solution to our many points of difference with European nations was wholly in accord with the ideas of Jefferson, who throughout the controversy sought to avoid a war.[45] It was in this spirit that he had delegated Monroe and Pinkney as commissioners to Britain in 1806 to negotiate a treaty. This episode we shall now examine, since Tench Coxe had an indirect interest in it.

A cessation of impressment of our sailors and acknowledgment of neutral commerce by broken voyages were the

[43] *Ibid.*, p. 18.

[44] *Ibid.*, p. 34.   (Italics in original.)

[45] See Mahan, I, 52, 74, 186, 188, who in discussing the background of the War of 1812 is critical of "the Jeffersonian horror of war." This noted student of naval history and strategy maintains that the lesson of the War is that a large navy was not necessary to attack the British with success—a view which, as we have just seen, Coxe did not agree with.

two principal objects of Monroe and Pinkney in their negotiations with Lords Holland and Auckland, the British Commissioners. While a treaty was concluded on December 31, 1806, it was to all intents and purposes worthless from the point of view of the American demands. A copy of this treaty Monroe and Pinkney forwarded to Madison, January 3, 1807, setting forth in an accompanying letter explanations of its defects.[46]

Writing of the third article by which trade with British possessions in India was confined to direct voyages from and to American ports, they pointed out that this was accepted in preference to no agreement at all. The British East India Company monopolized this trade and was unwilling to grant Americans further concessions in it. By the fifth article, trade of the two countries was placed on a most-favored-nation basis. Yet they were unable to get Britain to remove a discriminatory duty amounting to two and one-half per cent *ad valorem* on exports to us. Trade with the British West Indies was by the sixth article left for future settlement: they could do no better under the existing circumstances. As to trade with enemy colonies (the eleventh article), they were able to better the British proposal of requiring the goods to be landed and stored for one month, then exported in another vessel after payment of a duty of at least four per cent. Instead, they induced Britain to agree to the payment of a one per cent duty on European goods re-exported after landing, and two per cent on West Indian goods. Concerning the important question of impressments, they could only write that, "we are sorry to add that this treaty contains no provisions against the impressment of our seamen."[47] Furthermore, there was no assurance that Britain would

[46] Pinkney and Monroe to Madison, January 3, 1807, *American State Papers, Foreign Relations*, III, 142-147; for a copy of the Treaty, *ibid.*, 147-151.

[47] *Ibid.*, p. 146.

abide by even this faulty treaty. They must know before-
hand, the Commissioners advised Monroe and Pinkney,
whether America proposed to abide by the Berlin decree
of Napoleon, promulgated while the treaty was being
drafted (November 21, 1806). Acquiescence, they
warned, would mean a cancellation of the treaty. To this
Monroe replied that the question then became one of a
declaration of war upon France or a treaty with Britain.
To this he could not agree.

These explanations of Monroe and Pinkney were of no
use. Exactly one month after their receipt, Madison informed them that the President would never enter into any
agreement which ignored impressments.[48]

This deadlock prompted Coxe to express the view that
" I am of the opinion that the less we do the better, with
foreign nations, at this time." The foreign situation, he
continued in a letter to John Dickinson, "*inclines me
strongly to the cultivation of our interior.*"[49] To Madison
he wrote similarly: "*It appears to me that the less we do
with foreign powers, at this crisis of violent resentments
among them, the better.*"[50] A treaty with Britain, while
desirable, was not expedient. These opinions Coxe drew
out at length in an essay dated February, 1807, and entitled, " On the State of External Affairs in February
1807," a copy of which he sent to Madison.[51]

[48] Madison to Monroe and Pinkney, February 3, 1807, *ibid.*, p. 153.
[49] Coxe to John Dickinson, February 11, 1807, MS, Autograph Collection. (Underscoring in original.)
[50] Coxe to Madison, February 13, 1807, MS, Madison Papers, XXXI.
(Underscoring in original.)
[51] See Madison Papers, XXXI. The manuscript is sixteen pages in
length and apparently was never published. See also, Coxe to Madison,
February 15, 1807, enclosing notes (not found in MSS) on the foreign
trade situation and other pressing problems. MS, Madison Papers, XXXI.
In a letter to Madison, February 20, 1807, Coxe forwarded a copy of an
essay on the French decree, no doubt referring to that of November 21,
1806. He had already, he wrote, sent copies to Jefferson, Gallatin, and
certain members of Congress. MS, Madison Papers, XXXI.

The tenor of this essay is the position Coxe had earlier taken, that we should at all costs avoid a war. Conciliation, not aggression, he asserted, should be our policy. The fact that the negotiations of Monroe and Pinkney had broken down should not trouble us; some good might be derived in the end from that development. For our part, we should examine each of our diverse interests, to insure their protection in any future course of action. Specifically, he had the following recommendations to offer for Madison's consideration: first, he would limit resort to treaties "for a time" to what justice alone required. On this point Coxe was not explicit. Second, he advised that the utmost care be taken of our revenue. Restrictions on the imports of British goods as well as the growth of local manufactures made this necessary; these things reduced the possible revenue from import du ies. Third, we should stimulate internal commerce through encouraging manufactures. In this way agriculture and fisheries could be supported in an emergency. Fourth, import duties on foreign goods not made of American raw materials should be raised—such things as malt liquors, grain and fruit spirits, cordage, woolens, linens, silks, fish products, and coarse potteries. In this way we could both get more revenue and expand the markets for our agricultural surplus. This idea is similar to that in Coxe's *Thoughts on the Subject of Naval Power*. Having made these proposals, Coxe suggested that we ignore the British threat not to abide by the treaty. America, he wrote, could not "in good conscience" make war on France; for that nation was no more guilty of initiating attacks upon us than was England. War was of no use, Coxe repeated emphatically, and concluded that we had before us only the attainment of "a neutrality the most correct, and peaceful measures for redress of injuries."

Apparently pleased with the interest which Coxe thus displayed in the foreign affairs of the nation at this critical time, Madison on March 27, 1807 sent him a letter, marked " private and confidential," in which he requested that Coxe without delay express his opinions on the treaty just concluded. In particular, he wrote, " it is thought highly advisable to avail the Executive of such observations on those [clauses] relating to commerce and navigation as your intelligence and experience on those subjects will enable you to afford." [52]

Coxe's reply was a seventeen-page manuscript entitled, " Considerations relative to certain articles of the treaty prepared in 1806." [53] He began it with the assertion that " It is an important preliminary to every treaty to possess the mind fully with the idea, that it is made with a view to the *national* interests." [54] On such a criterion, this treaty should obtain for us reparations for past damages and assurances that we should be given respectful treatment in the future. What America and its representatives would approve, he pointed out, " is an important question of practical execution, whatever may be *the right theory of political economy for the United States.*" [55] In developing this thesis Coxe was not consistent, which was unfortunate, considering the critical situation facing the government. America, he wrote, could be made self-sustaining; but he did not develop the idea. On the contrary, he declared that the prohibition of commercial pursuits provided for in the treaty was not expedient; competition, on the other hand, would stimulate subsistence and wealth. Yet he had to acknowledge that commerce was already shackled by prohibitions and restrictions. Under the circumstances, a nation not disposed to duplicate such policies might " buy

[52] Madison to Coxe, March 27, 1807, MS, Madison Papers, XXXI.

[53] To be found in the Madison Papers, XXXI. It is unsigned, though accompanied by an undated letter of Coxe. Hereinafter referred to as Coxe, " Considerations," the pagination being that of the MS.

[54] Coxe, " Considerations," p. 1. (The word " national " is underscored in original.)

[55] *Ibid.*, p. 3. (Underscoring in original.)

off foreign prohibitions, by seeming to give to foreign nations apparent privileges in their trade, tho those privileges are in fact but parts of that freedom of trade, which the general national interests, well understood, may be found to require." [56] He considered this idea especially applicable to Anglo-American commerce. Precisely what Coxe had in mind when he wrote this is not clear, particularly when a comparison is made with the contents of several supplementary papers which he sent to Madison along with the "Considerations." In a paper marked "number three," Coxe wrote that we should threaten Britain with our capacity to become self-sustaining, if she restricted the outlet for our goods. Citing cotton as an example, he said we must manufacture it ourselves, if Europe refused to take it. A long list of local manufactures followed, with the assertion that "Manufactures (cotton water spinning being excepted) are more progressive here on a medium than in any other country." [57] In a paper marked "number four," he stressed the fact that we could not continue to buy British manufactures, if our food and raw materials were prohibited. He said that abstinence from the purchase of British goods for two or three years would be a great blow to England, and inferred that this should be our policy.[58]

[56] *Ibid.*, pp. 4-5. In a letter earlier written to William Jones, a member of Congress from Pennsylvania, Coxe suggested that the economic implications of the Napoleonic debacle be viewed in the abstract. Assuming freedom of trade on our part, we could then buy cheap and sell dear: "Our internal industry would flourish & would be on a broad & stable bottom . . .," he wrote. Such a program, he had to admit, was not possible; we should, none the less, seek its adoption. Coxe to Jones, February 2, 1802, MS, Autograph Collection. In another letter to Jones, January 3, 1802, *ibid.*, Coxe declared that the existing discriminations against foreign nations were useless. He recommended strict adherence to a policy of *quid pro quo.*

[57] See paper "number three," in Madison Papers, XXXI. In a letter to Madison, April 2, 1807, Coxe sent two more papers relating to the treaty. MS, Madison Papers, XXXII. These are missing from the collection.

[58] See paper "number four" in Madison Papers, XXXI.

These observations can hardly have been of much assistance to Madison. They were set down in a haphazard fashion, and showed Coxe's unwillingness to be precise. To have written of freedom of trade, self-sufficiency, and embargoes, all at the same time, only added to the existing confusion and hesitancy of the government. The haste which Madison impressed upon him perhaps accounts for Coxe's disjointed work. As he himself pointed out, the question before the country was one of " practical execution," and not one of what constituted a proper theory. For his part, however, he seems to have confused the two miserably.

Where Coxe did touch on specific provisions of the treaty he shows disapproval. The narrow limitations on American trade with British India ought to be, he thought, supplanted by a more liberal provision giving us the right to dispose at will of goods obtained from that source.[59] In return for this, the extra duty of 10 per cent on goods brought in foreign ships, provided for in the treaty, could have been cancelled.[60] Nor did he approve of the selfish attitude of Britain toward our trade with her colonial empire. He said that American territory was open to the British, but that, if Britain did not reciprocate, we ought to keep out her goods entering our country via Canada.[61]

The unfavorable reception which Coxe accorded the treaty was hardly necessary to influence the Administration in casting it aside. The fact that it did not settle the impressment issue was in itself enough to induce Jefferson to withhold it from the Senate.[62]

[59] Coxe, " Considerations," pp. 7-8. Madison on May 20, 1807, wrote Monroe and Pinkney that this provision could not stand. See *American State Papers, Foreign Relations*, III, 166-173.

[60] Coxe, " Considerations," p. 12.

[61] *Ibid.*, pp. 9-11. Gallatin in some notes on the treaty, written for Jefferson, also disapproved the illiberal manner in which Britain regulated our commerce with her colonies. *The Writings of Gallatin*, ed. Henry Adams, I, 284.

[62] Coxe made no mention of impressments in his " Considerations."

Jefferson had just tucked away the treaty of 1806 as useless when America was made the victim of a flagrant violation of her rights in her own waters. On June 22, 1807 the American frigate *Chesapeake* was fired upon and searched by the *Leopard* of the British navy. Such an outrage naturally prompted a nation-wide denunciation of the British.[63] The President immediately issued a proclamation closing our ports to all armed vessels of Britain.[64] The situation became so tense that Gallatin concluded that "war is inevitable." [65] He sent Jefferson a memorandum outlining preparatory measures.[66] In a letter to Madison, Coxe expressed views similar to Gallatin's.[67] Although he had hitherto advised the way of peace, he was now doubtful of its practicability.

This new position Coxe presented at greater length in an essay entitled, *An Examination of the Conduct of Great Britain, respecting neutrals,* published in Philadelphia, 1807, over the signature of " Juriscola." [68] Taken as a

In a letter to Madison, written during the year 1807, he spoke of having sent a paper on that subject to all of our seaports. MS, Madison Papers, XXXIII.

[63] McMaster, III, 253-263.

[64] The proclamation was issued on June 25, 1807. In a letter to Madison, July 6, 1807, Coxe wrote that the proclamation was being favorably received in Philadelphia. MS, Madison Papers, XXXII. He had earlier written Madison of a public meeting in Philadelphia protesting against the unwarranted attack on the *Chesapeake*. Coxe to Madison, June 30 and July 2, 1807, MS, Madison Papers, XXXII.

[65] Gallatin to Joseph H. Nicholson, July 17, 1807, *The Writings of Gallatin*, I, 338.

[66] Gallatin to Jefferson, July 25, 1807, *ibid.*, 341 ff.

[67] Coxe to Madison, 1807, MS, Madison Papers, XXXIII; see also Coxe to Madison, March 27, 1807, *ibid.*, XXXI.

[68] A second edition, marked by greater use of italics, was published in Boston in 1808. Publication of this essay was not, however, prompted by the *Chesapeake-Leopard* affair; in a letter to Madison, June 14,1807, Coxe wrote of his intention to prepare a pamphlet on the subject of neutrality. MS, Madison Papers, XXXII. In another letter to Madison, May 22, 1807, he complained that the Federalists would not publish a paper on the same subject by him. *Ibid.* The Library of Congress possesses

whole, the essay constitutes a severe indictment of the British people, charging them with having pursued a policy of destroying the legitimate commerce of America. To reinforce his argument, Coxe recalled the treaties which Britain concluded in 1793 with Russia, Spain, Prussia, and Austria, all with the purpose of annihilating trade with France. In the case of Russia, he added, there was a tacit understanding as early as the autumn of 1792 with that end in view. While the attacks of the French upon our commerce were not to be ignored, France at any rate was to be absolved from having instituted the practice.[69]

Passing next to an examination of a proper course of action for America, Coxe declared for a restoration of the law of nations; in the meantime, if need be, we could attack England economically. If she then made war on us, as some said she would,[70] then let us fight her: " We shall do much better than in the revolutionary war," Coxe optimistically predicted.[71] In any event, he concluded, " It is a sound maxim of our political economy, that *so far as we cannot trade abroad, we shall certainly manufacture at home.*" [72]

---

autographed copies of the first and second editions of Coxe's *Examination.* In the copy of the second edition several minor corrections were written in with a pen.

[69] Coxe, *An Examination of the Conduct of Great Britain, respecting neutrals*, pp. 6-23. Edward Channing, *The Jeffersonian System, 1801-1811*, p. 195, points out that the assignment of original responsibility for attacks upon our commerce is difficult to make. See also, James W. Gerard, "French Spoilations Before 1801," *Magazine of American History*, XII, 34-35.

[70] In *An Inquiry into the present state of the foreign relations of the Union*, p. 65, an " Independent American " wrote that the Non-Intercourse Act was " an incipient war measure." This writer criticized at length what he termed " the pretty theoretical impossibilities " of Jefferson. *Ibid.*, p. 19.

[71] Coxe, *An Examination of the Conduct of Great Britain, respecting neutrals*, pp. 42-43.

[72] *Ibid.*, p. 73. (Italics in original.)

In a letter to President Jefferson, written later in the same year (1807), Coxe also wrote in favor of an economic attack on Britain.[73] British naval despotism, he reasoned, rested upon that country's commercial monopoly. Instead of attempting in the first instance to match the former, we should seek to strike at the latter through regulations requiring foreign nations to bring us their goods in their own ships.[74] Furthermore, we could keep out British rum, among other things, and restrict the application of our system of drawbacks. If we were to arm, let it be upon land, Coxe again advised Jefferson. Jefferson, in reply, agreed that an equalization of naval power by attacking the British commercial monopoly was a sound proposition.[75]

This desire to equalize naval power was, however, more of a theory than an immediate expedient. Continued attacks upon our commerce, and British hesitancy in redressing the *Chesapeake-Leopard* wrong, demanded action. This came on December 18, 1807 when Congress enacted an embargo on all American commerce. Four days later it became operative with no time limit.[76] In a letter to

[73] Coxe to Jefferson, September 5, 1807, MS, Jefferson Papers, CLXX. Coxe enclosed to Jefferson a copy of his *Thoughts on the Subject of Naval Power*.

[74] The plea of Coxe here is for a navigation system after the fashion of that of Britain. In 1817 Congress adopted the idea by enacting that imports must be confined to American ships or to those of the countries producing the goods. The same law also confined the coasting trade to Americans. See Rabbeno, p. 156. Commenting upon this measure in an article entitled "United States," written for Abraham Rees' *Cyclopaedia* (1818), Coxe declared that it was modeled after the British navigation acts. Coxe, it may be noted here, repeated in 1814 the above suggestion that British naval supremacy could be weakened through restrictions upon her merchant marine. This he did in an article, "The Balance of Naval Power," which appeared in *The Democratic Press*, Philadelphia, September 24, 1814.

[75] Jefferson to Coxe, September 21, 1807, MS, Jefferson Papers, CLXXI.

[76] Supplementary measures to reinforce its effectiveness were passed the

Madison, March 24, 1808, Coxe estimated that business amounting to $261,000,000 would be arrested by the measure, which he thought to be a good one. It was therefore imperative, he wrote further, that we find local employment for our capital and skill. His suggestion was that we concentrate on manufactures and internal improvements.[77]

Prior to the enactment of the Embargo, American manufactures had received but scant protection; revisions of the Tariff of 1789 had not been drastically upward. Some progress had been made in the establishment of new manufactures, but the bulk of capital and enterprise of the country, not employed in agriculture, went into commerce. The temporary cessation of hostilities during the Peace of Amiens (1802) did, however, prompt a re-examination of the extent to which Congress should foster home manufactures. Those already established were threatened by heavy importation of foreign goods. In 1803 a House Committee on Commerce and Manufactures reported in favor of a revision of tariff duties whereby greater protection could be accorded manufactures, without increasing the revenue.[78]

Coxe found the report of this Committee defective in several particulars. These he set forth in *An Essay on the Manufacturing Interest of the United States; with remarks on the Report of the Committee of Commerce and Manufactures.*[79] The report of the Committee

---

following January, February, and April. See McMaster III, 281, 296, 298; L. M. Sears, *Jefferson and the Embargo*, pp. 60-61.

[77] Coxe to Madison, March 24, 1808, MS, Madison Papers, XXXIV.

[78] McMaster, III, 497.

[79] Signed, " By a Member of the Society of Artists & Manufacturers of Philadelphia," Philadelphia, 1804. Copy in The American Philosophical Society Pamphlets, Vol. 678. This Society was incorporated in March, 1803, with Dr. Rush as President and Coxe as Vice-President. See Scharf and Wescott, I, 515. Coxe was also at this time President of the Board of the Pennsylvania Society for the Encouragement of Manufactures and the Useful Arts, established in 1787. See *A Communication from the Penn-*

was, he declared, "only a confession of a want of information on the subject of manufactures."[80] Criticizing the national government, he listed the principal recommendations of Hamilton's *Report on Manufactures*, noting that little had been accomplished.[81] The manufacturers and merchants of America were still seeking independence from Britain. Citing the examples of Edward III of England and Colbert of France, Coxe asserted that much could have been done to foster our manufactures.[82] Heavy duties, he thought, must be levied upon foreign goods.[83] Congress, however, did not heed the advice of Coxe; instead, it provided for an additional duty of 2½ per cent.[84] The enactment of the Embargo three years later was, therefore, a windfall protection to American manufactures. Its stimulation of new industries was phenomenal.[85] As we shall see in the following chapter, the cotton industry, especially, underwent a great expansion.

In a letter to Madison, May, 1810, intended as a com-

sylvania Society for the Encouragement of Manufactures and the Useful Arts, Philadelphia, 1804, containing a list of officers elected January 20, 1804. Duane Pamphlets, Vol. 96, No. 2.

[80] Coxe, *Essay on the Manufacturing Interest of the United States*, p. 21.

[81] *Ibid.*, p. 20.

[82] *Ibid.*, pp. 23, 26. The admiration which Coxe here showed for the economic statesmanship of Edward III, and which many others have also expressed, including competent students of his reign, must in the light of the work of the late Professor George Unwin be considered undeserved. After a thorough study, Unwin concluded that "the part played by Edward in fostering English industry is reduced to comparatively small proportions." See "The Economic Policy of Edward III," *Studies in Economic History: The Collected Papers of George Unwin*, ed. R. H. Tawney, pp. 119-122.

[83] Coxe, *Essay on the Manufacturing Interest of the United States*, p. 19.

[84] McMaster, III, 497.

[85] Gallatin, *Report on Manufactures*, April 17, 1810, *American State Papers, Finance*, II, 425-431; McMaster, III, pp. 500 ff.; Sears, chaps. vi-viii; Rolla M. Tryon, *Household Manufactures in the United States, 1640-1860*, pp. 142 ff.

mentary upon Gallatin's *Report on Manufactures* of that year,[86] Coxe reasserted his belief that restrictions on American trade must force us into manufacturing.[87] The only objection that could be made to this was, he thought, the supposition that manufacturers were not friendly to a republican form of government, to which he could not agree. Merchants were " not so decidedly characterized." [88] In the past our manufactures had not been aided by large duties; only a revenue impost had been levied. But it was now time for America " to consider, foster, and promote manufactures on a system, for they depend much on each other. The stupendous mills for carding cotton and wool require the manufactory of wire to exempt them from foreign checks—so of steel, necessary to many manufactures and tools of manufactures." [89] It was to be hoped, he concluded, that during the prevailing crisis our manufactures would prosper and expand.

In a letter accompanying his *Report on Manufactures,* Secretary Gallatin suggested to Congress that it would be wise and feasible to have the United States marshals and their assistants collect information on our manufactures; [90] that Congress should provide for such a study in the next (third) census. On May 1, 1810 this request was granted, and the task of assimilating this material was committed

[86] Gallatin, *Report, American State Papers, Finance,* II, 425-431.

[87] Coxe to Madison, May, 1810, MS, Madison Papers, XLI. In a letter of January 25, 1810, to Madison, Coxe wrote of having begun a collection of documents on tonnage, shipping, and commerce. *Ibid.,* XL.

[88] The distinction which Coxe here drew between manufacturers and merchants was hardly a valid one. The fact is that the merchants were the founders, in a large measure, of our industrial system. At this time many of them were diverting their capital to manufactures in order to escape the disordered state of commerce. See Victor S. Clark, *History of Manufactures in the United States, 1607-1860,* pp. 442, 448-449; L. M. Sears, " Philadelphia and the Embargo: 1808," *Annual Report of the American Historical Association, 1920,* p. 253.

[89] Coxe to Madison, May, 1810, MS, Madison Papers, XLI. Gallatin wrote similarly. See his *Report.*

[90] Gallatin, *Report, American State Papers, Finance,* II, p. 425.

to Coxe by Gallatin on June 26, 1812.[91] By May of the following year Coxe had completed a classification of the data on a geographical basis and had written a lengthy introduction. The work was separately published in Philadelphia, in 1814, under the title, *A Statement of the Arts and Manufactures of the United States of America for the year 1810: Digested and Prepared by Tench Coxe, Esquire, of Philadelphia.*[92]

Whatever claim Coxe possesses to recognition as a statistician rests largely upon this *Statement*. In compiling it he initiated a long series of similar studies which, since his time, have been considerably expanded and improved upon. His own work is, of course, subject to criticism when judged in the light of modern statistical practice and census technique. But as one critic has pointed out in commenting upon this first industrial census of America,

Congress had no conception of the difficulties of the task ordained. . . . This first industrial census was undertaken without even the formality of a schedule, or definite instructions to the marshals, and necessarily forms no true measure of the industrial resources of the country at the time. Whatever utility the figures possess was imparted by Tench Coxe. . . .[93]

[91] The returns were sent to the Treasury Department in November, 1811. The inability of a member of the House Committee on Commerce and Manufactures to prepare a digest of them led Rep. Seybert of Pennsylvania to move that provision be made for the appointment of a competent person to do the work. See J. Leander Bishop, *A History of American Manufactures from 1608 to 1860*, II, 160.

[92] Hereinafter referred to as, Coxe, *Statement*. It was also printed in *American State Papers, Finance*, II, 666-812.

[93] S. N. D. North, " Manufactures in the Federal Census," *The Federal Census: Critical Essays by members of the American Economic Association*, March, 1899 (" Publications of the American Economic Association," New Series [1899]), p. 259. See also, C. Ford Worthington, " The Statistics of Manufacturing Cities," *ibid.*, p. 329, wherein he states that Coxe's work is " more curious than valuable "; and, *North American Review* (1815), I, 234-247, being a critical review.

In his preface to the statistics of the *Statement,* Coxe
sought to define the relation of manufactures to agriculture, foreign commerce, fisheries, and national defence.
In this way he was once again enabled to put before the
public his ideas concerning the importance of manufactures to the American economy. The wonder is that the
growing importance of manufactures did not prompt Coxe
to publish such a study earlier. He had, as we have seen,
performed such a service in 1789; [94] but the ideas then expressed could certainly have been restated with profit in
light of the far-reaching economic implications of the
Napoleonic struggle.

The first concern of Coxe in his *Statement* was the
controversial question of the relation of manufactures to
the landed interest. He had previously written more than
once on this subject.[95] Here he sought to show again that
manufactures were beneficial to agriculture. He did so not
by theory, but by the use of two concrete instances. The
first was " an examination into the state of manufactures, in four sparsely settled districts of our country,
which in 1810, had been recently laid out, according to
the nature of the places, for future establishments as
counties." [96] These districts were in the northwestern section of his native state of Pennsylvania. There he found
that the presence of raw materials had occasioned a considerable growth of manufactures, for otherwise difficulty
of access to eastern markets would have hampered progress considerably. The second instance was the state of
Ohio, admitted to the Union in 1810. There cloth was
manufactured, leather tanned, and indeed, machines of
iron for carding and spinning of wool constructed. If this
state were to have its raw materials transported to the
Atlantic coast to be exchanged for supplies, its growth, he

[94] See above, chap. iii.
[95] *Ibid.*
[96] Coxe, *Statement,* pp. v-vi.

thought, would be hindered and its present population involved " in much distress, if not ruin." [97]

Viewing the country at large, Coxe declared that European restrictions on trade had greatly stimulated the development of manufactures, even in the southern states.[98] Indeed, the demand of manufacturers of flax, wool, hemp, hides and skins of domestic animals, and various metals, had exceeded " all the abilities of the planters, farmers, landholders and miners, to supply those five descriptions of raw materials." He considered this a " momentous fact," and left his readers to infer that the landed interest was neglecting a great opportunity to profit.[99] Examining in some detail the production of each of these commodities, as well as several others, he found that " It is an impressive fact, that manufactures in America outrun agriculture in most instances. This is a conclusive truth." [100] Nor could it be argued that these industries were " forced "; on the contrary, they had come into existence with only the aid of " incidental protection." [101] The

[97] *Ibid.*, p. vii.

[98] *Ibid.*, p. ix, footnote.

[99] *Ibid.*, p. ix. Coxe put the importation of these materials at between forty and fifty million pounds in each of several years preceding the returns. This was not the first time that Coxe accused the farmers of negligence. In his " Reflections on the state of the Union in the year M,DCC,XCII," *View*, p. 359, he wrote that American farming was " generally speaking, the least understood, or the least economically and attentively pursued, of any of the occupations which engage the citizens of the United States." He had previously, *ibid.*, p. 358, listed numerous deficiencies which characterized American farmers. He none the less believed that there would be considerable improvements in the future. But, as he himself saw in 1810, progress was slow. John Taylor, the great palladin of agriculture in America at this time, wrote that American agriculture was quite backward. See his *Arator*, pp. 7-10. This Taylor wrote before 1810. *Ibid.*, p. 217.

[100] Coxe, *Statement*, pp. xii-xix.

[101] *Ibid.*, p. xix. In a letter to Madison, September 2, 1813, Coxe reiterated his belief that America had not forced her manufactures. When Peace came British manufacturers would flock to us as did their merchants after the Peace of 1783, he added. MS, Madison Papers, LIII.

Embargo and other non-intercourse measures did afford local manufactures extreme protection; but they were enacted as a part of the foreign policy of the country and not with a view to the deliberate promotion of manufactures.

The relation of manufactures to the commercial interest next engaged the attention of Coxe. He found it to be a mutually beneficial one. In England an extensive commerce was supported by the export of finished goods and the import of raw materials.[102] In our particular case, " The richest object of commercial enterprise . . . is the trade of those countries, which do no manufacturing." [103] Nor need we necessarily confine ourselves to such markets: " Even the manufacturing nations will be induced to purchase our goods, *which can be made with the vast advantage of labor-saving machinery, operating upon raw materials exempted from the duties and other charges of importation.*" [104]

Great as were the prospects in foreign commerce, Coxe considered them of lesser importance than interstate commerce. The latter was safe and certain. Mindful of the secessionist ideas of several New Englanders in their opposition to the Embargo, Coxe digressed at this point to emphasize the importance of maintaining intact the Federal union:

> It is an evident and important fact that this material and increasing exchange of raw productions, fuel and provisions, for finished manufactures, between the producing and manufacturing states, has become *a decisive consideration, for the continuance of the federal union*—a connexion *vital* to the general commerce of the American people. *The manifest difficulty of securing justice in commercial affairs, even by the whole of the United States, affords conclusive evidence, that each of any two possible*

[102] Coxe, *Statement*, p. xx.
[103] *Ibid.*, p. xxi.
[104] *Ibid.* (Italics in original.)

sections, into which they might be severed, would fail to maintain the standing of a trading nation.[105]

Passing next to manufactures and the fisheries, Coxe dismissed this connexion by reference to the fact that the products of the fisheries were used by manufacturers. Furthermore, the larger ships of the fisheries could enter the coastwise trade made possible by manufactures, if they were idle.[106]

In conclusion, Coxe took up manufactures in their relation to national defence—a subject of peculiar importance at that time. Here he properly observed that the encouragement of the manufacture of military supplies was a wise policy, especially since foreign nations had been known to restrict their export of this kind of manufactures. Coxe wrote on this subject with nearly nine years of experience as Purveyor of Public Supplies. As a large purchaser of military supplies for the government in that capacity he knew whereof he wrote. It was his belief that in the manufacture of military equipment we had made greater progress than in any other branch since 1775.[107]

The remainder of Coxe's long preface is devoted to miscellaneous observations upon the American economy, in each of which he tried to show further possibilities for American manufacturers.[108] In particular, he wrote at length on the subject of cotton and labor-saving machinery used in its manufacture. As the following chapter will show, this was a subject that had always been uppermost in his mind.

Writing to Madison soon after the enactment of the

---

[105] *Ibid.* (Italics in original.)
[106] *Ibid.*, p. xxii.
[107] *Ibid.*, p. xxiii.
[108] Coxe, *Statement.* See, for example, wool, pp. xxix-xxxi; iron, xxxi-xxxii; hemp, xxxiii-xxxiv; flax, xxxiv; hides and skins, xxxv; maple sugar, xxxvi-xxxvii; grape-wine, xl; etc.

Embargo, Coxe suggested as alternatives to foreign commerce not only the development of manufactures, but also the promotion of internal improvements.[109] The importance of canals and turnpikes to internal commerce was apparent to Coxe as early as 1788.[110] During the period under consideration, great progress was made in internal improvements.[111] These, in conjunction with the growth of manufactures, brought America closer to the ideal of a national economy. As Gallatin aptly wrote in 1816, " The people have now more general objects of attachments with which their pride and political opinions are connected. They are more Americans; they feel and act more as a nation. . . ." [112]   In short, the foundations of what was afterwards termed " The American System " had been laid.[113] The voice of Coxe ceased to be one crying in the wilderness.

[109] See Coxe to Madison, March 24, 1808, MS, Madison Papers, XXXIV.

[110] Coxe, " Address to the Friends of American Manufactures," *Pennsylvania Gazette*, October 29, 1788; also, Coxe to Madison, June 18, 1789, MS, Madison Papers, XI.

[111] McMaster, III, 461-495.

[112] Gallatin to Mathew Lyon, May 7, 1816, *The Writings of Gallatin*, I, 700.

[113] Rabbeno, pp. 115-116; see also Walter B. Smith and Arthur H. Cole, *Fluctuations in American Business, 1790-1860* ("Harvard Economic Studies," L), pp. 37-38.

CHAPTER V

THE AMERICAN COTTON CULTURE AND MANUFACTURE

The distinction of being the first enthusiastic advocate of cotton culture in the United States has been justly accorded Tench Coxe.[1] In 1786, at a time of great political and economic uncertainty, he seized upon the idea that in the cultivation and manufacture, too, of cotton America had the basis of a vast economic expansion. He worked persistently to bring others to a similar understanding; it was his conviction that " The subject of the cotton culture, commerce and manufacture can never cease to be of primary interest to any man who understands and feels concern on the means of promoting the wealth of the United States." [2] In 1819 he could, with pardonable pride, inform Madison that, " Never did my anticipations of any subject in our affairs issue in a conformity of subsequent events so considerable as in this case." [3] The purpose of this chapter is to examine the circumstances which prompted Coxe to think and write as he did.

The cultivation, and to a certain extent, the manufacture, of cotton was known to Americans even before the Revolution. As a raw material, it could be had in greater abundance than any other, flax excepted.[4] The supply,

[1] White, p. 49; M. B. Hammond, *The Cotton Culture and Cotton Trade* ("Publications of the American Economic Association," New Series, 1897, No. 1), pp. 12-13; William R. Bagnall, *Samuel Slater and the Early Development of Cotton Manufacture in the United States*, pp. 10-11; J. Leander Bishop, *A History of American Manufactures from 1608 to 1860*, I, 355; McMaster, I, 296-297.

[2] Coxe to Madison, July 5, 1817, MS, Madison Papers, LXIV.

[3] Coxe to Madison, February 2, 1819, MS, Madison Papers, LXVI.

[4] Clark, p. 83. He states that the colonies in 1768 imported 452,463 pounds of cotton, of which they re-exported to Britain 64,822 pounds; of that retained, Massachusetts manufactured (domestically) about 200,000 pounds.

however, was largely of foreign origin, especially in the
northern colonies. The New England colonies, for example, are reported to have imported from the British
Islands 54,409 pounds in 1678.[5] Connecticut in 1640 had
especially fitted out a vessel to import " cotton-wooll." [6]
But in this section the manufacture (domestically) of
woolen cloth predominated, a business so progressive that
the home government in 1699 saw fit to forbid inter-
plantation shipments of woolen goods.[7] Cotton goods
where used were mostly of East Indian manufacture.[8] In
the southern colonies the supply of raw cotton was more
domestic than foreign in origin. Cotton cultivation in
what is now Louisiana and Texas had been observed very
early (1536) by the Spanish explorer, De Vica.[9] Virginia
had cultivated it in small quantities from the outset; [10]
the founders of Georgia had intended its cultivation.[11]
South Carolina at one time provided a bounty of three
pence per pound on all exported.[12] As in the northern
colonies, cotton was manufactured in households, often
mixed with other materials, such as wool.[13] What is of

[5] Clark, p. 83. See also Weeden, I, 176; *ibid.*, II, 659, 681.
[6] Bishop, I, 49.
[7] Weeden, I, 388; also, *ibid.*, II, 679, referring to widespread use of
homespun woolen cloth.
[8] Clark, p. 21.
[9] Hammond, p. 4; James A. B. Scherer, *Cotton as a World Power,*
p. 116.
[10] Hammond, p. 4; Bishop, I, 28; Clark, p. 83.   Jefferson in his
" Notes on Virginia," written in 1781, listed cotton among the staple
crops of Virginia. See *The Writings of Thomas Jefferson,* II, 54. Bagnall, pp. 9-10, and G. Emerson, *Cotton in the Middle States,* p. 3,
ascribe the first culture of cotton to the eastern shore of Maryland.
[11] Bishop, I, 351.
[12] Giesecke, p. 73. He states that seven bags, valued at twenty-five
pounds sterling were exported in 1748. See also Clark, p. 84; E. J.
Donnell, *History of Cotton,* p. 8; cf., however, Bagnall, p. 10, where it
is stated that cotton was not grown in South Carolina or Georgia prior to
1788. Bagnall must have had in mind the growth of cotton as a money
crop.
[13] Victor S. Clark, " Colonial Manufactures," *The South in the Build-*

greater importance, however, is the fact that the fitness of the soil in the southern colonies for cotton culture was known before the outbreak of the Revolution.[14] Several writers made this observation,[15] among them the grandfather of Tench Coxe, Colonel Daniel Coxe. The latter in his *Carolana*, first published in 1722, wrote that "Cotton grows wild in the pod and in great plenty; may be managed and improved as in our islands, and turned to as great account; and in time perhaps manufactured either in this country or in Great Britain, which will render it a commodity still more valuable." [16]

The severance of commercial relations with Great Britain at the outbreak of the Revolution gave a feeble impulse to American cotton culture and manufacture. As the war progressed the customary market outlets of the staple crops of the South—tobacco, rice, and indigo—were narrowed.[17] Cotton culture attracted the attention of the planters. Its introduction was also advantageous because it afforded employment for the slaves. Furthermore, cotton could be expected to find a domestic market, since in every part of

---

ing of the Nation, V, 309-310; Tryon, pp. 70-71; James L. Watkins, *King Cotton: A Historical and Statistical Review, 1790-1908*, p. 11; Harriet L. Herring, " Early Industrial Development in the South," *Annals of the American Academy of Political and Social Science*, CLIII, 3; August Kohn, *The Cotton Mills of South Carolina*, pp. 6-7.

[14] Hammond, pp. 5-6; Clark, p. 85.

[15] Bishop, I, 351.

[16] Daniel Coxe, *A Description of the English Province of Carolana* . . . ("Historical Collections of Louisiana, ed. B. F. French, II), p. 262.

[17] Hammond, pp. 14-15. As Hammond points out, the British began to import indigo more cheaply from the East Indies. Tobacco, from the earliest times a commodity of commanding importance, had already sorely depleted the fertility of the soil. See also, Samuel Batchelder, *Introduction and Early Progress of the Cotton Manufacture in the United States*, p. 20; letter of Joshua Gilpin to Louis McLane, Secretary of the Treasury, May 1, 1832, *McLane Report*, 22d Cong., 1st sess., H. Doc. No. 308, VII, Part 2, p. 842; Leila Sellers, *Charleston Business on the Eve of the American Revolution*, pp. 167, 168.

America manufactures were being advocated as a measure of retaliation against the mother country. In fact, according to Hamilton, cotton could and should be manufactured in the South. Replying to the " Westchester Farmer " in 1775, Hamilton wrote that:

> Several of the southern colonies are so favorable to it [cotton], that with due cultivation, in a couple of years, they would afford enough to clothe the whole continent.
>
> As to the expense of bringing it by land, the best way will be, to manufacture it where it grows, and afterwards to transport it to the other colonies. Upon this plan, I apprehend, the expense would not be greater than to build and equip large ships to import the manufactures of Great Britain from thence.[18]

The idea that a local market could be had for southern cotton was, however, somewhat premature. Aside from an increase in household manufactures, only one real effort was made at this time to establish American manufacture of cotton. This was the United Company of Philadelphia for Promoting American Manufactures, instituted in 1775. It was a joint-stock undertaking, with shares of ten Pounds Sterling each, formed to manufacture linen, woolen, and cotton cloth.[19] Benjamin Rush, the outstanding medical man in the colonies at the time, was elected its president. At a meeting of the subscribers, held in Carpenters' Hall, March 16, 1775, Rush addressed those present on the necessity of manufactures in this country and the immediate prospects of the United Company. He assured his audience that cotton could be had from the southern colonies as well as from the West Indies.[20] In reply to

[18] Hamilton, "The Farmer Refuted," February, 1775, *The Works of Alexander Hamilton*, ed. John C. Hamilton, II, 113-114.

[19] See plan of the Company, *Pennsylvania Packet*, Philadelphia, March 6, 1775, and *Pennsylvania Magazine* (March, 1775), I, 140-141. See also, Goodman, p. 46, and William R. Bagnall, *The Textile Industries of the United States*, I, 63-73.

[20] Philadelphia had early gained a reputation as a market for cotton,

those critics who said that it would be cheaper to purchase our cloth from England, Rush hinted at the arrival of a spinning machine from that country, whereby we could produce as cheaply as they could.[21] But the United Company, though it got off to a good start, was short-lived. In the first year of its existence, it employed some four hundred women in spinning,[22] most of the work being done at home. The Company possessed the first spinning-jenny seen in America,[23] obtained from England in violation of an Act of Parliament forbidding the exportation of machinery.[24] In 1777, however, when the British entered Philadelphia, the United Company ceased operations.[25] Although an attempt was made in 1780 to form an association of a similar nature in Worcester, Massachusetts,[26] the local manufacture of cotton progressed no further until 1787.

Meantime there appeared in Great Britain the remarkable series of inventions which made possible the machine manufacture of cotton on a large scale. This was the impetus to extensive cotton culture in the South, not events in America. The inventive genius of Kay, Wyatt, Ark-

---

roller gins having been set up there before the Revolution. Hammond, p. 114. See also, Clark, p. 84, pointing out that Philadelphia was "a seat for the manufacture of the primitive gins that preceded Whitney's invention." According to Bishop, I, 353, cotton was at this time grown in the neighborhood of Philadelphia. By "neighborhood" Bishop must have meant Maryland and New Jersey.

[21] See Speech, reprinted in *The American Museum* (1789), V, 581-584.

[22] Domestic cotton, costing 2/- per lb. was used, according to Donnell, p. 13.

[23] It had twenty-four spindles. An engraving of the machine by Christopher Tully, who introduced it, is to be found in *The Pennsylvania Magazine* (April, 1775), I, opposite p. 158. The jenny was invented by James Hargreaves; his patent was taken out in 1770. Edward Baines, *History of the Cotton Manufacture in Great Britain*, pp. 155-163.

[24] The exportation of machinery, plans, or models was forbidden by an Act passed in 1774. Clark, p. 260.

[25] Clark, p. 183.

[26] Bishop, I, 396. The association raised a subscription to obtain a jenny. See also, Weeden, II, 848.

wright, Hargreaves, Crompton, and others revolutionized cotton manufacture and, in time, the whole British economy. With the dissolution of the Arkwright patent on spinning machinery in 1785, the industry underwent a tremendous expansion.[27] The consumption of cotton, needless to say, increased *pari passu*, the increase from 1780 to 1790 being, according to Baines, five-fold.[28]

To this market and its potentialities the average American appears to have been oblivious. The expansion in the cultivation of cotton during the years immediately following the Peace was slight. Indeed, a regular exportation of southern cotton to the British Isles did not begin until 1784.[29] In that year the paltry quantity of eight bags was landed at Liverpool, only to be seized by the customs authorities on the ground that the Americans could not have raised so much cotton. Given assurances to the contrary, the importation was permitted, and the cotton was sold to the mill of Messrs. Strutt & Co. of Derby—a concern notable in the annals of American economic development, since it then employed as an apprentice Samuel Slater.[30] The British were not looking to America for a supply of cotton; they relied upon the West Indian Islands, India, and South America.[31] There was need for recognition in America of the profit in extensive cultivation of cotton, but the idea rapidly took hold.

[27] Baines, pp. 192, 214.

[28] *Ibid.*, pp. 214-215.

[29] Hammond, p. 231. As Hammond points out, though there are no actual records of the fact, cotton must have been exported from the South before the Revolution; that is, cotton of domestic origin. Edward Spencer, *A Sketch of the History of Manufactures in Maryland*, p. 21, refers to the export of three barrels of home-grown cotton from New York in 1770. Some of this cotton, he says, was from the Counties of St. Mary and Talbot in Maryland, and Accomac and Southampton in Virginia. Our knowledge of early exports of cotton is at best scanty. W. B. Dana, *Cotton from Seed to Loom*, pp. 20-22, lists the supposed early instances of the export of cotton from America.

[30] Hammond, p. 231; see below for an account of Slater's part in founding the American cotton manufacture.

[31] Baines, p. 304; Hammond, pp. 234-235, 237.

While attending the Annapolis Convention of 1786, Tench Coxe and James Madison, observing the cultivation of cotton in the neighboring gardens, agreed that it was a plant of great economic worth to the southern states. Writing later of this episode, Coxe pointed out that the capacity of " the country south of Annapolis, in Maryland " for cotton culture was not widely known in 1786:

Circumstances in the family horticulture of the writer . . ., arising among relations resident in Talbot County, had possessed him of the information that cotton wool was constantly and familiarly raised there, in the little gardening of the children and domestics. It is distinctly remembered, that the impressions of early youth had matured, in the year 1786, into pleasing convictions, that the United States, in its extensive regions south of Anne Arundel, and Talbot, would certainly become a great cotton-producing country. This expectation was rendered the more deeply interesting, because European inventions of labour-saving machinery, for the carding and spinning of this raw material, were known to the writer to have occurred, though they were, at that time, very imperfectly understood, and not possessed in the United States.[32]

Coxe never lost an opportunity after this to bring before influential minds the prospects of cotton culture in the South, even though the country during the next three years was engrossed in a great movement of constitutional reform. For example, addressing the Philadelphia Society for Political Enquiries in May, 1787, Coxe made it the occasion to say that the southern states might cultivate cotton with great profit. It sold in the West Indies for nine pence Sterling per pound before the Revolution; now

[32] Tench Coxe, *A Memoir of February, 1817, Upon the Subject of the Cotton Wool Cultivation, the Cotton Trade, and the Cotton Manufactories of the United States of America,* in The American Philosophical Society Pamphlets, Vol. 33, No. 6, p. 1. Coxe's reference to relatives in Talbot County, Maryland, was to those on his mother's side. See above, chap. i.

with the great advance being made abroad in its manufacture, its price had advanced fifty per cent. "This article," he contended, "must be worth the attention of the southern planters." [33]

Shortly after the delivery of this address, Coxe was asked to assist in the formation of a new society to encourage manufactures in Philadelphia. The large importations of English goods following the Peace, with the accompanying export of specie, prompted several leading merchants of that city to revive the idea back of the defunct United Company. They gathered at the University of Pennsylvania to hear Coxe speak upon the subject of American manufactures. [34] In addressing them Coxe again pointed out the striking possibility of extensive cotton culture and manufacture in this country. Familiar with the abortive efforts of the United Company, he was yet hopeful that success could be achieved. Since 1775 many improvements had been made in textile machinery abroad, of which America should take advantage. [35] "It is much to be desired," he declared, "that the southern planters would adopt the cultivation of an article from which the best informed manufacturers calculate the greatest profits, and on which some established factories depend." [36] As he later wrote, cotton was not then grown as a crop, nor

[33] Coxe, "An Enquiry into the principles, on which a commercial system for the United States of America should be founded . . . ," *View*, p. 20. There is no positive evidence for the statement of McMaster, I, 297, that Coxe "stood up before the Federal Convention and begged southern delegates to go home and urge their people to cultivate it [cotton]."

[34] The first meeting occurred on August 9, 1787, followed by another five days later. See *Pennsylvania Packet*, August 11, 18, 23, 1787; *Pennsylvania Journal*, August 15, 1787; *Pennsylvania Herald*, August 11, 1787.

[35] Coxe, "An Address to an assembly of friends of American manufactures, convened for the purpose of establishing a Society for the encouragement of Manufacture and the Useful Arts, in the University of Pennsylvania, on Thursday, the 9th of August, 1787," *View*, pp. 39-41.

[36] *Ibid.*, p. 44.

were machines to work it known of here: " Such was the real inadvertence, on the part of the intelligent cultivators of the south, to the natural advantages of our soil and climate; such the unacquaintance of the ingenious and energetic mechanicians of the whole union with the form and value of labour-saving machinery." [37]

Coxe advocated, therefore, not only the extension of cotton culture but also the American manufacture of the raw material. Both were to be the initial steps in the development of an American national economy, to the advocacy of which his address was chiefly devoted.[38] Since in the beginning the manufacture outstripped the cultivation of cotton, we shall first examine it.

Immediately following Coxe's address at the University of Pennsylvania, there was organized by those present The Pennsylvania Society for the Encouragement of Manufactures and the Useful Arts.[39] To manage its manufacturing operations, a " manufacturing committee " was created, with Coxe a member.[40] Financial support was to be had from a " manufacturing fund " derived from subscriptions of not less than £10 each,[41] in transferable shares. In order to carry out the project outlined by Coxe of manufacturing cloth with labor-saving machinery, the Society during the following month (November, 1787) offered " a gold medal of the value of twenty dollars for the most useful engine or machine, to be moved by water,

[37] Coxe, *Memoir of February, 1817*, p. 2.

[38] See above, chap. iii.

[39] See Plan of the Society, *The American Museum* (1787), II, pp. 167 ff.

[40] See Plan. Notice of elections to office was carried in the *Pennsylvania Herald*, September 8, 1787. Thomas Mifflin was the Society's president.

[41] According to the *Pennsylvania Gazette*, August 22, 1787, the number of subscriptions totaled 853. Two years later the Pennsylvania Assembly subscribed to 100 shares at £10 each. See An Act to Assist the Cotton Manufactures of this State, passed March 26, 1789, *The Statutes at Large of Pennsylvania from 1682 to 1801*, XIII, 239-240.

fire, or otherwise, by which the ordinary labor of hands in manufacturing cotton, wool, flax, or hemp, should be better saved than by any then in use in this State." [42] The Society's determination in this respect was noteworthy; during the same month British agents in Philadelphia purchased and reshipped to England three machines for spinning cotton and one for carding. These had been "clandestinely shipped from Liverpool to Philad[a] packed in Queen's ware crates and casks, to elude discovery. . . ." [43] The task before the Society was accordingly no easy one.

To assist them, it is related of Coxe that some time during 1787 he "made a contract with an English emigrant in Philadelphia to return to his native country, and there secure brass models of the Arkwright machinery." [44] These models were to be sent to France and thence, with the help of Jefferson, to this country. The following year, however, the models were discovered on the eve of shipment and seized by the customs authorities, since their export was forbidden by the Act of 1774.[45] Whether this

[42] Quoted in Donnell, pp. 43-44.

[43] See Phineas Bond to Lord Carmarthen, November 20, 1787, in "Letters of Phineas Bond, British Consul at Philadelphia, to the Foreign Office of Great Britain, 1787, 1788, 1789," *Annual Report of the American Historical Association, 1896,* I, 552-553. This effort on the part of the British to forestall the development of cotton manufactures here no doubt prompted the Pennsylvania Assembly to pass an Act, March 29, 1788, whereby "the exportation of machines, and enticing artizans from this State" was forbidden. See *Pennsylvania Statutes at Large,* XIII, 58-62.

[44] Simpson, p. 267. Davis, II, 265, credits Coxe with having obtained machinery for the Pennsylvania Society.

[45] Simpson, p. 267. White, p. 71 n, describes the episode: Tench Coxe "entered into a bond with a person who engaged to send him, from London, complete brass models of Arkwright's patents; the machinery was completed and packed, but was detected by the examining officer, and forfeited, according to the existing laws of Great Britain, to prevent the exportation of machinery." According to McMaster, I, 297, and Donnell, p. 14, Coxe undertook to acquire machines soon after the Revolution, but his models were confiscated by the British in 1786. The present writer has been unable to check these statements.

is an accurate account of the episode is not certain. At any rate, according to Mathew Carey, himself an ardent advocate of American manufactures, machines were obtained from abroad in 1787. In the March, 1788, issue of his *American Museum* Carey wrote that:

The manufacturing society of this city have at length obtained two complete machines for carding and spinning cotton, of which one cards forty pounds of cotton per day, and the other spins fifty threads at a time. We feel infinite pleasure in communicating this agreeable intelligence to the public, and we have no doubt, that by application to the society, private persons or companies will be informed how they may be supplied with them. As they are of the greatest consequence to this country, we beg leave to suggest the propriety of gentlemen in every town in the state joining to procure one of each. Five lads of fifteen years of age, and a girl of twelve, may tend four spinning and carding machines, which will card and spin 12,000 lb. of cotton per annum.[46]

Furthermore, by 1788 Americans were in possession of the principles of European labor-saving machinery, applicable to cotton manufacture;[47] there were also foreign artisans competent to construct the machines. In an undated letter to Benjamin Franklin, probably written during 1788, Coxe informed his correspondent that " Machines saving labor in the proportion of about fifty to one have been made here [e. g. Philadelphia] by European Artists. They yield a profit of 6d to 8d per yard and [the cloth is] sold by the single piece at 3/3 per yard, 1/2 ell wide or near it." [48] These machines, he added, were on

[46] *The American Museum*, III, 286; see also, *ibid.*, IV, 342 n. The Pennsylvania Assembly in 1788 paid one John Hague the sum of £100 for " introducing into this State a useful machine for carding cotton." See *Pennsylvania Statutes at Large*, XIII, 138-139.

[47] Coxe, " Address to the friends of American manufactures," *The American Museum* (1788), IV, 342. This address also appeared in the *Pennsylvania Gazette*, October 29, 1788. In the *Museum* Carey ascribes it to Coxe.

[48] Coxe to Franklin, n. d., MS, Franklin Collection, LXVIII, Part 1.

a smaller scale than those used in England, but they could and would be enlarged. In 1789 Phineas Bond, the British Consul at Philadelphia, noted in a letter to the Duke of Leeds that progress was being made in that city in the construction of textile machinery.[49] In the *Pennsylvania Gazette*, July 1, 1789, it was reported that several Baltimoreans had ordered from Philadelphia a complete set of machinery to manufacture cotton cloth.[50]

Whether the Pennsylvania Society had by then obtained machinery of the Arkwright type is, however, problematical.[51] Coxe on September 17, 1789 wrote Madison of having succeeded, with the assistance of Jefferson, in obtaining models of English machinery; these may have been of the latest design, but he did not say so. In his letter he informed Madison that:

> This affair in which you were good enough to make me known to him [Jefferson] is now decided on. I find it necessary to regain the papers which were deposited with him on that occasion, as they have not been wanted. The plan was to gain sketches and models from a country in the vicinity of France, which would very much assist the manufactures of the United States. I em-

---

In this letter Coxe speaks of South Carolina planters having put in all the cotton seed they could obtain; in a letter to Madison, July 23, 1788, MS, Madison Papers, IX, he says the same thing. The price of cotton in Philadelphia, as given in the letter to Franklin, is the same as that furnished Madison in a letter to him, June 11, 1788. MS, Madison Papers, IX. It is therefore likely that Coxe wrote Franklin sometime during 1788.

[49] Phineas Bond to the Duke of Leeds, November 10, 1789, *The Letters of Phineas Bond*, I, 653.

[50] The writer added that Philadelphia machine builders had become very skilled in their work, and that costs were reduced sixty per cent.

[51] Clark, p. 534, states that the machines used by the Society were of the jenny type, though he admits that Arkwright machines may have been used. His position is borne out by entries in the manuscript Account Book of the Society for the years 1788-1790, preserved in the Library of Congress. There, under date of June 27, 1789, it is noted that eleven Pounds Sterling was " paid in full for the 70 spindle jenny." Also, on July 1, 1789, a purchase of 32 jenny spindles is listed.

barked 120 Guineas in the pursuit, and the business is completed. I mention this much that when you ask the favor of Mr. Jefferson to procure the papers to be transmitted, which I beg you will receive of him for me, you may be able to explain to him *confidentially* that the object which I took the liberty to trouble him and you with was in some degree connected with the public interests.[52]

An insight into the manufacturing operations of the Pennsylvania Society is to be had from a report of its Manufacturing Committee to the Board of Managers. It stated that on August 23, 1788, the circulating capital of the Society amounted (in specie) to £874-0-4; the fixed, £453-10-2. Four jennies of 40, 44, 60, and 80 spindles were in operation. The first loom was used beginning April 12; since that time the number had been increased to twenty-six. Imperfect models of machinery and obstructions by foreign agents were noted. However, by August 23, 4527 yards of cotton goods had been manufactured; linen and corduroy goods made in addition thereto brought the total to 7111 yards of goods. Between August 23 and November 1 (1788), 2095 yards of cotton cloth was manufactured, aside from other cloth. In a report of the Board of Managers, signed by Tench Coxe and George Clymer, it was stated that the value of the cloth sold between April 12, 1788 and August 23, 1788, was £448-5-11½, with a profit of £72-4-9½, or at a rate of thirty per cent per annum. Raw cotton could be obtained at from two shillings to 2/3 per lb. An increased supply from the South was mentioned, though it was sug-

[52] Coxe to Madison, September 17, 1789, MS, Madison Papers, XII. Coxe gives no clue as to the nature of the papers which he mentions. The underscored word is in the original. William Bingham, it may be noted, also sought the assistance of Jefferson in obtaining machines or models from Europe. In a letter of September 25, 1789, Jefferson wrote him that a complete set of carding and spinning machines could be delivered five weeks from the date of order. He added that he would be happy to assist the Pennsylvania Society, of which Bingham was a member, in any way possible. MS, Jefferson Papers, LII.

gested that since water machines had not been obtained, it was preferable to get cotton yarn from India for the warp.[53] It was also encouragingly noted that the price of cotton machinery had fallen considerably. Finally, the request was made that all printers in the United States publish the two reports.[54]

The Society, it is thus evident, had a substantial beginning; but it was not long to continue operations. On the night of March 24, 1790, the building that housed the undertaking was destroyed by fire, probably of an incendiary origin.[55] The entire contents, machinery included, were lost.

This disaster must have greatly disappointed Coxe. Only three days before its occurrence he had written Madison of the prospects of acquiring locally machinery to spin flax, hemp, and wool:

I have the satisfaction to inform you that the artist, who undertook to make the machine for spinning flax, hemp and wool by water has completed the model and that it is now in my hand ready for an application for a patent, which he will make as soon as the law shall pass. The drawings and description are prepared.

[53] This admission is an additional reason for believing that the Society was unsuccessful in obtaining Arkwright machinery.

[54] The two reports are printed together in the *Pennsylvania Gazette*, November 12, 1788. See also, *ibid.*, July 9, 1788, for an account of the Grand Federal Procession in Philadelphia, in celebration of the ratification of the Constitution by ten states. The Society was represented in the Procession by a large carriage, covered with cotton cloth made by its workers. On the carriage was the Society's largest spinning machine. The editor of the *Gazette*, it may be noted, took a very friendly attitude toward the work of the Society; he also wrote in favor of an extension of cotton culture in the southern states. See issues of December 10, 24, 31, 1788; January 7, July 1, September 9, 1789.

[55] Bishop, I, 409. The site was rented from William Bingham for forty pounds per annum. *Ibid.* On April 13, 1790, a memorial from a committee of the Society was addressed to the Supreme Executive Council of the State, stating that they believed the fire to have been a result of foul play. The Council proclaimed a reward of $300 for apprehension of the person or persons guilty. *Minutes of the Supreme Executive Council of Pennsylvania*, XVI, 326-327.

He has added another invention of wch he has deposited the drawing with me to make cordage 1½ in. diameter, and he has furnished me with a drawing of a two-part water engine to grind optical glasses or lenses, and to polish them when ground. This engine is capable of grinding and polishing above 1000 glasses in a day and requires but one man and a small constant stream. He also has furnished me with the great movements of Arkwright's cotton spinning mill, and some of the lesser ones, but this material is more perfectly manufactured by Milne's improvement on Arkwright's machinery now established in France. Mr. Bingham informs me that Mr. Jefferson wrote him that this mill might be got in France for 1200 livres, or 2000 silver crowns of that kingdom.[56]

Following this account of his interest in machinery, Coxe informed Madison of the great value which he attached to the mechanical improvements:

To procure and record the drawings and descriptions of machinery and apparatus in the arts and philosophical science appears to me a very great object. It is manifest that without depending inconveniently upon manual labor we may, by mechanism and a knowledge of the value of sensible objects and their effects upon each other, save great sums of money, raise our character as an intelligent nation, and encrease the comforts of human life and the most pure and dignified enjoyments of the mind of man. No man has a higher confidence than I, in the talents of my countrymen and their ability to attain these things by their native strength of mind.[57]

In a circular communication to other societies of its type, sent out in 1804, reference was made by the Manufacturing Committee of the Pennsylvania Society to its

[56] Coxe to Madison, March 21, 1790, MS, Madison Papers, XII. It is probable that the " artist " to whom Coxe refers was a Mr. Parkinson, later (1791, see below) recommended by Hamilton to the New Jersey Society for the Encouragement of Useful Manufactures as " an ingenious Mechanic." He, it appears, about this time demonstrated to Coxe a machine to spin flax. See Davis, I, 399, 400.

[57] Coxe to Madison, March 21, 1790, MS, Madison Papers, XII.

misfortune of 1790. None the less, they declared, " We have the satisfaction to observe that the exertions made by the Manufacturing Committee in 1787 and 1788, contributed greatly to the obtaining and *displaying before the public* the real existence of the precious machinery for preparing, carding and spinning cotton." [58] Mindful of their own sad experience, they advised that caution be taken against similar fires " in the labor-saving manufactories."

Though forced to cease its manufacturing operations, the Pennsylvania Society of 1787 was not an entire failure. As an example of what could be done in this country to establish machine-manufactures, it served a useful purpose. [59] The Hartford (Connecticut) woolen manufactory, begun in April, 1788 with a capital of £2150, was no doubt modelled after the manufacturing project of the Pennsylvania Society. [60] This concern, however, met an end that was probably in store for the Pennsylvania Society, too. It failed to prove profitable owing to an insufficient capital, the high price of raw material, and machinery much inferior to that used in England. [61] Another effort, more successful, to manufacture cloth with machinery appeared in the Beverly cotton mill erected in Massachusetts " at some time after August,

[58] *A Communication from the Pennsylvania Society for the Encouragement of Manufactures and the Useful Arts,* Philadelphia, 1804, Tench Coxe, President, Duane Pamphlets, Vol. 96, No. 2, pp. 4-5. (Italics in original.)

[59] Bishop, I, 404, says its short-lived manufacturing operations were of greater influence than any other undertaking " in giving impulse to the cultivation and manufacture of cotton in the United States."

[60] See Davis, II, 258, 266, 268, 275; also, the Constitution of the Baltimore Manufacturing Society, *The American Museum* (1789), V, 595; that of the New York Manufacturing Society, *ibid.,* pp. 325-326; and that of the Delaware Society for the Encouragement and Promotion of Manufactories of America, *ibid.,* p. 174.

[61] See Elisha Colt to John Chester, August 20, 1791, Hamilton Manuscripts, XII. Elisha Colt was associated with Peter Colt and Jeremiah Wadsworth in the business. See also, Davis, II, 266-269.

1788." [62] It is likely that the incentive for its establishment was derived from the successful construction here or acquisition in England of textile machinery by the Barr brothers and Thomas Somers.[63] In common with other projects of its type, the Beverly mill met with many setbacks,[64] yet it managed to survive until 1807. The interference of the Embargo with trade destroyed its market, as well as that of other industrial undertakings in Essex County.[65]

These attempts to manufacture cotton cloth, while indicative of widespread interest, cannot be said to have laid the foundations of a permanent cotton industry in America. Their initiators are deserving of recognition for their faith and determination; but credit for instituting a successful cotton manufacture must be accorded to Samuel Slater, the youthful, "plain practical mechanic," [66] who came to this country from England toward the end of 1789. Equipped with seven years of experience with the

[62] Robert S. Rantoul, "The First Cotton Mill in America," *Historical Collections of the Essex Institute*, XXXIII, 11. There was an experiment to manufacture cotton at Beverly a few months earlier. The *Pennsylvania Gazette*, May 28, 1788, published a Boston news item, dated May 1, 1788, in which the operation of a jenny and carding machine at Beverly was reported. The distinction accorded the Beverly mill by Rantoul as the first to manufacture cotton in America is difficult to establish when we remember that the factory of the Pennsylvania Society was in actual operation before August, 1788. Indeed, according to Kohn, p. 8, a cotton factory was erected near Charleston, S. C., in 1787. "When the true history of the cotton mills is written it will be found that South Carolina was probably the very first State to undertake the development of cotton manufacturing," Kohn declares. *Ibid.*, p. 6. But neither this statement nor that of Rantoul seems to take into account the success of the Pawtucket mill, with which Slater was associated.

[63] See Rantoul, pp. 8-9; Bishop, 398-401; White, p. 57; Bagnall, *Textile Industries*, pp. 89-100.

[64] Rantoul, p. 24; letter of George Cabot, a member of the firm, to Hamilton, September 6, 1791, Hamilton Manuscripts, XII; Davis, II, 270 ff.

[65] Clark, pp. 534-535.

[66] White, p. 10. White was a personal friend of Slater. *Ibid.*, pp. 11, 30.

firm of Jedediah Strutt, an associate of the famed Arkwright, young Slater left his native land secretly, bent
upon trying his hand in the cotton manufacturing business in this country.[67] It is related of him that he was
prompted to make this memorable decision through having read in a newspaper of the steps taken by Pennsylvania to foster cotton manufactures. Moses Brown, who
employed Slater at Pawtucket, Rhode Island, to initiate
the cotton textile industry in America, explained it thus
in 1791:

> The publication of their grant [Pennsylvania's] to a certain
> person for a certain machine in this [cotton] manufactory reaching
> England [and] coming to the knowledge of the workmen at
> Arkwright's mills occasioned the workman before mentioned
> [Samuel Slater], privately coming to America and perfecting the
> first water spinning in the United States that I have heard of,
> 'tho I am informed a company from England are now about to
> erect mills near New York for which machinery is making at
> Newhaven.[68]

[67] For an account of Slater's life, see in addition to White: Bagnall,
Samuel Slater; F. L. Lewton, "Samuel Slater and the Oldest Cotton
Machinery in the United States," *Annual Report*, Smithsonian Institu-
tion (1926), pp. 505-512; D. H. Gilpatrick, "Samuel Slater, Father of
American Manufactures," *Proceedings of the South Carolina Historical
Association* (1932), pp. 23-34; S. Slater & Sons, Inc., *The Slater Mills
at Webster*; and Rev. John L. Blake, "Samuel Slater," Freeman Hunt's
Lives of American Merchants, I, 451-472.

[68] Moses Brown to John Dexter, July 22, 1791, Hamilton Manuscripts, XI. Brown may have had reference to the grant of £100 made
by the Pennsylvania Legislature to one John Hague for introducing into
that state a cotton-carding machine. See *Pennsylvania Gazette*, December 10, 1788, and above. In S. Slater & Sons, Inc., pp. 4-7, it is stated
that an advertisement of the Philadelphia Society in a local newspaper,
"offering a reward for the invention of textile machinery, to accomplish
what Arkwright had done . . . ," was read by Slater, prompting him to
come to America. A Glasgow worker, signing himself as "A Hosier,"
addressed a letter to "The Manager or Partner of a Company for Weaving Cotton Cloth late got up or erected in Philadelphia," no doubt referring to the Pennsylvania Society. This letter was dated July 6, 1790.
In it the writer urged that financial assistance be provided for workers
desirous of settling in America; their poverty, he wrote, prevented their

Arriving in Pawtucket in January, 1790, Slater found that the machines which Brown had assembled, in partnership with his son-in-law William Almy, were of no use, and that he himself would have to begin afresh. After having devoted nearly twelve months to the task, he was able to set in operation two frames of 72 spindles of the Arkwright type, along with several accessory machines.[69] It was only then that, to quote the words of Moses Brown, "we could get a single warp of cotton perfected." [70] By the first of January, 1791, 4556 yards of cloth had been made; during the next ten months, production increased to 7823 yards.[71] The concern also offered yarn for sale, for which there appears to have been only a small demand.[72] In later years the firm, of which Slater became a partner, continued to expand, always remaining in the lead until the War of 1812 brought in larger competitors, notably Francis Lowell.[73] In the interim other attempts were made to establish cot-

---

coming to America. "O remember," he plaintively concluded, "the Poor Hard Wrought half starved workmen in Britain." He enclosed some samples of British cotton goods. This letter is to be found in the Hamilton Manuscripts, VIII. It may have been handed to Hamilton by Coxe.

[69] White, p. 23; Bishop, I, 403. Coxe, in his "Summary View of the State of Pennsylvania," written during the middle of 1790, spoke of Pennsylvania's possessing an Arkwright water-mill for spinning cotton yarn. See *View*, p. 69. He does not say what success was had in its use. On December 30, 1791, William Pollard of Philadelphia obtained a patent for a water-frame to spin cotton, but it failed to work satisfactorily. See White, p. 183; also, *The United States Chronicle*, Providence, June 17, 1790. Clark, p. 535, writes of an unsuccessful attempt to use Arkwright machinery in Philadelphia in the year 1796. The first permanently successful Arkwright mill in that city was not erected until 1810, he declares, adding that Philadelphia had hitherto been backward in mill machinery. *Ibid.*, p. 537.

[70] Brown to Dexter, July 22, 1791, Hamilton Manuscripts, XI.

[71] *Ibid.*

[72] Caroline F. Ware, *The Early New England Cotton Manufacture*, pp. 31 ff.

[73] *Ibid.*, p. 19.

ton manufactories.[74] Many of these were unsuccessful, a notable example being the bold project of Hamilton and others to establish the New Jersey Society for establishing Useful Manufactures.

This last, as we have said, was an effort on Hamilton's part to give tangible form to his thesis in the *Report on Manufactures*.[75] Several of the Society's directors wrote Hamilton on August 9, 1791 for assistance in obtaining workmen and artists competent to manufacture and print cotton cloth.[76] This was not difficult, for Hamilton and Coxe were already in contact with such men. Thomas Marshall had written Hamilton that he had had " immediate tuition " under Sir Richard Arkwright, entering his employ in 1786. Marshall was, he assured Hamilton, fully acquainted with every improvement made by Arkwright and could establish a complete cotton manufactory.[77] Another desirous of employment was William Pearce, who came to America in July, 1791, assisted financially by William Seton of the Bank of New York and Thomas Jefferson.[78] Pearce went immediately to Coxe, bearing a letter from Jefferson. Writing to Jefferson about

[74] President Ezra Stiles of Yale mentioned in his *Diary* several cotton manufactories visited by him in New England. See *The Literary Diary of Ezra Stiles*, ed. Franklin B. Dexter, III (1782-1795), 508, 524, 525, 562. Consult also Bagnall, I, 166-201. In the South, too, the manufacture of cotton goods with reasonably up-to-date machinery was attempted. Coxe in his " Reflections on the State of the Union in the year 1792," *View*, p. 303, wrote of an association in Virginia, one in the territory south of the Ohio, and a company in the western district of South Carolina, which " have provided themselves with carding and spinning machinery on the British plans to manufacture their native cotton." The company in South Carolina had a subscription of twenty-five thousand dollars, Coxe wrote; that, considered in relation to the population there, was " an indication of zeal not equalled in any middle or northern state. . . ." *Ibid.*, p. 305; see also, Kohn, pp. 8-9.

[75] See above, chap. iii.

[76] See letter of Low, Duer, Constable and others to Hamilton, August 9, 1791, Hamilton Manuscripts, XII.

[77] Thomas Marshall to Hamilton, July 19, 1791, *ibid.*, XI.

[78] Davis, I, 401.

him, July 13, 1791, Coxe said that " It is Mr. Pearce's intention to proceed immediately to make the frames necessary to set up his machinery, which he says he can exhibit at work in a week's time." [79] These two men, along with several others, were recommended by Hamilton to the New Jersey Society.[80] In time the Society came to possess a considerable quantity of textile machinery,[81] but its manufacturing operations were marked by one failure after another.[82] The firm of Almy, Brown & Slater did, on one occasion, refer to it as a competitor producing a very inferior grade of yarn.[83]

In 1800, according to one writer,[84] the organized cotton industry of America was represented by " the factory at Beverly, and 7 Arkwright mills, 4 within a few miles of Providence and 3 in Connecticut." They had probably less than 2000 spindles and consumed between 50,000 and 100,000 pounds of cotton annually. Between 1800 and 1804, however, the number of mills in Rhode Island, Massachusetts, and Connecticut more than doubled.[85] This

[79] Coxe to Jefferson, July 13, 1791, MS, Jefferson Papers, LXV. See also, Davis, I, 401.

[80] Ibid., pp. 399-400, reproducing the letter of Hamilton. Included among those recommended was Parkinson, who had a machine to spin flax.

[81] Ibid., pp. 471-472; Bagnall, I, 181.

[82] Davis, I, 492-497. Its operations ceased in 1795.

[83] Ware, p. 21. Davis, I, 495, reproduces an advertisement of December, 1795, of goods offered for sale by the Society.

[84] Clark, p. 535.

[85] Ibid. See also Report of the Committee appointed to prepare a report on the state of manufactures in the United States generally, and particularly in the State of Pennsylvania, at the time of the establishment of this Society, and of their progressive increase and improvement to the present time. Published by order of the Board, Tench Coxe, President (1804), Duane Pamphlets, Vol. 96, No. 3. The Report was printed in the Philadelphia Evening Post, March 13, 1804, with an introductory note by Coxe, who probably wrote it. The Society was that established in August, 1787. See above. On July 17, 1802, Coxe wrote Thos. M. Willing in quest of any papers of the Society in his possession, adding that a collection of them was being made. Coxe to Willing, MS, Gratz Collection, box 4, case 1.

growth took place in spite of the enormous attraction of
capital to commerce. It is to be accounted for, in part, by
the migration to America of skilled artisans of Slater's
type,[86] many of whom are known to have gone to him
for assistance and advice.[87]

The development of machinery here and abroad to
manufacture cotton cloth was, of course, significant to
prospective growers of cotton in the southern states.
"Without cotton, the newly acquired machines will be
of no value; with abundance of raw material, they may
perform wonders," Carey wrote in March, 1788.[88] During the same month the editor of the *Pennsylvania Gazette*
addressed a plea to southern planters to cultivate cotton.
The prices of tobacco, rice, and wheat had fallen because
of overproduction; diversification, he argued, could be
had by planting cotton.[89] There were also other advantages to be had by the cultivation of cotton, as the editor
learned from a Charleston correspondent the following
month. One slave, according to this informant, could
manage seven acres of cotton; slaves cultivating cotton
would live longer than those engaged in the wet rice
fields. What was more important, their value would rise.
Speaking of the possible demand for cotton, the writer
asserted that "It is well known that the cotton manufactories in Great Britain will take any quantity that this

[86] See W. E. Lingelbach, "Historical Investigation and the Commercial History of the Napoleonic Era," *American Historical Review*, XIX,
278.

[87] White, p. 249.

[88] *The American Museum*, III, 286.

[89] See issue of March 19, 1788. The editor credited a correspondent,
perhaps Tench Coxe, with this idea, and suggested that it be republished
in all southern newspapers. *The Virginia Gazette and Weekly Advertiser*
of April 10, 1788, reprinted the item as requested. Southern members
of Congress in the debates on the Tariff of 1789 several times referred
to a decline in the price of tobacco, rice, and indigo. *Annals of Congress*,
1st Cong., 1st sess., pp. 155, 263, 265. See also, George Rogers Taylor, "Wholesale Commodity Prices at Charleston, South Carolina, 1732-
1791," *Journal of Economic and Business History*, IV, 356-377.

State can raise, as they are deemed by good judges to be now only in their infancy." [90] Coxe wrote of the enhanced importance of cotton to the southern economy to Madison, June 11, 1788, as follows:

> I remember you were struck with the probable benefits from cotton to the United States. The acquisition of machines has increased its importance. It supports its price in Europe and consequently in the W. Indies. A fair experiment has been made here [e. g. Philadelphia], and I can now assure you after careful examination and a fair calculation that the Cotton Manufacture will be always a profitable branch at 2/6 per lb. (2/3 of a dollar) for cotton, and the first cost and charges of English or French goods as the price of ours. The South Carolinians have just put in all the seed they could procure, and I have no doubt will find a profit in it. The concourse of people attending the Convention will give you a good opportunity of making enquiries into the present extent of the cultivation, the extension of it, if any this year, the probable quantity put in, and the comparative quality of it. I should suppose that near the salts, where the injuries from frost are rare and inconsiderable, the situation would be favorable.[91]

Continuing, Coxe referred to the wealth being acquired in the Barbadoes through cotton culture. " Every Barbadian speaks of it with rapture. I hope in one or two years every Virginian and southern citizen of America will do the same," he affirmed.

The Convention mentioned by Coxe in his letter was the one in Richmond called to pass on the proposed Federal Constitution. Madison at the time Coxe wrote him was waging a desperate struggle for ratification, yet Coxe wanted him to learn from members of the Convention the status of cotton culture in Virginia. Thrilled over the acquisition of labor-saving machines and aware of the demand likely to arise for cotton—he gave little heed to

[90] *Pennsylvania Gazette*, April 23, 1788.
[91] Coxe to Madison, June 11, 1788, MS, Madison Papers, IX.

the English demand—Coxe could not refrain from troubling his friend. Indeed, Coxe had himself just called the attention of the Virginia Convention to the possibility of cotton culture in their farming operations. In his letter to them he stressed the importance of cotton, "which must be the great American raw material for piece goods." [92]

Writing to Madison, July 23, 1788, Coxe again mentioned the matter:

> I forgot to ask you if you had time to make any enquiries or observations upon the subject of cotton planting in Virginia. I have seen a letter of Gen[l] Pinckney's, in which he mentions that he and Mr. E. Rutledge have put in 25 acres on a farm they own, and that Gen[l] Moultrie has put in 50 acres. He adds that they have planted all the seed they could procure in the different parishes, that were fit for that cultivation.[93]

Madison, on July 30, 1788, finally gave Coxe the much-desired reply. "From the few enquiries I had an opportunity of making on the subject of cotton," he wrote, " I found that it enters as far into the culture of the present year in Virginia, as seed could be got for the purpose." He added that he had communicated Coxe's observations to a friend, whom he was sure would make use of them.[94]

Other reports from the South at the same time indicated that similar attention was being given cotton. In South Carolina planters were reported to have carried on profitable experiments with it.[95] From Savannah, Richard

[92] Coxe, "Address to the honourable the members of the convention of Virginia" (June, 1788), *The American Museum*, III, 545.

[93] Coxe to Madison, July 23, 1788, MS, Madison Papers, IX.

[94] Madison to Coxe, July 30, 1788, *ibid*. In the October, 1788, issue of *The American Museum*, the editor, Mathew Carey, informed his readers that "From incontrovertible evidence, it appears, that a considerable quantity of cotton seed was purchased in Virginia by British agents, and burned, in order, if possible," to stay the development of cotton manufactures in America. *The American Museum*, III, 343 n.

[95] *Ibid*. (April, 1788), p. 391; *Pennsylvania Gazette*, April 23, 1788.

Teake wrote Thomas Proctor of Philadelphia that Georgia could supply all cotton needed for manufacturing purposes in the northern states. For his part, he proposed to raise five thousand pounds of seed, having already experimented with the plant on a large scale.[96]

But Teake and others were confronted with the difficulty of preparing the raw cotton for the market by removal of the seed. Primitive gins used for this purpose were inadequate.[97] Accordingly, neither the firm of Almy, Brown & Slater nor that at Beverly made much use of southern cotton in their early operations.[98] As to quantity, the domestic crop of 1790 has been estimated at a million and a half pounds, and the domestic consumption, for the same year, at about five million pounds.[99] The difference was imported principally from the West Indies and Brazil. Prior to December 1, 1790, cotton was imported duty-free; thereafter it was charged three cents per lb., provision to this effect having been made in the Tariff Act of 1789.[100]

Contrary to the accepted view,[101] Coxe was not respon-

[96] Teake to Proctor, December 11, 1788, reprinted in White, pp. 348-349. According to James L. Watkins, p. 96, Teake (he misspells the name as "Leake") sent some samples of Georgia cotton to the Pennsylvania Society.

[97] Hammond, pp. 22-23. A hand-mill, after the fashion of those used in India for centuries, was used in the South to gin the Sea-Island cotton. It was not applicable to the upland variety.

[98] It is probable, too, that the Pennsylvania Society used little southern cotton. Its Account Book for 1788-1790 contains entries of several purchases of cotton, some of which is termed "fine cotton." No clue, however, is furnished as to its source.

[99] Hammond, p. 233. He puts the crop of 1789 at one million pounds. According to the customs returns, 139,316 pounds were exported between October 1, 1790, and September 30, 1791; during the next ensuing twelve months the amount exported was 138,328 pounds, plus 100 bushels of Georgia cotton seed. See Coxe, *View*, p. 418. Britain in 1790 imported 31,447,605 pounds of cotton. Baines, p. 215.

[100] Act of 1789, *Tariff Acts Passed by the Congress of the United States from 1789 to 1909*, 61st Cong., 2d sess., H. Doc. No. 671, p. 15.

[101] Hammond, p. 20, and Scherer, p. 179, state erroneously that Coxe was responsible for this duty.

sible for this duty, which was an unwise burden on the
new industry.[102] In a letter to Madison, June 18, 1789,
Coxe wrote that he had "strongly" recommended to
several members of Congress that cotton be duty-free;
for "it is the only article to which labor-saving machines
can be applied, and it may be encreased by the planters
and importers to any quantity, while wool is limited and
flax is unfit for winter uses."[103] Madison explained in
reply that "The duty was a concession to S. C. and Georg[a]
who complained of sacrifices in almost every other article.
It has unluckily happened in a variety of instances that
compromises between local views have been made at the
expense of the general interest."[104]

Southern cotton was not only limited in supply; it was
also of a quality too poor to permit much use of it by
the early manufacturers. Moses Brown, writing to John
Dexter in 1791, averred that cotton culture in the South
"is as imperfect and more so, than the Manufacturing
when raised."[105] He attributed this to "promiscuous
gathering and saving of this article from the podd in
which it grows. . . ." Suitable cotton for his machines,
Brown continued, had to be imported from the West
Indies, subject to the three cent duty—"a circumstance
truly mortifying."[106] His firm did, however, use some

[102] Hamilton, *Report on Manufactures*, wrote that the duty was "undoubtedly a very serious impediment to the progress" of our cotton
manufactures. *American State Papers, Finance*, I, 141. He advised repeal
of the duty. *Ibid.*, p. 142.
[103] Coxe to Madison, June 18, 1789, MS, Madison Papers, XI. See
also Coxe, *Observations on the Agriculture, Manufactures and Commerce
of the United States*, p. 33, where he recommends the free importation
of cotton.
[104] Madison to Coxe, June 24, 1789, MS, Madison Papers, IX. In
1795 the cotton interest was threatened with a total loss of its foreign
market. By Article 12 of Jay's Treaty the exportation of cotton was
forbidden during the duration of Britain's war with France; this the
Senate refused to accept. Hammond, p. 21; Bemis, pp. 258-259, 332.
[105] Moses Brown to John Dexter, July 22, 1791, Hamilton Manuscripts, XI.
[106] *Ibid.*

southern cotton, maintaining an agent to buy it.[107] The
Beverly firm used no southern cotton,[108] but relied instead
on fine cotton from abroad, finding that it could be more
profitably worked up by their crude machinery. The use
of bad materials, it was asserted, meant a total loss.[109]

The invention of the cotton gin by Eli Whitney in 1793
was of revolutionary importance to the cotton growers of
the South. Thereafter a much enlarged supply of cotton,
of improved quality, was produced. The cultivation of
the upland variety in particular was greatly extended,
since the gin was especially applicable to it.[110] The extension of cotton culture served both to perpetuate the
institution of slavery and to prevent the South from
developing a diversified economy for many years to come.

Writing to Robert L. Livingston, the American Minis-
ter to France, June 18, 1802, Coxe remarked that the

---

[107] Ware, p. 22.

[108] See George Cabot to Hamilton, September 6, 1791, Cole, *Industrial
and Commercial Correspondence*, p. 64. Cabot was part owner of the
concern. In its petition to the state for assistance, 1790, it stated that
fish were exchanged for the West Indian cotton. Rantoul, p. 7.

[109] Cabot to Hamilton, September 6, 1791, Cole, *Industrial and Commercial Correspondence*, p. 64. In his *Report on Manufactures*, pp. 141-
142, Hamilton took cognizance of the alleged inferiority of southern
cotton. He expressed the belief that its quality could be improved. To
foster both the culture and manufacture of cotton in America, Hamilton
recommended a bounty of one cent per yard on cloth of domestic manufacture, plus one cent per lb. weight of the raw material, if it were grown
domestically. *Report*, p. 142. This was in accordance with a suggestion
made in April, 1791, by Moses Brown. The latter at that time sought
the support of the Beverly concern in obtaining from Congress an increase in the duty on foreign cloth, the proceeds of which were to be
paid out as a bounty partly " for raising and saving cotton in the Southern States, of a quality and clearness suitable to be wrought by machines
and partly as a bounty on cotton goods of the kind manufactured in the
United States." Quoted in Donnell, p. 53.

[110] Hammond, p. 23. Long-staple, or Sea-Island, cotton was introduced
into the South in 1786. Its success led the uplanders to try their hand,
though they found they could only raise successfully the short-staple
variety. Difficulties in ginning the short-staple variety prevented an extensive culture of it until after Whitney's invention. *Ibid.*, p. 16.

production of raw cotton was rapidly increasing but was
" unobserved." [111] What he had in mind was the question of markets for the crop.[112] He informed Livingston that the exports for the year 1800 were nearly 21 million pounds, of which 4 million was of foreign growth. The crop of 1801 was believed to have been 25 million pounds; and that of 1802 would be between 28 and 30 million pounds.[113] The poorest acre of land yielded above 400 pounds; the best nearly 1000 pounds, with the average 600 to 800 pounds. Water-ginning was used. In a word, cotton was, according to Coxe, " the first American raw material." As such, the matter of markets for it was likely to become a serious one.

On this score Coxe had several clever suggestions to offer Livingston for consideration. He asked Livingston to publicize the idea among Europeans that their tropical colonies could best be devoted to sugar, coffee, ginger, pimentoes, and the like, rather than to cotton, which should be obtained from us. Livingston could also stress the value of labor-saving machinery to European manufacturers of cotton cloth. The expansion of output so obtained would lead to a greater demand for our cotton. Coxe, of course, knew that if more cloth were made, a market would have to be found for it, too. He therefore told Livingston that it would be worthwhile to induce a preference for cloth made of cotton rather than of wool, hemp, or flax. Woolen cloth, in particular, Coxe pointed out, was inferior to that made of cotton, since it was sub-

[111] Coxe to Livingston, June 18, 1802, MS, Roberts Collection, Haverford College.
[112] In a letter to William Jones, February 12, 1802, Coxe said he was " satisfied, that we have yet little idea of the value of cotton to our navigation, trade and manufactures. . . ." Letter in Autograph Collection, Historical Society of Pennsylvania.
[113] In both instances Coxe underestimated the size of the crop. For 1801 it was 48 million pounds; for 1802, 55 million pounds. See Hammond, Appendix I.

ject to moths and shrinkage, and difficult to clean. For our part, he continued,

It has been found our interest here to create a rivalship between the British Lancashire *cotton* spinners and weavers and the British Yorkshire *woolen* spinners and weavers, in order that the latter, working on wool of foreign countries, may lose our custom, in favor of the former, who consume much of our *cotton*: and that the woolen manufacturers and their capital may, in self-defence, turn to the manufacture of cotton goods.[114]

Progress in this direction would mean a greater consumption of our cotton. Less attention would be given to cattle and grains, thus enabling the price of these to be maintained.

The emphasis which Coxe placed here upon a foreign market for our cotton is not, however, to be taken as indicating a lack of interest in the development of the American cotton manufacture with its demand for the raw material. On the contrary, he admitted to Livingston that the growth of cotton manufactures in America was much to be desired. This, as we have seen, had all along been in his mind. Writing in 1804, following a period of large importations of British goods, Coxe even went so far as to argue that we should manufacture all of the cotton cloth we used:

To send 20,000,000 pounds of cotton to England, at 16 cents per pound, and to pay them for manufacturing it into cloathing for us, at an average of 160 cents per pound, will be found to be paying too much for that which might be done, within ourselves, if the national industry were properly directed. . . . If to erect machinery to spin and weave such a quantity of cotton,

[114] Coxe to Livingston, June 18, 1802, MS, Roberts Collection. (Underscoring in original.) Later, 1806-1807, Coxe agitated in favor of the exclusion of Indian piece-goods because they were not made of our cotton. See Coxe, *Thoughts on the Subject of Naval Power in the United States,* pp. 16-17; Coxe, " Considerations relative to certain articles of the Treaty prepared in 1806," in Madison Papers, XXXI; and Coxe to Madison, May 20 and July 31, 1807, MSS, Madison Papers, XXXII.

and to teach the people these arts, should be the labour of 20 years, the most stupid reasoner would naturally conclude, that it was time to make a beginning; for if we remain as we are, and pursue the same conduct we have done for the last twenty years, we shall then be obliged to employ England to spin and weave for us 40 million lbs. of cotton, for which they will charge for manufacturing (say 160 cents).[115]

Ignoring the question of necessary capital, Coxe proceeded to point out that cotton cloth of the finer varieties might be made by the sons of " large gentell families." [116] In addition, there were many lawyers who could give up their profession to supervise manufacturing plants. There would still remain, he added, enough lawyers for our purposes, provided " questions of accounts " were submitted to arbitration by juries of five persons chosen by the litigants.[117] " But, of all things," he concluded, " the political economist will attend to the proper employment of the fair sex." They, too, could manufacture quality cloth. The number available for such purposes he estimated to be one million.[118]

Capital, which Coxe failed to mention in his argument, was being drawn into a lucrative neutral commerce. Yet, as we have seen above, cotton manufacturing continued to develop. In 1806 it reached a peak for the period prior to 1809-1810.[119] The expansion was financed largely by the profits of the business.[120] When the Embargo was

---

[115] Coxe, *An Essay on the Manufacturing Interest of the United States,* p. 12. See above, chap. iv. The argument here presented by Coxe was one that was to be frequently enunciated in the 1880's by southern advocates of a local cotton manufacture. See Broadus Mitchell, *The Rise of Cotton Mills in the South* (" Johns Hopkins University Studies in Historical and Political Science," Series XXXIX, No. 2), pp. 115-117.

[116] Coxe, *An Essay on the Manufacturing Interest of the United States,* p. 14.

[117] *Ibid.,* p. 15.

[118] *Ibid.,* p. 15.

[119] Clive Day, " The Early Development of the American Cotton Manufacture," *Quarterly Journal of Economics,* XXXIX, 463.

[120] Clark, pp. 367, 369.

enacted in December, 1807, the industry was already firmly established,[121] though there was a recession then and in 1808.[122] In 1809 there were fifty mills under construction in New England alone,[123] and the number continued to grow.[124] For the most part the business was confined to the manufacture of yarn; weaving was still a household industry.[125] A western demand for cloth, however, prompted some firms to combine weaving with their spinning operations.[126] The war period brought into being large firms engaged in mass production, by which weaving and spinning were simultaneously undertaken.[127] A secure home market, plus capital from commercial quarters, facilitated this development.[128] Another factor of equal importance was the perfection of the power-loom by Francis C. Lowell and his assistants. Visiting England in 1810-1811, Lowell carefully observed their machinery; on his return he was able to duplicate it, and in 1813 founded the Boston Manufacturing Company at Wal-

[121] *Ibid.*, p. 536.

[122] Day, p. 463. He produces tables showing the course of the industry's development at this time. Almy and Brown, the selling agency of Almy, Brown & Slater, experienced a slump in their sales during 1808-1809, for the Embargo meant a curtailment of purchasing power among the commercial classes. The southern demand, however, sustained the firm, as well as many of its competitors. Ware, pp. 39, 40, 41, 46-48. Coxe, it may be noted here, in the early part of 1808 joined with Mathew Carey in founding the Philadelphia Manufacturing Society, which was expected to manufacture textiles. Scharf and Wescott, I, 531.

[123] Clark, p. 536.

[124] Day, p. 452. See also, letter of Samuel Slater to Louis McLane, 1832, *McLane Report*, 22d Cong., 1st sess., H. Doc. No. 308., VII, Part 1, pp. 927-928.

[125] Clark, p. 539.

[126] Ware, p. 50. Almy, Brown & Slater did some weaving. Coxe as Purveyor of Public Supplies at one time purchased 40,000 yards of their cloth. Clark, p. 625.

[127] Ware, p. 60.

[128] Clark, pp. 536, 539-541; Melvin T. Copeland, *The Cotton Manufacturing Industry of the United States* ("Harvard Economic Studies," VIII), pp. 4-5.

tham, Massachusetts. With a paid-in capital of $300,000 this company was unprecedented in size.[129] Weaving henceforth became increasingly a factory operation.[130]

Although the War of 1812 and the restrictions on trade that preceded it occasioned a phenomenal growth of the American cotton manufacture, the problem of how to face the growing surplus of the raw material still perplexed Coxe, not without reason. While the domestic demand had greatly increased,[131] it alone could not sustain the price received by the southern planter.[132] Furthermore, following the Embargo, Indian cotton growers began to ship heavily to the British market; this advantage enabled them, up to 1818, to send more cotton to England than did America.[133] In short, the situation of the American cotton growers seemed likely to become critical. Alert to this fact, Coxe in 1813 reverted to the possibility of our manufacturing the whole crop ourselves. In a digest of American arts and manufactures, prepared for Secretary Gallatin in that year and published in 1814, Coxe estimated that 1,160,000 spindles would be required to work up the maximum of our exports of cotton in any one previous year—sixty-four million pounds.[134] There would be needed 210,000 workers; the necessary capital he put at 70 million dollars, noting that the accumulation of capital from profits of the business had already been considerable. The value of the surplus, if thus disposed of, would, according to Coxe, be increased from 8 or 9

[129] Ware, pp. 63-64; Bagnall, *Samuel Slater*, pp. 60-61; Clark, p. 450.
[130] Tryon, p. 247.
[131] Watkins, pp. 13-14, estimates that the domestic consumption doubled between 1800 and 1810; during the War it increased by 70%.
[132] Hammond, p. 240.
[133] *Ibid.*, p. 246. See also, Levi Woodbury, *Report on the Production and Consumption of Cotton in the United States*, 24th Cong., 1st sess., Ex. Doc., No. 146, p. 9.
[134] Coxe, *A Statement of the Arts and Manufactures of the United States of America*, p. x.

million to 75 million dollars: "Such are the benefits, which agriculture and the country at large may derive from the manufacture of *our only redundant raw material*." [135] In support of the practicability of this idea Coxe cited the remarkable progress of the cotton industry in Massachusetts and Rhode Island.[136] The large supply of cotton, together with the fact that it was adapted to machine-manufacture, would soon make it our greatest manufacture.[137] Furthermore, we had an advantage over foreign competitors in that the transportation costs of cotton were lower for us.[138] Again, their goods coming to us must, in the case of the coarse varieties, bear an additional 70 per cent charge on manufacturing costs, and for the finer varieties, 50 per cent, to get into our markets.[139]

The conviction that America should manufacture all of her cotton was again expressed by Coxe in 1817. In *A Memoir of February, 1817, upon the subject of the cotton wool cultivation, the cotton trade, and the cotton manufactories of the United States of America*,[140] he viewed with anxiety the increasing cultivation of cotton for ex-

[135] *Ibid.*, pp. x-xi. (Italics his.)

[136] *Ibid.*, p. xi. In a letter to Madison, September 2, 1813, Coxe wrote that he had been informed that six million dollars was employed in the cotton industry located in a radius of twenty miles around Providence, R. I. MS, Madison Papers, LIII.

[137] Coxe, *Statement*, p. xxviii.

[138] Clark, p. 319, discussing this point with the assistance of statistics not available to Coxe when he wrote, gives a different conclusion: "The immediate competitive advantage American mill-owners derived from home supplies was moderate. Cotton freights from New Orleans to New England and Old England ports, during the early part of the century, were one cent and one penny a pound respectively, a difference of about a cent a pound in favor of domestic manufactures," he writes.

[139] Coxe, *Statement*, p. xxix.

[140] The copy here used is to be found in the American Philosophical Society Pamphlets, Vol. 33, No. 6. On p. 16 n of the Memoir it is stated that the Memoir was ordered printed by the Philadelphia Society for the Promotion of American Manufactures, August 28, 1817. This Society, according to Bishop, II, 118, was instituted in 1805.

port in other countries, especially India. Enclosing a copy of the essay to Madison, Coxe wrote as follows:

It is above thirty years since I submitted to you on our return from the convention at Annapolis, that the garden cultivation of cotton on the Chesapeake bay convinced me that we would one day become great producers and cultivators of cotton. You decidedly confirmed the hope, and we now raise for ourselves and others probably 100 millions of pounds of clean cotton, and have land to spare for more millions than the world can consume. I have had this subject under my observation and consideration, in a favorable position, during those thirty years. A very important crisis seems to approach in the American culture, sale, and employment of it. The memoir which I have now the honor to submit to your perusal, exhibits the principal facts and considerations, which appear to constitute this crisis.[141]

In the *Memoir* Coxe first traced his interest in the subject of cotton culture. He next emphasized the importance of the crop to our economy, with a view to centering attention upon the vital matter of markets for it. The cotton crop he estimated to be 111 million pounds, involving about a million acres of land and the employment for three months each year of one-seventh of our population.[142] The area of cultivation extended to the 38th degree, north and south latitude, which meant that other nations in this region could compete with our producers of cotton. "Men of observation and reflection will quickly perceive the possibility of this inconvenience to the *southern agriculture* of the United States," he wrote.[143] Already we were meeting competition at the hands of Indian growers; Britain, he thought, would continue to foster this source of cheap cotton, for there were tremen-

---

[141] Coxe to Madison, February 8, 1817, MS, Madison Papers, LXIV. See also, Coxe to Madison, February 25, July 5, and September 25, 1817, *ibid.*

[142] Coxe, *Memoir*, pp. 3, 7.

[143] *Ibid.*, p. 3. (Italics his.)

dous profits to prompt such imports.[144] Furthermore, Africa, South America, Italy, Turkey, Greece, and other regions were potential cotton producers.[145] If they became so to any great extent, the price of cotton must necessarily fall. America, therefore, should take action: our cotton should be manufactured in our own mills. The government, he concluded, should interest itself in the project.[146]

In a continuation to his *Memoir*, written in August, 1817, Coxe reaffirmed the above observations and conclusion. He added that unless we did manufacture our cotton, in both mills and households, falling prices for it would occasion a reversion in part to rice, tobacco, grain, and the like, thereby sinking the prices of these, too.[147]

During the following year, Coxe again wrote of the threats to our cotton growers. This essay he entitled, *An addition, of December 1818, to the memoir, of February and August 1817, on the subject of the cotton culture, the cotton commerce, and the cotton manufacture*

[144] *Ibid.*, p. 7. The first importation of Indian cotton by Britain, he declared, was in 1798; this initial cargo brought a profit of £50,000. *Ibid.*, p. 16. On Indian competition, see also, Coxe to Madison, February 25, July 5, and September 25, 1817, MSS, Madison Papers, LXIV.

[145] Coxe, *Memoir*, p. 7. Brazil was already producing cotton for export. See Hammond, pp. 30, 235-236; Woodbury, p. 7; Baines, p. 305.

[146] Coxe, *Memoir*, pp. 7-10.

[147] The continuation is subjoined to the *Memoir of February, 1817*. See *ibid.*, p. 15. Coxe during this year also wrote an article entitled the "United States," for incorporation in *The Cyclopaedia; or, Universal Dictionary of Arts, Sciences, and Literature,* of which Abraham Rees was the editor. It appeared in 1818. Coxe devoted by far the greater portion of his article to a reiteration of the contents of his *Memoir*. He also deplored what he termed "the limited degree of notice" accorded labor-saving machinery in this country, pointing especially to the use of steam-power. Coxe, "United States," *The Cyclopaedia*, XXXIX (no pagination); also Coxe to Madison, February 2, 1819, MS, Madison Papers, LXVI, wherein Coxe informed Madison of this article. Madison, in reply, praised it. Madison to Coxe, February 12, 1819, *ibid.* He also made it available to Jefferson. Madison to Jefferson, February 12, 1819, *ibid.*

of the United States, most respectfully submitting a suggestion, for consideration only, of a specific measure for securing to the planters of cotton a market for their crops.[148] In it he wrote once more of Indian competition, calling attention to the fact that now that steam navigation was a fact, Indian cotton could be shipped to England more cheaply than could ours. Moreover, the British were sending their cloth, made cheaply by machinery, to India; this, he expected, would lead India to concentrate upon cotton culture—to our detriment, of course.[149] Predicting a crisis in the cotton markets the following year (1819),[150] Coxe renewed his plea for the development of cotton manufactures in America: " Home machine manufactures, and home house-hold manufactures are the only supports to the price of our cotton, within our command," he declared.[151] To effect this end, he was willing to cast aside the principle that manufactures should not be forced by prohibitions or heavy duties.[152] Finally, Coxe offered the more practical suggestion that the cotton planters put in a smaller crop during 1819, and supplement their income by cultivating sugar cane, vineyards, or olives.[153]

Writing to Madison, February 2, 1819, Coxe noted with delight that the price of cotton was being maintained at a steady level, owing largely, he thought, to the

[148] The copy here used is to be found in the Library of Congress, Rare Book Room.

[149] Coxe, *Addition of December, 1818*, pp. 1-3. He put the import into England of Indian cotton at 220,000 bales for the year 1818, compared with our greatest export in any one year, to England, of 135,000 bales. *Ibid.*, p. 4.

[150] *Ibid.*, p. 10.

[151] *Ibid.*, p. 6.

[152] *Ibid.*, pp. 5-6. In 1818 Congress enacted ·that the 25% duty on cotton cloth was to continue in force until 1826, and not expire in 1819 as provided for in the Tariff Act of 1816. Taussig, p. 24.

[153] Coxe, *Addition of December, 1818*, pp. 13-14. The value of the cotton crop in 1817 was, he wrote, 40 million dollars. *Ibid.*, p. 6.

"wonderful power of machinery."[154] For this reason, perhaps, the planters failed to heed his advice that the crop should be curtailed. At any rate, the crop of 1819-1820 was of unprecedented size; the surplus so created brought an immediate fall in the price received, from 24 cents in 1818-1819 to 17 cents in 1820.[155] A contributing factor was the collapse of the whole price structure of the country, beginning towards the end of 1818.[156] It had been founded upon an unwise expansion of credit, in many instances through the issuance of irredeemable paper currency. A policy of credit contraction initiated by the Second Bank of the United States in August, 1818, to curb the demand for specie, much of which was intended for export, led to numerous bank failures. The ensuing debâcle was marked by unemployment, bankruptcies, idle capital, and great social distress.[157] Many cotton manufacturers, especially those of Philadelphia, were ruined.[158] In fact, the prices of cotton cloth had already fallen ruinously, owing to the dumping policy of British manufacturers,[159] and to accumulation of large stocks by domestic manufacturers during the War, in anticipation of a continued price rise.[160]

[154] Coxe to Madison, February 2, 1819, MS, Madison Papers, LXVI.

[155] Watkins, p. 14. The prices of other farm exports also tumbled, due largely to good European harvests in 1818. See Smith and Cole, *Fluctuations in American Business, 1790-1860*, pp. 20, 29, 31. These writers state that the price of cotton fell from 33 cents to 20 cents within a period of nine months, in 1818-1819. *Ibid.*, p. 20.

[156] Bolles, p. 329; Taussig, pp. 19-21.

[157] Samuel Rezneck, "The Depression of 1819-1822, A Social History," *American Historical Review*, XXXIX, 29-35; Smith and Cole, pp. 21, 27, 29.

[158] See *Niles' Weekly Register* (1819), XVII, 117-119; Clark, p. 379; and Hammond, p. 245. There were 1808 commitments to prison for debt in Philadelphia County during 1819. Rezneck, p. 32.

[159] White, pp. 232-233; Clark, p. 379; Bagnall, p. 59.

[160] Clark, p. 379. The Tariff of 1816 was passed with a view to according relief from foreign competition; it had southern support. Taussig, p. 30.

In November, 1819, Coxe wrote out for the benefit of President Monroe his views upon the recession in economic activity. He was perhaps prompted by a desire to assist the President in the formulation of his impending annual message to Congress. Comprising seven pages of manuscript, Coxe's contribution bore the grandiose title of "An Inquiry into the causes of the disorders in the private business of the civilized world; with a *particular view to the case of the United States, and especially of the manufacturing branch of its national industry.*" [161] In an introductory letter accompanying the essay, Coxe wrote that the powers of machinery and science had brought about a surplus of goods, glutted markets, and unemployment of manual workers.[162] This observation is interesting as an anticipation of the recent technocratic theories about the depression of 1929-35. It was made, it should be remembered, at a time when machine techniques were only beginning to be applied extensively in America. In his "Inquiry" proper, Coxe noted the rapid economic expansion which the country had lately undergone. During this period many who were not qualified undertook to manufacture, he wrote, mentioning as examples, lawyers, teachers, and physicians.[163] During this development credits had been too unwisely extended; now that they were curtailed, there were bankruptcies on all sides. Failures were numerous among those manufacturers who relied upon hand power and who, after the Peace, had to face the competition of European machine-made cloth.[164]

[161] To be found in the Monroe Papers, XVIII. (Italics his.)

[162] Coxe to Monroe, November 18, 1819, MS, Monroe Papers, XVIII. John Melish, in his *The Necessity of Protecting and Encouraging the Manufactures of the United States, in a letter to President James Monroe,* estimated the number of unemployed to be a half-million. See p. 10. James Flint, *Letters from America* (Edinburgh, 1822), p. 248, gave a similar estimate. Cited in Rezneck, p. 31 n.

[163] Coxe, "Inquiry," p. 3. He apparently forgot his own suggestion, made in 1804, that lawyers could manage cotton mills. See above.

[164] *Ibid.,* p. 4. However, in his letter to Monroe, Coxe discounted the importance of heavy importations in bringing on the crisis.

In the case of those introducing machinery, costs of production had been cheapened, he wrote; this, he thought, also contributed to the crisis.[165] In short, Coxe detected temporary as well as permanent causes of the crisis.

In his third annual message to Congress, December 7, 1819, President Monroe sought to minimize the intensity of the recession. There was, he said, a surplus of produce for export; moreover, the currency situation had improved. But trade, commerce and manufactures, he was forced to admit, were embarrassed by the fall in prices and by dumping.[166]

But this view of the country's difficulties, as many contemporary writers noted, was too superficial.[167] Cessation of economic activity, they wrote, was widespread and calamitous in its results. Their explanations of the causes were numerous. Some blamed the bankers for an unwise overexpansion of credit; others wrote that the country was experiencing the natural aftermath of a war. Again, it was said that there was not sufficient protection accorded our manufacturers. To Mathew Carey, the trouble lay in the fact that the American economy was unbalanced: there were too many farmers.[168] Had Coxe taken greater pains in examining the causes of the recession, we may be sure that he would not have omitted a similar observation, but here, as in other instances, he wrote too hastily.

During 1820 general business conditions showed definite improvement, and by 1821 recovery was well under way.[169] In the cotton industry, technical improvements

---

[165] *Ibid.*, p. 6. As an example of the technical progress which he believed to have taken place, Coxe cited the fact that wool could be sheared from a sheep's back and made into a suit of clothes in a few hours time. *Ibid.*, p. 7. This doubtless was an exaggeration.

[166] Richardson, II, 54, 61.

[167] Rezneck, pp. 38-39.

[168] See *ibid.*, pp. 34-41, for an excellent account of the explanations offered by contemporary writers.

[169] Clark, p. 379; Ware, p. 79.

had been stimulated by the recession. From 1820 to 1831 the industry expanded greatly, the number of spindles quadrupling, and the number of factory looms increasing tenfold.[170] In 1823 the industry was exporting its product.[171] Furthermore, after 1818 the importation of Indian cotton into England fell off, by 1820 amounting to only one-sixth of that bought from this country.[172] Indeed, statistics of our cotton exports show only stagnation, rather than retrogression, for the period up to the year 1820.[173] Although the volume of cotton exports increased after that date, the price received by the planter did not; for a decade after 1820 the price of cotton continued to fall.[174]

To Coxe, the cause of this fall lay in the fact that the culture of cotton was being overdone. Apparently convinced that his proposition of our manufacturing the whole crop was impracticable, he abandoned it in 1819 in favor of the advocacy of further diversification in southern agriculture. In that year, writing as "A Friend to the National Industry," he published in *The Daily National Intelligencer* of Washington a series of seven articles on vine culture.[175] "No principle of action in the business and industry of the United States has been so beneficial to them as the adoption of new objects of culture by the

[170] Clark, pp. 380, 544; Ware, pp. 79-81.

[171] Ware, pp. 189-190. As she points out, however, "Probably no more than five or six per cent of the total output left the country in any year before 1840." *Ibid.*, p. 190.

[172] Hammond, p. 246. In a trade circular of Maury & Latham of Liverpool, dated October 23, 1820, it was stated that the import of American cotton for the year ending October 21, 1820, amounted to 410,347 bales, compared with 330,680 bales for the previous year. See Circular in Madison Papers (Printed Material), LXXIX.

[173] Hammond, Appendix I.

[174] *Ibid.*, p. 246.

[175] See issues of November 6, 10, 13, 16, 19, and December 2, 14, 1819. The full title was, "On the Grape Vine, with its wines, brandies, salt, and dried fruit." (Hereinafter referred to as, Coxe, "On the Grape Vine.")

planters and farmers, whose old objects of culture were likely to become redundant, and to fall in price," he wrote.[176] Already he had pointed out in his *Memoir* and elsewhere the value of crop diversification to support agricultural prices; it was time for another step in this direction to prevent overproduction of cotton, particularly in view of possible competition in foreign markets of other producers of the raw material.[177] The new turn which agriculture—"the Colossus of our country"[178]—now must be given was, Coxe wrote at length, the introduction of vine culture. The region for such an undertaking he defined as "between the sites of the vineyards of the Lower Schuylkill, Southwark, of Pennsylvania, Butler of Pennsylvania, Glasgow, of Kentucky, New Vevay, of Indiana, and Harmony, of the same state, on the north, and the coasts of the Gulf of Mexico," on the south.[179] The remainder of his articles is given over to an account of vine culture in other countries, especially France; to details of how the vine should be propagated here, with reference to experiments then under way; and to a plea for widespread circulation among our farmers of tracts on the technical phases of the subject.[180] "The subject," he wrote, "is too important to be longer neglected or postponed. The times require the extension, diversification, and improvement of our agriculture, as one of the

[176] *Ibid.*   [177] *Ibid.*   [178] *Ibid.*   [179] *Ibid.*

[180] *Ibid.* The work of Messrs. Parmentier and Chaptal, *Sur la culture de la Vigne, &c* (Paris, 1801, 2 vols.), particularly struck his attention as worthy of translation and adaptation to our needs. See Coxe, "On the Grape Vine," November 10 and December 2 issues. Coxe also would have Assistant U. S. Marshals report on vine culture in this country. November 16 issue. For references to two early attempts to introduce vine culture on a large scale, one in Kentucky and one in Pennsylvania, see Davis, II, 284, 286; consult also Bishop, I, 276-277; Thomas Cooper, *Some Information Respecting America*, pp. 70, 128-129; W. Winterbotham, *An Historical, Geographical, Commercial and Philosophical View of the United States of America*, III, 449-487. Coxe had written at some length on the subject in his *Statement* of 1810, pp. xvii-xviii, xl.

surest remedies for the momentary disorders of the body politic." [181]

In a letter written the following year to his old friend, James Madison, Coxe expressed the view that our capacity for vine culture " is actually much more valuable than what cotton has yet proved in money." [182] Moreover, " It is a matter of the deepest importance to our agriculture to strike out new objects of cultivation to prevent redundance." [183] To spread this idea he would like to have a pamphlet made of his essays on vine culture. In the past, he informed Madison, it had been his custom to publish and distribute free of charge his essays. On one occasion he spent a thousand dollars in such useful work; now, however, he did not have the cash to continue the policy.[184]

In the same letter Coxe also discussed in a cursory manner the question of protection to manufactures. On this point he wrote that " I remain convinced that they are not, in general, in need of more protection " than that afforded by a tariff for revenue purposes. Proof of this he saw in the fact that we exported no iron, hides, skins, flax, hemp, silk, wool rags, or lead during the last returned year. Yet, Coxe continued, " It is to be considered, whether upon mere agricultural policy, we ought not to force the manufacture of any landed production, of which we cannot find consumers abroad." [185] He had cotton in mind, of course. Unfortunately, Coxe was not

[181] Coxe, " On the Grape Vine," December 2, 1819. A request that anyone who knew about the cultivation of the grape vine contribute to the discussion brought at least one reply. An anonymous writer in the issues of December 17, 23, 1819, agreed substantially with the ideas of Coxe, and referred to his own experience.

[182] Coxe to Madison, March 7, 1820, MS, Madison Papers, LXVII. He also spoke of having agitated the subject among the French exiles of 1814-1815.

[183] Ibid.

[184] Ibid.

[185] Ibid.

clear in his analysis here, for he goes on to point out that our agricultural population " cannot wisely be burdened to promote more rapidly our great and growing manufactures." [186] We may conclude that he was in doubt on this score.

Madison, long a friend to the agrarian interests, wrote in reply that he wished " heartily " that Coxe's essays on vine culture would engage the public attention; but he could not bring himself to believe that vine culture would exceed in worth the culture of cotton.[187] In regard to the development of manufactures, Madison wrote that he thought the greatest obstacle had been overlooked. This he found to be the fact that the sale of imported manufactures was greatly assisted by generous credit facilities provided by foreigners, whereas the domestic goods were not sold on credit to any great extent.[188] We have no record of Coxe's views on this point. It may be inferred, however, that he took the differentials which he earlier set up in favor of the sale of domestic goods as covering such circumstances.[189] With experience as a merchant he

[186] *Ibid.*

[187] Madison to Coxe, March 20, 1820, MS, Madison Papers, LXVII. Frederick List, it is interesting to note, also doubted the ability of vine culture to offset the decline in the price of cotton. In his *Outlines of American Political Economy* . . . (Philadelphia, 1827), List advised that the wise policy for the South to pursue would be to develop manufactures of their cotton: " After having started the machineries, the inhabitants of the South would even enjoy peculiar advantages: first, they would apply their labourers from the prime of their youth to a certain branch of business, and their skill would be secured to the manufactory for their whole lifetime; secondly, for the spinning mills they could turn the labour of the females and of the children, who are now of very little use to them, to a better account; thirdly, they would have the cotton cheaper, and the South American market nearer; fourthly, they could dye with home-raised colour-plants, particularly indigo, without any preparation." See *ibid.*, in Margaret E. Hirst, *Life of Frederick List and Selections from his Writings*, pp. 265-270.

[188] Madison to Coxe, March 20, 1820, MS, Madison Papers, LXVII.

[189] See above, chap. iii.

certainly could not have been unaware of the basis of Madison's contention.

We have set forth in some detail in this chapter the story of the introduction on a large scale of cotton culture into the American economy, and the establishment of the cotton manufacture here. The former, credit for which must in a large measure be ascribed to Tench Coxe, was significant in that its consequences were to mold our political development throughout the greater part of the nineteenth century. This was because cotton, slavery, and territorial expansion became inextricably interwoven.[190] The latter two, deriving their *raison d'être* from the first, constituted a source of increasing friction between the North and the South prior to the final break.

The upshot of the whole was that the attractive picture painted by Tench Coxe in 1787 of a happy consolidation of economic interests[191] did not materialize without a struggle—a violent, bloody one. To be sure, the southern states became producers of raw materials, cotton in particular, the western states, purveyors of foodstuffs, and the northern states were well on the road to manufacturing enterprise. Against such a background a plea for consolidation through the mutual exchange of each other's output was appropriate. But its peaceful achievement, as Coxe would have had it, was rendered impossible owing to the existence of slavery—an institution in the first instance insured by the introduction of cotton culture and the invention of the gin. In concluding this chapter, therefore, it is appropriate to mention the interest of Tench Coxe in the problem of slavery.

As has been pointed out, Coxe was no friend to the institution of slavery, having become in 1787 an active

---

[190] The importance of the gin in making possible a tremendous expansion in cotton culture, and thereby sustaining the institution of slavery, is not to be overlooked. D. A. Tompkins, *History of Mecklenburg County*, I, 96, 98, 100.

[191] See above, chap. iii.

member of the Pennsylvania Society for promoting its abolition.[192] The use of slaves in introducing and extending cotton culture in the South never prompted him to change his views, either. In his " Examination of the Constitution of the United States of America, . . ." written in 1787, he noted with approbation that Article whereby the importation of slaves was to be forbidden after 1807. It laid, he thought, " A solid foundation . . . for exploding the principles of negro slavery. . . ."[193] Writing to Madison in 1801 he expressed concern over the maintenance of the institution. Slaves (he called them " blacks ") should be dispersed through settlement on new lands.[194] In what manner, he did not say. Later, in his *Essay on the Manufacturing Interest of the United States* (1804), he wrote that different kinds of tillage were needed in the South to solve the slavery problem. Southerners were, he declared, " placed betwixt Sylla and Charybdes without a pilot."[195]

Important, however, as was the problem of slavery in relation to his pet subject of cotton culture, Coxe does not appear to have given extended consideration to it until the Missouri question arose in 1820. The expansion of slavery into new territory then became a matter of national concern. In a letter to Madison, March 7, 1820, Coxe agreed with the southern position that Congress had no right to impose restrictions on the admission of new states into the Union. The slaves, he again asserted, should be dispersed as a measure preparatory to gradual abolition. He did not think that the movement for African colonization could do more than reduce their number. Accompanying his letter was an article of his dealing with the question of slavery.[196]

[192] See above, chap. i.
[193] Coxe, " Examination," Duane Pamphlets, Vol. 96, No. 3, p. 16.
[194] Coxe to Madison, 1801, MS, Madison Papers, XXIII.
[195] Coxe, *Essay on the Manufacturing Interest*, p. 13.
[196] Coxe, to Madison, March 7, 1820, MS, Madison Papers, LXVII.

In this article Coxe wrote of the problem of emancipation. He would attempt a solution by creating what he termed "the new Africa," to be established by setting aside twenty million acres of our territory in the South. Upon it would be settled "all those, who now are, and who shall hereafter, gradually and lawfully, become free." The states, where possible, should provide for emancipation; loans, donations, and bequests would support the emancipated ones so colonized.[197] This plan, it must be admitted, was certainly not very helpful.[198]

In a series of articles appearing in *The Democratic Press*, November 25, 1820 to January 9, 1821, Coxe reiterated his plea for a dispersion of the slaves.[199] He again took the southern view, too, when he wrote that slaves were not citizens, and that they were private property.

The article, captioned "Civilization," appeared in *The National Recorder*, Philadelphia, February 20, 1820, pp. 132-133, over the signature of "Columbus."

[197] Coxe, *The National Recorder, ibid.*

[198] Madison, however, wrote Coxe that he had for many years thought the use of our vacant lands of great value "as a gradual cure for the portentious evil" of slavery. Madison to Coxe, March 20, 1820, MS, Madison Papers, LXVII. Benjamin Lundy, in *A Plan for the Gradual Abolition of Slavery in the United States without Danger or Loss to the Citizens of the South* (Baltimore, 1825), presented a plan somewhat similar to Coxe's. He proposed that colonies of slaves be established after the fashion of those of the Rappites. The slaves would be purchased at a price of $300 each, and states presumably providing the necessary funds. Profits of the colonies would be used to pay the debt so created. Five years, Lundy thought, would be needed to effect repayment. In the meanwhile, the poor whites would take the place of the slave on the plantations. A copy of this pamphlet is to be found in the Madison Papers, Printed Material, LXXVI.

[199] Coxe, over the signature "A Democratic Federalist," on "Considerations respecting the Helots of the United States, African and Indian, native and alien, and their descendants of the whole and mixed blood." In *The Democratic Press*, issues of November 25, 28, December 2, 5, 9, 13, 22, 25, 28, 29, and 30, 1820; January 4 and 9, 1821: a total of thirteen numbers. For identification, see Coxe to Madison, December 28, 1820, and January 8, 1821, MSS, Madison Papers, LXVIII. In those letters he calls Madison's attention to the series of articles. He also spoke of an essay addressed to the Quakers "in their ecclesiastical stile."

It thus appears that the problem of slavery baffled Coxe. He was never a defender of the institution; his suggestions for its reform, however, can hardly be termed practicable. That he did not give greater attention to the development of manufactures in the South, especially the cotton industry, is to be regretted. The most that can be said for him in this connection is that he recognized that the development of manufactures was imperative, if the inland and western counties of the southern states were to prosper.[200] Unfortunately, he merely stated this truth, and did not work for a widespread acceptance of it.

[200] See Coxe, " Reflections on the State of the American Union in the year M,DCC,XCII," *View*, p. 296. His prescience is borne out by the fact that this section has developed a cotton textile industry to the point where its output is greater than that of any other region in the United States. See Ben F. Lemert, *The Cotton Textile Industry of the Southern Appalachian Piedmont*, p. 3.

CHAPTER VI

CONCLUSION

The keynote of the economic thought of Tench Coxe is his persistent advocacy of the idea of a balanced national economy, by which he meant the joint and harmonious pursuit of agriculture, manufacturing, and commerce. To his mind, "The right application of the national industry, is the surest and greatest of the means to promote the wealth of nations."[1] Already possessed of a foreign commerce, America, Coxe contended, should develop manufactures in order that her agrarian pursuits might have a sure and substantial support. Agriculture, he found, was increasing to superabundance. This fact, coupled with the inadequacy of local transportation facilities and the possibility of disruptions to our markets abroad through wars and restrictive measures on the part of other nations, prompted him to declare for " a national system."[2] His program, therefore, was not a result of mere theorizing; on the contrary, it was grounded in a recognition of the prodigious natural resources of America and an unbounded faith in the capacity of the people to utilize them. " In a country thus circumstanced," he wrote in 1794, " producing the great raw materials for manufactures, and possessing unlimited powers by water and resources of fuel, subject also to considerable charges upon the importation of foreign fabrics, *to neglect manufactures would have been highly criminal.*"[3]

[1] Coxe, *A Statement of the Arts and Manufactures of the United States of America for the year 1810*, p. liv.

[2] The expression, "a national system," was used by Coxe in his " Address to an assembly of friends of American manufactures " (August, 1787). See *View*, p. 34. Hamilton, justifying the adoption of the Federal Constitution on economic grounds, declared that we must erect " one great American system." *The Federalist*, No. xi, ed. Bourne, I, 78.

[3] Coxe, " A Concise general view of the United States," *View*, p. 98. (Italics his.)

190

Centering his attention upon those who believed that America could more profitably remain a nation of farmers, and who thought the scarcity of industrial laborers would prevent manufactures, Coxe replied with a glowing tribute to "*the peculiar value of labor-saving machinery to a nation of moderate numbers dwelling in a country of redundant soil. . . .*"[4] Learning in 1786 of the extensive use made of machinery in England, he thereafter lost no opportunity to stress its possible value to the American economy. Moreover, he personally interested himself in obtaining from abroad models and designs of textile machinery, and offered praise and encouragement to our own inventors. Finally, to clinch his argument that manufactures could be developed here, Coxe frequently referred to the desirability of attracting skilled foreign workmen to America. Such persons, he thought, might also bring with them some capital.

Coxe's first, and what is perhaps his best, statement of the idea of a balanced national economy was given in an address read before the Philadelphia Society for Political Enquiries, May 11, 1787. The arguments then advanced were reasserted in the speech before an assembly of friends of American manufactures on August ninth of the same year, in the same city. In both instances the immediate background was the political and economic disintegration that followed the Peace of Paris. Active participation by Coxe in the movement for adoption of the Federal Constitution came next, for he knew that there must first be created an effective national government, if the economic needs of the country were to be met.

Once the new Constitution had been adopted and the national government set up, an opportunity was given

[4] Coxe, *Statement of the Arts and Manufactures of the United States,* p. xxiv. See also *ibid.*, p. lix: "*Machinery and processes to effect manufactures, so as to leave manual industry for other employments, are of a degree of importance to the United States, proportioned to the smallness of the average population on a square mile.*" (Italics his.)

Coxe to participate officially in the formulation of a program strikingly in accord with his convictions. Hamilton
personally appointed him his assistant in the Treasury
Department, from which issued the notable series of reports. What part Coxe took in the drafting of the one
on manufactures is uncertain; it cannot be denied, however, that the arguments presented in the *Report* have
much in common with ideas earlier expressed by Coxe.

But neither Hamilton nor Coxe was able to progress
very far in gaining popular support for the program of
manufactures. Within two years after submission to Congress of the *Report on Manufactures*, the commerce of
the country expanded tremendously, so that the development of manufactures was in a large measure neglected.
The long war between Great Britain and France, beginning in 1793, was responsible for the expansion. Although
some progress was achieved in establishing manufactures,
particularly of cotton, the attention of the country was
for several years thereafter focussed on the lucrative neutral commerce. In time, however, it proved increasingly
difficult to pursue, owing to the imposition of numerous
restrictions by both foreign governments and our own.
In 1807 commerce was brought to a virtual standstill.
The accumulation of profits which had taken place meanwhile then made possible a great spurt in manufacturing
enterprise. America definitely embarked on the road to
industrialization.

Throughout the whole of the Napoleonic struggle,
Coxe never deviated from his first position, namely, that
America should make herself self-sufficient, especially as
regards manufactures. The neutral commerce he acknowledged to be profitable, but at the same time it was uncertain and likely to result in war. Security of the national
interest, he frequently observed, required that we foster
a diversified economy. We could then avoid the horrors
and cost of war. Furthermore, we should be in a position to make the most of our productive capacity.

Originality in advancing the idea of a properly proportioned economy cannot be ascribed to Tench Coxe, though he can be said to have been among the first to examine in some detail its applicability to the United States after the Revolution. Alexander Hamilton at the age of eighteen, in his replies to the "Westchester Farmer," gave what appears to be its first statement.[5] In these essays Hamilton expressed at length the conviction that, "If we were to turn our attention from external to internal commerce, we should give greater stability and more lasting prosperity to our country than she can possibly have otherwise."[6] The full implications of the idea of a national economy, however, were not examined; in fact, Hamilton wrote more in a spirit of retaliation to British colonial policy than with a view to proposing a program based on purely local advantages.[7] That Hamilton should have written of cotton culture and manufacture as a basis for domestic commerce can doubtless be accounted for in the light of his early youth, spent in the British West Indies, where cotton was cultivated and shipped to Britain for manufacture. Tench Coxe, for his part, advanced the same idea in a spirit different from forthright retaliation. Coxe, of course, derived no satisfaction from a continuance after the Peace of selfish commercialism on the part of the British; at the same time, he thought in terms of

[5] See Hamilton, "A Full Vindication" (December, 1774), and "The Farmer Refuted" (February, 1775), *The Works of Alexander Hamilton,* ed. John C. Hamilton, II, especially pp. 12, 111-115.

[6] *Ibid.,* p. 112.

[7] Cf., however, William Hill, "The First Stages of the Tariff Policy of the United States," *Publications of the American Economic Association,* VIII, 87-88. Hill maintains that Hamilton had a detached viewpoint; that the spirit of feeling against Britain had not become bitter when Hamilton wrote. The fact is that it was the narrow colonial policy of the British which prompted Hamilton to write as he did; local considerations appear to have entered his mind only insofar as they bolstered his argument for retaliation by the creation of a national economy.

the wealth-producing capacity of America and the dictates of common-sense to capitalize upon it.[8] In short, his was a long-range program for America.

Again, there is little evidence of doctrinal indebtedness to other writers in the writings of Tench Coxe. His use of quotations and citations is so infrequent as to lead one to believe that he thought as did List: " The best book on political economy which one can read in that country [America] is life itself." [9] Indeed, American writers upon the subject of economics were, in Coxe's time, few and far between.[10] Abroad the number was, of course, large. Of these Coxe referred to two by name, in each instance to substantiate his plea for manufactures. In 1793 he cited David Hume in support of the contention that manufactures promoted agriculture; he added that following Hume other writers, whose names he did not give, had argued similarly.[11] In the second instance, 1804, Coxe quoted passages from James Anderson's *Observations*, relating to the interdependence of commerce, manufactures, and agriculture.[12] The impression, however, that

[8] Coxe in his *A Brief Examination of Lord Sheffield's Observations on the Commerce of the United States*, had a choice opportunity to write in a spirit of hostility to British interests; yet his treatment is remarkably free of such sentiment. His advocacy of home manufactures was, it is true, an assault upon British dominance; but it was also highly in accord with the needs of America which were, as we have said, uppermost in his mind.

[9] Quoted in Hirst, p. 37.

[10] See Chas. F. Dunbar, "Economic Science in America, 1776-1876," *North American Review*, CXXII, 134.

[11] Coxe, " Some Ideas concerning the creation of manufacturing towns and villages on the River Susquehannah," *View*, p. 384 n. Coxe's citation is merely the word, " Hume." Presumably, he had reference to Hume's *Political Discourses* (1752).

[12] Coxe, *Essay on the Manufacturing Interest of the United States*, p. 10. Anderson's work, *Observations on the Means of Exciting a Spirit of National Industry*, was written in part in 1775. It consists of a series of letters to a London friend. In these Anderson advocated the extension of sheep raising in Scotland and the development of a woolen manu-

Coxe was acquainted with the English classical economics of Adam Smith and others is not to be had from his writings. Coxe's economic principles, so far as they can be inferred from his essays, ran entirely counter to those of the so-called Classicists. This group of writers made much of governmental passivity, diminishing returns, overpopulation, the international immobility of labor and capital,[13] and the rise of rents. Coxe, with an entirely different background, wrote in an optimistic way—fully justified—of the time " When *returning* œconomy, and the fall of rents and provisions shall have reduced the expenses of living, when our increasing farms shall have poured in their addition of raw materials. . . ."[14] Likewise, he referred often to the need of attracting to our shores foreign labor and capital. The implication that these factors were mobile was not unwarranted; foreign labor and capital greatly assisted American economic development.[15] Coxe differed from the Classicists also as to government intervention. " To excite the citizens to industry, without deviating into slavery or oppression on the one hand, or suffering them to sink into idleness and consequent barbarism on the other, is the standard by

facture to use the raw material so obtained. He had in view particularly the improvement of the economic status of the Scot Highlanders, Coxe's quotation is from pp. 348-349 of the Edinburgh edition (1777). On pages 9-10 of his *Essay* Coxe also quoted from a certain " I. Lang." The writer has been unable to identify this citation. From Coxe's quotation it seems that " Lang " was an American; he, too, wrote in favor of a national economy.

[13] The international immobility of labor and capital formed the basis of the distinction made by the Classicists between internal and international trade; it was also the foundation of their law of comparative costs. See James W. Angell, *The Theory of International Prices*, pp. 66, 363.

[14] Coxe, " An enquiry into the principles on which a commercial system for the United States of America should be founded," *View*, p. 25. (Italics his.)

[15] For the export of capital to America, see C. K. Hobson, *The Export of Capital*, pp. 89, 97, 110; for emigration of British workers, see Arthur Redford, *Labor Migration in England, 1800-50*, chap. x.

which the great statesman ought to be estimated," he wrote.[16] Coxe's position with respect to the regulation of trade was neither that of a free trader nor of an out-and-out protectionist. At times, it is true, as in 1789, 1804, and 1808, he entertained pronouncedly protectionist views; but in general his preference was for a revenue tariff with incidental protection. His plan was, he wrote in 1787, " to *foster and encourage,* but *not to force manufactures.*"[17] Although extreme protectionist sentiment ultimately became triumphant in his native state, he retained his former opinion, writing Madison to that effect in 1820. Further evidence of the moderate views entertained by Coxe in regard to the control of commerce is to be found in his opinion that America in its then existing circumstances should not possess a favorable balance of trade in specie. Instead, she should import tools and other products that would facilitate in a direct way her economic development.[18] In 1806, in a letter written to Jefferson, he went so far as to assert that we should import implements to manufacture with, and not manufactures.[19] But this, however, was more of an *obiter dictum* than a settled principle on his part.

The emphasis which Coxe placed upon a proportioned development of America's productive capacity and the marked optimism which characterizes his writings in contrast with the pessimism of the Classicists, entitle him, in common with Alexander Hamilton, to rank as a precursor

[16] Coxe, *An Essay on the Manufacturing Interest of the United States,* p. 5. He added that " The statesman, worthy of being called such, also avoids to make distinctions, or give preference to any species of industry—The smith, who fabricates the plough, is equal, in his eye, to the peasant or farmer, who directs its course along the glebe—The miller is not exalted above the weaver, who weaves the bolting cloth— They are equally necessary, both to each other and to the State." *Ibid.*

[17] Coxe, " Address," *View,* p. 45 n.   (Italics his.)

[18] Coxe, " Reflections on the State of the Union in the year M,DCC,-XCII," *View,* p. 333.

[19] Coxe to Jefferson, May 22, 1806, MS, Jefferson Papers, CLIX.

of the "American Nationalist School." This group of
writers came into prominence during and after our second
war with Great Britain; included in their number were
Mathew Carey, his son Henry Charles Carey, Frederick
List, Daniel Raymond, John Rae, and Hezekiah Niles.

The first of this group, Mathew Carey, acknowledged
himself to be a follower of Hamilton.[20] Born in Ireland,
Carey came to this country as a young man deeply embit-
tered against the British. This feeling he reflected in a
plea that America develop a self-sufficing economy—that
the new nation should concentrate on manufacturing enterprise and not import British manufactures. Finding the
essays of Tench Coxe to his liking, Carey published several of them in his *American Museum*. It is probable that
he was influenced by their contents, though we cannot be
certain. Although the two were friends, available evidence does not point to any mutual exchange of views.
Their economic opinions, none the less, have much in
common, particularly as they relate to the idea of a national economy.[21] Carey was more extreme than Coxe in
his advocacy of manufactures; he also advocated a greater
degree of protection to them than did Coxe.[22] Coxe, as
our study has shown, was as much a friend to agriculture
as to manufactures. He frequently pointed out the importance of diversification to agriculture as well as to
the whole economy. In short, he would sustain the price
of agricultural produce by both crop diversification and
the development of a home market through the growth
of manufactures. This principle Coxe emphasized in a

[20] Rowe, *Mathew Carey*, p. 114.
[21] For an excellent presentation of Carey's economic opinions, see
Rowe.
[22] Carey accorded agriculture and commerce secondary importance only.
Rowe, p. 53. He acknowledged the existence of a differential in favor
of our manufactures due to transportation costs and the like; but he
thought more protection was needed, relying upon internal competition
to keep prices within reasonable limits. *Ibid.*, pp. 52, 56.

14

classical way by publicizing the importance of cotton culture to the southern planters. He thereby established his
name in the annals of American agriculture. The services
of Mathew Carey, on the other hand, were more limited
in their scope.[23]

Henry Charles Carey excelled both his father and Coxe
in his presentation of the case for a balanced national
economy. He, too, was decidedly more nationalistic than
Coxe. Again, his writings are marked by a greater attention to economic theory, since it was his purpose to take
deliberate issue, as did List, with the classical economists
of England.[24]

Frederick List, a resident in this country for five years
(1825-1830),[25] was the foremost spokesman of the American School. His famous *National System of Political
Economy* (1841) contains the most convincing presentation of the theory of a national economy. The work is
in no small measure a product of scholarly reflection upon
observations made during List's stay in America.[26] List,
as has been pointed out,[27] apparently made deliberate use
of Daniel Raymond's *Thoughts on Political Economy*
(Baltimore, 1820). Both writers openly disavowed the
English classical economics; both emphasized the mani-
fold development of the productive capacity of the na-

[23] In 1835, two months before his death, Carey did, however, write a
pamphlet imploring the South to consider remedies for the overproduction of cotton. Rowe, p. 106.

[24] See Kaplan, p. 30 and *passim*.

[25] For an account of List's sojourn in America, see Hirst, chap. ii.

[26] See Sidney Sherwood, *Tendencies in American Economic Thought*
(" Johns Hopkins University Studies in Historical and Political Science,"
15th Series, XII), p. 16; Rabbeno, *American Commercial Policy*, pp. 344-
345; Chas. P. Neill, *Daniel Raymond, An Early Chapter in the History
of Economic Theory in the United States* (" Johns Hopkins University
Studies in Historical and Political Science," 15th Series, VI), pp. 58-63;
Hirst, pp. 111-122.

[27] Neill, chap., iv. In particular the idea of the importance of developing the productive power of the nation rather than an immediate
accumulation of goods is common to both writers.

tion. Their work, in the latter respect, is similar to that of Coxe. The idea of historical stages in the economic development of a nation and the necessity of governmental policies appropriate to each, which has been declared by one writer[28] to be the most important part of List's theory, was also stated by Coxe. In his *Essay on the Manufacturing Interest of the United States* . . . (1804), Coxe wrote that:

The first progress of men towards the perfection of the social system is from a hunting to a pastoral life: but this progress is not in the nature of things, or produced by necessity; it is brought about by the enlightened rulers of a nation, to whom Providence has consigned the task of altering the condition of society. Hence, if no enlightened statesman appears in a nation, the people may continue, as the aborigines of this country have done, hunters and warriors for thousands of years; in whom, even the example of their conquerors has not been able to produce any considerable change in their manner of life. . . . The same may be said of a nation [which] has progressed to a state of agriculture, and that *cluster* of necessary arts which administer to its wants. No step further can be made by them in the finer arts, which administer to the comforts of polished society, but by the direction of the legislature.[29]

Population, Coxe added, is in proportion to the advancement made. But unlike List, he was not prepared to make

[28] Rabbeno, pp. 347-348.
[29] Coxe, *Essay on the Manufacturing Interest of the United States,* p. 25. (Italics his.) See also, *ibid.*, p. 11. List, writing of his stay in America, admitted that " Here it first became clear to me that nations pass through different stages of economic development." Quoted in Hirst, p. 37. Miss Hirst, *ibid.*, pp. 122-123, points out that List's conception of economic stages was anticipated by Rau in his *Studies in Economics* (1820). Benjamin Franklin, as early as 1751, had an inkling of the idea when he wrote of hunting, pastoral, agricultural, and manufacturing societies. See W. A. Wetzell, *Benjamin Franklin as an Economist* ("Johns Hopkins University Studies in Historical and Political Science," 13th Series IX ,, p. 25. For List's theory see his *National System of Political Economy*, p. 72.

manufactures the supreme economic activity of a nation—
certainly not of America. Instead, Coxe placed manufactures on a par with agriculture and commerce where the
country was extensive and adapted to all.[30] Where these
conditions did not prevail and a choice had therefore to
be made between agriculture and manufactures as the
principal industry of the nation, he favored manufactures.[31] But America, as he knew, did not face such a
choice; our problem was to balance agriculture with manufactures and to expand each harmoniously. To this extent
only did Coxe glorify manufactures.

Hezekiah Niles and John Rae, too, had something in
common with Tench Coxe. This is especially true of
Niles, whose writings in favor of manufactures and protection were voluminous.[32] In this connection it is interesting to note that although Niles on at least one occasion
disavowed any intention " to build up a *forced* or *arti-
ficial system* . . . ,"[33] he none the less was more of a
protectionist than Coxe. John Rae, born in Scotland but
a resident of Canada and the United States for many
years, wrote largely as a theorist.[34] His profound discussion of the processes of capital formation and his emphasis upon invention in the utilization of natural resources entitle him to rank as an economist of superior
ability. His rejection of the cosmopolitanism of the English in favor of the development of a national economy in

[30] Coxe, *Essay*, p. 6.

[31] Coxe, *Observations on the Agriculture, Manufactures and Commerce
of the United States*, pp. 18-19. See above, chap. iii.

[32] See R. G. Stone, *Hezekiah Niles as an Economist* (" Johns Hopkins
University Studies in Historical and Political Science," Series LI, No. 5),
chap. iii.

[33] *Niles' Weekly Register* (1827), XXXII, 49. (Italics in original.)
Niles began to write in favor of home industry in 1805, adopting at that
time the term, " national system." In 1811 he definitely arrayed himself
with the protectionists. Stone, p. 7.

[34] John Rae, *The Sociological Theory of Capital, being a complete reprint of the New Principles of Political Economy, 1834*. Edited with biographical sketch and notes by Charles Whitney Mixter.

America compels one to include him among the American School and to liken his thought to that of Coxe.

That Tench Coxe has not received due recognition as a forerunner of the American Nationalist School is to be accounted for, certainly in part, by his political entanglements. A desire to retrieve his personal finances, it seems, led him to take an active interest in politics. Querulous in disposition and possessed of a record for inconsistency in political allegiance, Coxe enjoyed little success as a politician.[35] His repeated attempts to gain appointment in the service of the government, productive as they were of discord, brought only meagre results. The basis for an underestimation of his ability as a student of economic problems must thereby have been created.

Our emphasis in this study of the life and thought of Coxe has been upon his place in the economic development of America. When one considers his work in publicizing the possibility of an American cotton culture and manufacture, it must be admitted that his part in advancing the economic interests of the country was notable. Equally creditable, too, was his plea for the general development of manufactures. That happy combination of economic pursuits—the idea of a balanced national economy—upon which Coxe and the American School wrote at length, has, however, yet to be attained. When Coxe wrote, the difficulty was one of developing a manufacturing enterprise to counterbalance agriculture; today we are confronted with the task of coordinating those two great branches of the national industry. That, in fact, was the avowed object of the Roosevelt Administration when it enacted the Agricultural Adjustment Act. The decision of the Supreme Court declaring that measure unconstitutional raises the question as to whether the neces-

[35] Richard Hildreth, *The History of the United States of America*, V, 378, characterizes Coxe as "a mousing politician and temporizing busybody, though a man of considerable financial knowledge and ability. . . ."

sary coordination can be obtained within the spirit and letter of the Federal Constitution.

Nor is this problem one peculiar to America alone. In Great Britain, the traditional dependence of the country's economy upon foreign markets has been subjected to serious attention. The belief that increasing reliance should be placed upon British agriculture—that the British economy should be balanced in terms of its own constituent elements—has had both governmental and private support. Elsewhere in Europe, notably in Germany and Italy, the ordering of the national economy is being sought by a new form of government, namely, fascism or the corporative state. In these countries, it seems, the spontaneous achievement of a harmony of economic interests is not taken for granted; on the contrary, it is sought by intervention of varying degrees by the state. In this respect the development is analogous to that which has occurred in Russia since the Revolution of 1917.

BIBLIOGRAPHY

THE WRITINGS OF TENCH COXE [1]

1786

1. *Thoughts concerning the Bank of North America, with some facts relating to such establishments in other countries, respectfully submitted to the honorable the General Assembly of Pennsylvania, by one of their constituents. December 13, 1786.* Copy in Library of Congress, Rare Book Room, Miscellaneous Pamphlets, Vol. 1092.

1787

2. *An Enquiry into the principles on which a commercial system for the United States of America should be founded; to which are added some political observations connected with the subject,* Philadelphia. Copy in Library of Congress, Commercial Pamphlets, Vol. 3, No. 6.
3. Letters on the Federal Government, in *The American Museum* (September and October, 1787), II, 300-306 and 387-391; also in the *Pennsylvania Gazette*, October 24, 1787. In 1788 these essays were printed in pamphlet form by Zachariah Poulson, Jr., of Philadelphia, under the title: *An Examination of the Constitution of the United States of America, submitted to the people by the general convention, at Philadelphia, the 17th day of September, 1787, and since adopted and ratified by the conventions of eleven states. By an American Citizen. To which is added a speech by the Honorable James Wilson, Esquire, on the same subject.* Copy in Library of Congress, Duane Pamphlets, Vol. 96, No. 3.
4. Letter to the Honourable Richard Henry Lee, Esq., signed, "An American," in the *Pennsylvania Herald*, December 29, 1787; the *Pennsylvania Packet*, January 2, 1788; *Pennsylvania Gazette*, January 16, 1788; and *The American Museum* (January, 1788), III, 78-83.

1788

5. Address to the Minority of the Convention of Pennsylvania. Three numbers, in the *Pennsylvania Gazette*, No. 1, January 23, 1788,

---

[1] The list here presented is, of necessity, by no means complete. In the custom of his day, Coxe nearly always used a *nom de plume*. A complete list of his writings cannot therefore be had until the collection of his papers is made available to the student. With few exceptions, positive identification has been found for all of the items listed above. (See chapter footnotes.)

No. 2, January 30, 1788, No. 3, February 6, 1788; *Pennsylvania Packet*, No. 1, January 25, 1788, No. 2, January 31, 1788, No. 3, February 7, 1788. It was also printed in *The American Museum* (February, March, and April, 1788), III, 158-161, 242-245, and 365-367. In each instance the Address was signed, "A Freeman." It is ascribed to Tench Coxe by the editor of the *Museum*, Mathew Carey.

6. To the People of the United States, signed, "A Pennsylvanian." Four numbers, in the *Pennsylvania Gazette*, No. 1, February 6, 1788, No. 2, February 13, 1788, No. 3, February 20, 1788, and No. 4, February 27, 1788.

7. Address to the honourable the members of the Convention of Virginia, signed, "An American." In the *Pennsylvania Gazette*, May 21 and 28, 1788; and the *Virginia Gazette and Weekly Advertiser*, June 5, 1788. It was also printed in *The American Museum* (May and June, 1788), III, 426-433 and 544-548. Mathew Carey, editor of the *Museum*, ascribed it to Tench Coxe.

8. To the honorable the Convention of the State of New York, signed, "A Pennsylvanian." In the *Pennsylvania Gazette*, June 11, 1788.

9. To the Inhabitants of the Western Counties of Pennsylvania, signed, "A Friend of Society and Liberty." In the *Pennsylvania Gazette*, July 23, 1788.

10. To the People of the United States, and particularly to the Independent Electors of Pennsylvania, signed, "A Federal Centinel." In the *Pennsylvania Gazette*, September 10, 1788.

11. Thoughts on the present situation in the United States. In *The American Museum* (November, 1788), IV, 401-404. Ascribed to Tench Coxe, by Mathew Carey.

12. Address to the friends of American Manufactures—ascribed to Tench Coxe, Esq. In *The American Museum* (October, 1788), IV, 341-346; also in the *Pennsylvania Gazette*, October 29, 1788, over the signature of "An American Citizen."

1789

13. *Observations on the Agriculture, Manufactures and Commerce of the United States. In a letter to a Member of Congress. By a Citizen of the United States*, New York.

1791

14. *A Brief Examination of Lord Sheffield's Observations on the Commerce of the United States*, Philadelphia.

1792

15. *Reflexions on the State of the Union*, Philadelphia.

1794

16. Letter to an Inhabitant of Pittsburgh. In the *Pittsburgh Gazette*, September 20, 1794.

17. *A View of the United States of America, in a series of papers, written at various times, between the years 1787 and 1794*, Philadelphia. London and Dublin edition, 1795.

1795

18. An Examination of the pending Treaty with Great Britain, signed, "Juricola" [*sic*], and addressed "To the President of the United States of America." Four numbers, in the *Philadelphia Gazette*, July 31, August 4, 8, and 12, 1795.

1796

19. To the Electors of the President of the United States, signed, "Federalist." Ten numbers, in the *Gazette of the United States*, November 9, 11, 14, 15, 16, 17, 18, 21, 24, 25, 29, and 30, 1796.

1799

20. *An Authentic view of the progress of the state of Pennsylvania since the establishment of the independence of the United States*, Philadelphia. Printed as Appendix F to the report of the case of the Commonwealth vs. Tench Coxe, in Library of Congress, Hazard Pamphlets, Vol. 92.

21. *Facts Respecting the Bank of North America*, Philadelphia (1799?).

1800

22. To the Public. Letter of one page in *The Aurora*, October 6, 1800.

23. Address to the Editor, *The Aurora*, November 1, 1800.

24. *Strictures upon the letter imputed to Mr. Jefferson, addressed to Mr. Mazzei*, signed, "Greene," June, 1800. Copy in Library of Congress, Rare Book Room.

1801

25. *An important statement of facts relative to the invalidity of the pretensions formerly made upon the Pennsylvania lands, by the unincorporated companies of Connecticut claimants, and by those who claimed under those companies; in a letter from the secretary of the land-office, to the Pennsylvania Commissioners, intended to evince the liberality of the Government and land-holders of Pennsylvania, in the act of the 4th of April, 1799, and the releases of 120 to 180,000 acres under the same*, Lancaster, May, 1801. Copy in Library of Congress, Hazard Pamphlets, Vol. 108.

1804

26. *An Essay on the Manufacturing Interest of the United States; with remarks on some passages contained in the Report of the Committee of Commerce and Manufactures.* By a member of the Society of Artists and Manufactures of Philadelphia, Philadelphia. Copy in American Philosophical Society Pamphlets, Vol. 678.

27. *Report of the Committee appointed to prepare a report on the state of manufactures in the United States generally, and particularly in the State of Pennsylvania, at the time of the establishment of this Society and of their progressive increase and improvement to the present time. Published by order of the Board, Tench Coxe, President,* Philadelphia. Copy in the Library of Congress, Duane Pamphlets, Vol. 96, No. 3. It was also printed in the *Philadelphia Evening Post,* March 13, 1804.

1805

28. *An Exposition of some facts relative to the personal conduct and business of the office of Tench Coxe, Purveyor of Public Supplies, December 10, 1805, Philadelphia.* Copy in Library of Congress, Duane Pamphlets, Vol. 96, No. 4.

1806

29. *Thoughts on the Subject of Naval Power in the United States of America; and on certain means of encouraging and protecting their commerce and manufactures,* Philadelphia.

1807

30. *An Examination of the Conduct of Great Britain, respecting neutrals,* signed, " Juriscola," 1st ed., Philadelphia. Copy in the possession of Library of Congress is autographed.

1808

31. ———, 2d ed., with corrections and amendments, signed, " Juriscola," Boston.

1809

32. *A Memoir of the subject of a Navigation Act,* Philadelphia. No. copy found.

1814

33. Balance of Naval Power. In *The Democratic Press,* Philadelphia, September 24, 1814.

34. *A Statement of the Arts and Manufactures of the United States of America for the year 1810: Digested and Prepared by Tench Coxe, Esquire, of Philadelphia,* Philadelphia. Also to be found in *American State Papers, Finance,* II, 666-812.

1817

35. *A Memoir of February, 1817, upon the subject of the cotton wool cultivation, the cotton trade, and the cotton manufactories of the United States of America.* Ordered printed by the Philadelphia Society for the Promotion of American Manufactures, August 28, 1817. Copy in American Philosophical Society Pamphlets, Vol. 33, No. 6.

1818

36. Article on the " United States." In *The Cyclopaedia; or, Universal Dictionary of Arts, Sciences, and Literature*, Abraham Rees, ed., 1st American ed., rev., Philadelphia, 1818, Vol. 39.

37. *An Addition, of December 1818, to the memoir, of February and August 1817, on the subject of the cotton culture, the cotton commerce, and the cotton manufacture of the United States, most respectfully submitting a suggestion, for consideration only, of a specific measure for securing to the planters of cotton a market for their crops.* Copy in Library of Congress, Rare Book Room.

1819

38. On the Grape Vine, with its wines, brandies, salt, and dried fruits, signed, " A Friend to the National Industry." Seven numbers, in the *Daily National Intelligencer*, Washington, November 6, 10, 13, 16, 19, December 2, 14, 1819.

1820

39. Civilization, signed, " Columbus." In *The National Recorder*, February 26, 1820, Philadelphia, pp. 132-133.

1820–1821

40. Considerations respecting the Helots of the United States, African and Indian, native and alien, and their descendants of the whole and mixed blood, signed, " A Democratic Federalist." In *The Democratic Press*, issues of November 25, 28, December 2, 5, 9, 13, 22, 25, 28, 29, 30, 1820; January 4 and 9, 1821.

1823

41. To the Friends of the Principles of the Constitution of the United States, signed, " Sidney." In *The Democratic Press*, Philadelphia, January 6, 11, 16, 23, 28, 31, February 11 and 18, 1823.

No date:

42. *A Plan for encouraging Agriculture, and increasing the value of farms in the midland and more western counties of Pennsylvania, applicable to several other parts of that State, and to many parts of the United States.* Copy in Library of Congress, Miscellaneous Pamphlets, Vol. 1092, No. 8.

MANUSCRIPTS

(By Libraries)

LIBRARY OF CONGRESS

Papers of Thomas Jefferson.
Hamilton Manuscripts.
Papers of James Madison.
Papers of James Monroe.
Papers of James McHenry.
Private Letter Book of Robert Morris.
American Letters and Documents, 1652-1845. U. S. Miscellany.
Library of Congress Broadsides, Vol. 106.
Personal Papers, Miscellaneous.
Account Book (November 12, 1788, to March 20, 1790), of the Manu-
facturing Society of Philadelphia.

HISTORICAL SOCIETY OF PENNSYLVANIA

Autograph Collection.
Papers of James Wilson.
Gratz Collection.
Dreer Collection.
Papers of Major-General Edward Hand.
Papers of the Shippen Family.
Papers of Brigadier-General William Irvine.

LIBRARY COMPANY OF PHILADELPHIA (Ridgway Branch)

The Correspondence of Dr. Benjamin Rush.

HAVERFORD COLLEGE LIBRARY

Roberts Collection.

AMERICAN PHILOSOPHICAL SOCIETY

Franklin Collection.

UNITED STATES ARSENAL, SCHUYLKILL, PHILADELPHIA

Records of the Office of Purveyor of Public Supplies (held by Tench
Coxe, 1803-1812).

CORRESPONDENCE, DIARIES AND MEMOIRS

Adams, John, *The Works of,* Chas. F. Adams, ed., 10 vols., Boston, 1854.
Adams, John Quincy, *Memoirs of,* Chas. F. Adams, ed., 12 vols., Philadelphia, 1875.

Gallatin, Albert, *The Writings of,* Henry Adams, ed., 3 vols., Philadelphia, 1879.

Gibbs, George, *Memoirs of the Administration of Washington and John Adams* (edited from the papers of Oliver Wolcott, Secretary of the Treasury), 2 vols., New York, 1846.

Graydon, Alexander, *Memoirs of his Own Time, with Reminiscences of the Men and Events of the Revolution,* J. S. Littell, ed., Philadelphia, 1846.

Hamilton, Alexander, *The Works of,* Henry Cabot Lodge, ed., 12 vols., Federal ed., New York and London, 1904.

————, *The Works of,* John C. Hamilton, ed., 7 vols., New York, 1850.

————, *Industrial and Commercial Correspondence of,* Arthur H. Cole, ed., Chicago, 1928.

Hamilton, John C., *History of the Republic of the United States as Traced in the Writings of Alexander Hamilton,* 7 vols., Boston, 1879.

Hammond, M. B., " Correspondence of Eli Whitney relative to the Invention of the Cotton Gin," *American Historical Review* (1897), II, 90-127.

Hiltzheimer, Jacob, *Extracts from the Diary of, 1765-1798,* J. C. Parsons, ed., Philadelphia, 1893.

Jay, John, *The Correspondence and Public Papers of,* Henry P. Johnston, ed., 4 vols., New York, 1890.

Jameson, J. F., ed., " Letters of Phineas Bond, British Consul at Philadelphia, to the Foreign Office of Great Britain, 1787, 1788, 1789," *Annual Report of the American Historical Association, 1896,* I, pp. 513-659, 704-841.

Jefferson, Thomas, *Memoir, Correspondence, and Miscellanies from the papers of,* Thos. J. Randolph, ed., 4 vols., 2d ed., Boston, 1830.

————, *The Writings of,* Library ed., 20 vols., Washington, 1903.

————, *The Writings of,* Paul Leicester Ford, ed., 10 vols., New York and London, 1899.

Lee, Richard Henry, *The Letters of,* J. C. Ballagh, ed., 2 vols., New York, 1914.

Maclay, William, *The Journal of, 1789-1791,* New York, 1927.

Madison, James, *The Writings of,* Gaillard Hunt, ed., 9 vols., New York, 1900-1910.

Monroe, James, *The Writings of,* Murray S. Hamilton, ed., 4 vols., New York, 1898.

Smith, Josiah, *Diary of, 1780-1781,* Mabel L. Webber, annotator, " The South Carolina Historical and Genealogical Magazine," XXXIII and XXXIV.

Stiles, Ezra, *The Literary Diary of,* F. B. Dexter, ed., 3 vols., New York, 1901.

Ames, Fisher, *The Works of* (compiled by a number of his friends, to which are prefixed notices of his life and character), Boston, 1809.

CONTEMPORARY BOOKS AND PAMPHLETS

A Communication from the Pennsylvania Society for the Encouragement of Manufactures and the Useful Arts, Philadelphia, 1804. Library of Congress, Duane Pamphlets, Vol. 96, No. 2.

A List of Those Tories who took part with Great Britain and were attainted of High Treason, commonly called the Black List, Philadelphia, 1802. American Philosophical Society Pamphlets, Vol. 33.

Anderson, James, *Observations on the Means of Exciting a Spirit of National Industry* . . . , Edinburgh, 1777.

An Address to the Citizens of Philadelphia on the Great Advantages which arise from the trade of the western country to the state of Pennsylvania at large, and to the City of Philadelphia in particular. By Messrs. Tarascom, Junr., James Berthoud and Co., Philadelphia, 1806. Copy in the Library of Congress, Duane Pamphlets, Vol. 96, No. 10.

Allen, James, *Considerations on the Present State of the Intercourse between his Majesty's Sugar Colonies and the Dominions of the United States of America,* London, 1784.

Bingham, William, *A Letter from an American, now resident in London, to a member of Parliament, on the subject of the restraining proclamation; and containing strictures on Lord Sheffield's Pamphlet on the Commerce of the American States,* Philadelphia, 1784. Library of Congress, Duane Pamphlets, Vol. 86, No. 1.

Bishop, Abraham, *Connecticut Republicanism* . . . , Philadelphia, 1800.

Bourne, Edward G., ed., *The Federalist,* by Hamilton, Madison, and Jay, 2 vols., Washington and London, 1901. Universal Classics Library.

Brissot de Warville, J. P., *New Travels in the United States of America performed in 1788,* 2 vols., 2d ed., corrected, London, 1794.

[Carnac, Thomas], *Facts and arguments respecting the great utility of an extensive plan of inland navigation in America,* signed, "By a Friend to National Industry," Philadelphia, 1805. Library of Congress, Hazard Pamphlets, Vol. 92.

Chalmers, George, *Opinions on Interesting Subjects of Public Law and Commercial Policy, Arising from American Independence,* new ed., corrected, London, 1785.

Champion, Richard, *Considerations on the Present Situation of Great Britain and the United States of America, with a view to their future commercial connexions, containing remarks upon Lord Sheffield's Observations &c.,* 2d ed., London, 1784.

[Cooper, Thomas], *Some Information respecting America,* collected by Thomas Cooper, late of Manchester, London, 1794.

Coxe, Daniel, *View of Carolana,* London, 1722.

——, *A Description of the English Province of Carolana, by the Spanish called Florida, and by the French la Louisiane. As also of the great and famous river Meschacede or Mississippi, the five vast navigable lakes of fresh water, and the parts adjacent. To-*

gether with an account of the commodities of the growth and production of the said Province, "Historical Collections of Louisiana," B. F. French, ed., II, 221-276, Philadelphia, 1850.

Ein Pennsylvanischer Deutscher, *Ein Ernstlicher Ruf an die Deutschen in Pennsylvanen,* Lancaster, 1799.

Fennell, James, *Description of the Principles and Plan of Proposed Establishment of the Salt Works; for the Purpose of Supplying the United States with Home made Salt,* Philadelphia, 1798. American Philosophical Society Pamphlets, Vol. 678.

Ford, Paul Leicester, ed., *Pamphlets on the Constitution of the United States, published during its discussion by the people, 1787-1788,* Brooklyn, 1888.

———, *Essays on the Constitution of the United States, published during its discussion by the people, 1787-1788,* Brooklyn, 1892.

Henfrey, Benjamin, *A Plan with Proposals for forming a Company to work Mines in the United States and to Smelt and Refine the Ores whether of Copper, Lead, Tin, Silver, or Gold,* Philadelphia, 1797. American Philosophical Society Pamphlets, Vol. 678.

Hume, David, *Essays and Treatises on Several Subjects,* new ed., Edinburgh, 1825.

[Independent American], *An Inquiry into the present state of the foreign relations of the union, as affected by the late measures of the administration,* Philadelphia, 1806. Library of Congress, Miscellaneous Pamphlets, Vol. 1011, No. 2.

Jordan, G. W., *The Claims of the British West India Colonists to the right of obtaining necessary supplies from America, and of employing the necessary means of effectually obtaining those supplies under a limited and duly regulated intercourse, stated and vindicated. In answer to Lord Sheffield's Strictures,* London, 1804.

[Long, Edward], *A Free and Candid Review of a Tract entitled, "Observations on the commerce of the American States"; shewing the Pernicious Consequences, both to Great Britain, and to the British Sugar Islands, of the Systems recommended in that Tract,* London, 1784.

Marshall, John, *The Life of George Washington,* 4 vols., Philadelphia, 1805.

McMaster, J. B., and Stone, Fred. D., eds., *Pennsylvania and the Federal Constitution, 1787-1788,* Philadelphia, 1888.

Melish, John, *The Necessity of Protecting and Encouraging the Manufactures of the United States, in a letter to President James Monroe,* Philadelphia, 1818. American Philosophical Society Pamphlets, Vol. 33.

[Moore, C. C.], *An Inquiry into the Effects of our Foreign Carrying Trade upon the Agriculture, Population, and Morals of the Country,* by Columella, New York, 1806.

Morse, Jedediah, *The American Geography; or, a View of the Present Situation of the United States of America,* 3d ed., Dublin, 1792.

(Observator), *Thoughts on the Increasing Wealth and National Economy of the United States of America*, Washington, 1801. American Philosophical Society Pamphlets, Vol. 678.

Pitkin, Timothy, *A Statistical View of the Commerce of the United States of America &c.*, New Haven, 1835.

Report of the Case of the Commonwealth vs. Tench Coxe, Esq., on a motion for a Mandamus, in the Supreme Court of Pennsylvania: taken from the transcript of the fourth volume of Mr. Dallas's Reports, Philadelphia, 1803. Library of Congress, Hazard Pamphlets, Vol. 92.

Seybert, Adam, *Statistical Annals*, Philadelphia, 1818.

Sheffield, Lord, *Observations on the Commerce of the American States with Europe and the West Indies; including the general articles of import and export*, 1st ed., Philadelphia, 1783.

———, *ibid.*, 6th ed., enlarged, London, 1784.

———, *Strictures on the necessity of inviolably maintaining the navigation and colonial system of Great Britain*, 1st ed., London, 1804.

Tallyrand, Citizen, *Memoir Concerning the Commercial Relations of the United States with England* (trans.), London, 1806.

Taylor, John, *An Inquiry into the Principles and Policy of the Government of the United States*, Fredericksburg, Va., 1814.

———, *Arator; being a series of Agricultural Essays, practical and political: in sixty-one numbers*, 3d ed., revised and enlarged, Baltimore, 1817.

The Constitution of the Germantown Society for promoting domestic manufactures, Philadelphia, M,DCC,XC. Copy in the Library of Congress, Miscellaneous Pamphlets, Vol. 1092, No. 7.

To the Republican Citizens of the State of Pennsylvania, Lancaster, September 17, 1800. Signed by Tench Coxe, Timothy Matlock, Frederick A. Muhlenberg, Jacob Carpenter, and Samuel Bryan. Library of Congress, Political Pamphlets, Vol. 100.

To the Republicans of Pennsylvania, Philadelphia, August 31, 1799. Signed by Peter Muhlenberg, Samuel Miles, Tench Coxe, Michael Lieb, William Penrose, and A. J. Dallas. Library of Congress, Rare Book Room.

Tracy, Count Destutt de, *A Treatise on Political Economy*, Georgetown, 1817.

Webster, Pelatiah, *Political Essays on the Nature and Operation of Money, Public Finance, and other Subjects: Published during the American War, and continued up to the present year, 1791*, Philadelphia, 1791.

Winterbotham, W., *An Historical, Geographical, Commercial and Philosophical View of the United States of America*, 4 vols., New York, 1796.

NEWSPAPERS AND MAGAZINES

The Aurora (Philadelphia), 1804.
The Freeman's Journal (Philadelphia), 1804.
The National Gazette (Philadelphia), 1824.
The Pennsylvania Gazette (Philadelphia), 1787-1788.
The Pennsylvania Herald (Philadelphia), 1787.
The Pennsylvania Journal (Philadelphia), 1780, 1787.
The Pennsylvania Packet (Philadelphia), 1775, 1785, and 1787.
The Philadelphia Evening Post, 1804.
Poulson's American Daily Advertiser (Philadelphia), 1824.
The United States Chronicle (Providence), 1790.
Virginia Gazette and Weekly Advertiser (Richmond), 1788.
Virginia Independent Chronicle (Richmond), 1788.

The American Museum (Philadelphia), I-XII (1787-1792).
The Monthly Review (London), LXIX (1783); IX (1792).
Niles' Weekly Register (Baltimore), XVII (1819); XXXII (1827).
The Pennsylvania Magazine, I (1775).

OFFICIAL DOCUMENTS, STATE AND NATIONAL

American State Papers, Finance; Foreign Relations, Washington, 1832-1861.
Biographical Directory of the American Congress, 1774-1927, H. Doc. 783, Washington, 1928.
Documentary History of the Constitution of the United States of America, 1786-1870, 3 vols., Washington, 1894.
Journals of the Continental Congress, 1774-1789, Washington, 1904—.
McLane Report, 22d Cong., 1st sess., H. Doc. No. 308, VII, Parts 1 and 2.
Minutes of the Supreme Executive Council of Pennsylvania, XV and XVI, Harrisburg, 1853.
New Jersey Archives, First Series, X and XXX; Second Series, V.
Pennsylvania Archives, Second Series, XVIII; Third Series, XIV, XVI, XXIV, XXV, XXVI, XXVIII; Fourth Series III; Sixth Series, I, III, XIII.
Richardson, James D., ed., *A Compilation of the Messages and Papers of the Presidents*, 10 vols., Washington, 1896.
Tariff Acts passed by the Congress of the United States from 1789 to 1909, 61st Cong., 2d sess., H. Doc. No. 671.
The Statutes at large of Pennsylvania from 1682 to 1801, 18 vols., Harrisburg, 1908.
The Annals of Congress.
U. S. Statutes at Large.
Woodbury, Levi (Secretary of the Treasury), *Report on the Cotton Production and Consumption of the United States*, 24th Cong., 1st sess., Ex. Doc. No. 146 (1836).

SECONDARY WORKS

Adams, Henry, *History of the United States,* 9 vols., New York, 1921.
Adams, Henry Carter, *Taxation in the United States, 1789-1816,* " Johns Hopkins University Studies in Historical and Political Science," 2d Series, V-VI, Baltimore, 1884.
Adams, James Truslow, *Jeffersonian Principles,* Boston, 1928.
Alvord, Clarence W., *The Mississippi Valley in British Politics,* 2 vols., Cleveland, 1917.
Angell, James W., *The Theory of International Prices,* " Harvard Economic Studies," XXVIII, Cambridge, 1926.
Bagnall, William R., *Samuel Slater and the Early Development of the Cotton Manufacture in the United States,* Middletown, Conn., 1890.
———, *The Textile Industries of the United States,* I (1639-1810), Cambridge, 1893.
Baines, Edward, Jr., *History of the Cotton Manufacture in Great Britain,* London, 1835.
Bancroft, George, *History of the Formation of the Constitution of the United States of America,* 2 vols., New York, 1882.
Bassett, John Spencer, *The Federalist System,* " American Nation Series," XI, New York and London, 1906.
Batchelder, Samuel, *Introduction and Early Progress of the Cotton Manufacture in the United States,* Boston, 1863.
Beard, Charles A., *An Economic Interpretation of the Constitution of the United States,* New York, 1921.
———, *Economic Origins of Jeffersonian Democracy,* New York, 1915.
———, (with the collaboration of G. H. E. Smith), *The Idea of National Interest,* New York, 1934.
Becker, Carl, *The Eve of the Revolution,* " Yale Chronicles of America Series," XI, New Haven, 1918.
Bemis, S. F., *Jay's Treaty: A Study in Commerce and Diplomacy,* New York, 1923.
Beveridge, Albert J., *The Life of John Marshall,* 4 vols., Boston and New York, 1919.
Bishop, J. Leander, *A History of American Manufactures from 1608 to 1860,* 3 vols., 3d., rev., Philadelphia, 1868.
Bolles, Albert S., *The Financial History of the United States, from 1789 to 1860,* New York, 1883.
Brackenridge, H. M., *History of the Western Insurrection in Western Pennsylvania,* Pittsburgh, 1859.
Cannan, Edwin, *A History of the Theories of Production and Distribution in English Political Economy from 1776 to 1848,* 3d ed., London, 1924.
Chandler, Charles L., *Early Shipbuilding in Pennsylvania, 1683-1812,* Princeton, 1932.

Channing, Edward, *A History of the United States,* 6 vols., New York, 1905-1925.

———, *The Jeffersonian System, 1801-1811,* " American Nation Series," XII, New York, 1906.

Chinard, Gilbert, *Thomas Jefferson,* Boston, 1929.

Clark, Victor S., *History of Manufactures in the United States, 1607-1860,* Washington, 1916.

Clauder, Anna C., *American Commerce as Affected by the Wars of the French Revolution and Napoleon, 1793-1812,* Philadelphia, 1932.

Collections of the New York Historical Society, XXIII, 1890.

Conowingo, brochure issued by Stone & Webster, Inc., [1928].

Copeland, M. T., *The Cotton Manufacturing Industry of the United States,* " Harvard Economic Studies," VIII, Cambridge, 1912.

Crane, Verner W., *The Southern Frontier, 1670-1732,* Durham, 1928.

Dana, W. B., *Cotton from Seed to Loom,* New York, 1872.

Davis, Joseph S., *Essays in the Earlier History of American Corporations,* 2 vols., " Harvard Economic Studies," XVI, Cambridge, 1917.

DeBow, J. D. B., *The Industrial Resources of the Southern and Western States,* 3 vols., New Orleans, 1852-1853.

Dictionary of American Biography, 20 vols., New York, 1928-36.

Donnell, E. J., *History of Cotton,* New York, 1872.

Dunbar, Louise B., *A Study of " Monarchical " Tendencies in the United States from 1776-1801,* " University of Illinois Studies in the Social Sciences," X, Urbana, 1920.

Eiselen, Malcolm R., *Franklin's Political Theories,* New York, 1928.

———, *The Rise of Pennsylvania Protectionism,* Philadelphia, 1932.

Elliott, O. L., *The Tariff Controversy, 1789-1833,* Palo Alto, 1892.

Emerson, Gouverneur, *Cotton in the Middle States, with directions for its easy culture,* Philadelphia, 1862.

Encyclopaedia of the Social Sciences, 15 vols., New York, 1930-35.

Fisher, S. G., *Pennsylvania, Colony and Commonwealth,* Philadelphia, 1897.

Fiske, John, *The Critical Period of American History, 1783-1789,* Boston and New York, 1888.

Frazer, Leon, *English Opinion of the American Constitution and Government (1783-1798),* New York, 1915.

Freedley, Edwin T., *Philadelphia and its Manufactures,* Philadelphia, 1859.

Fuller, Grace P., *An Introduction to the History of Connecticut as a Manufacturing State,* " Smith College Studies in History," I, Northampton, 1915.

Giesecke, Albert A., *American Commercial Legislation before 1789,* Philadelphia, 1910.

Goodman, Nathan G., *Benjamin Rush, Physician and Citizen, 1746-1813,* Philadelphia, 1934.

Grayson, T. J., *Leaders and Periods of American Finance,* New York, 1932.

Grigsby, Hugh Blair, *The History of the Virginia Federal Convention of 1788*, 2 vols., "Collections of the Virginia Historical Society," New Series, IX and X, Richmond, 1890-1891.

Hammond, M. B., *The Cotton Industry. Part I, The Cotton Culture and the Cotton Trade*, "Publications of the American Economic Association," New Series, No. 1, 1-382, New York, 1897.

Harding, Samuel B., *Party Struggles over the Pennsylvania Constitution*, "Annual Report of the American Historical Association, 1894," pp. 371-402, Washington, 1895.

Heckscher, Eli, *The Continental System*, New York, 1922.

Henry, William Wirt, *Patrick Henry, Life, Correspondence and Speeches*, 3 vols., New York, 1891.

Hildreth, Richard, *The History of the United States of America*, 6 vols., New York, 1856.

Hirst, Margaret E., *Life of Frederick List and Selections from his Writings*, London, 1909.

Hunt, Freeman, ed., *Lives of American Merchants*, 2 vols., New York, 1858.

Hobson, C. K., *The Export of Capital*, New York, 1914.

Holdsworth, J. T., *Financing an Empire: History of Banking in Pennsylvania*, 4 vols., Chicago-Philadelphia, 1928.

Hobson, E. W., Jr., *Tench Coxe, His Activities*. (Typewritten essay for the degree of Master of Arts, in the Columbia University Library.)

Kaplan, A. D. H., *Henry Charles Carey*, "Johns Hopkins University Studies in Historical and Political Science," XLIX, Baltimore, 1931.

Kohn, August, *The Cotton Mills of South Carolina*, Charleston, 1907.

Lemert, Ben F., *The Cotton Textile Industry of the Southern Appalachian Piedmont*, Chapel Hill, 1933.

Lewis, Lawrence, *A History of the Bank of North America*, Philadelphia, 1882.

Lincoln, Charles H., *The Revolutionary Movement in Pennsylvania, 1760-1776*, Philadelphia, 1901.

List, Frederick, *The National System of Political Economy* (translated from the German by G. A. Matile, with a Preliminary Essay and Notes by Stephen Colwell), Philadelphia, 1856.

Mahan, A. T., *Sea Power in its Relations to the War of 1812*, 2 vols., Boston, 1905.

McLaughlin, A. C., *The Confederation and Constitution, 1783-1789*, "American Nation Series," X, New York, 1905.

McMaster, John Bach, *A History of the People of the United States*, 8 vols., New York, 1883-1913.

Meigs, Wm. M., *The Growth of the Constitution in the Federal Convention of 1787*, Philadelphia, 1900.

Mitchell, Broadus, *William Gregg*, Chapel Hill, 1928.

——, *The Rise of Cotton Mills in the South*, "Johns Hopkins University Studies in Historical and Political Science," XXXIX, Baltimore, 1921.

Montgomery, T. H., *A History of the University of Pennsylvania, 1749-1770*, Philadelphia, 1900.
Neill, Chas. P., *Daniel Raymond, An Early Chapter in the History of Economic Theory in the United States*, " Johns Hopkins University Studies in Historical and Political Science," 15th Series, VI, Baltimore, 1897.
Nelson, William, *New Jersey Biographical and Genealogical Notes*, " Collections of the New Jersey Historical Society", IX, Newark, 1916.
Nevins, Allan, *The American States During and After the Revolution, 1775-1789*, New York, 1924.
Newlin, C. M., *The Life and Writings of Hugh Henry Brackenridge*, Princeton, 1932.
North, S. N. D., "Manufactures in the Federal Census," *The Federal Census: Critical Essays by members of the American Economic Association*, March, 1899, " Publications of the American Economic Association," New Series, 1899.
Oliver, Frederick Scott, *Alexander Hamilton: An Essay on the American Union*, New York and London, 1907.
Palgrave's Dictionary of Political Economy, Henry Higgs, ed., 3 vols., London, 1926.
Rabbeno, Ugo, *The American Commercial Policy*, 2d ed., rev. (trans.), London, 1895.
Rae, John, *The Sociological Theory of Capital, being a complete reprint of the New Principles of Political Economy, 1834*, C. W. Mixter, ed., New York, 1905.
Redford, Arthur, *Labour Migration in England, 1800-50*, " University of Manchester Economic History Series," III, Manchester, 1926.
Richardson, Lyon N., *A History of Early American Magazines, 1741-1789*, New York, 1931.
Rowe, Kenneth W., *Mathew Carey*, " Johns Hopkins University Studies in Historical and Political Science," LI, Baltimore, 1933.
Sabine, Lorenzo, *Biographical Sketches of Loyalists of the American Revolution*, 2 vols., Boston, 1864.
Scharf, J. T., and Westcott, Thompson, *A History of Philadelphia*, 3 vols., Philadelphia, 1884.
Scherer, James A. B., *Cotton as a World Power*, New York, 1916.
Schlesinger, Arthur M., *The Colonial Merchants and the American Revolution, 1763-1776*, " Columbia University Studies," LXXVIII, New York, 1918.
———, *New Viewpoints in American History*, New York, 1925.
Schouler, James, *History of the United States of America*, 5 vols., New York, 1880.
Sears, Louis M., *Jefferson and the Embargo*, Durham, 1927.
Sellers, Leila, *Charleston Business on the Eve of the American Revolution*, Chapel Hill, 1934.
Sherwood, Sidney, *Tendencies in American Economic Thought*, " Johns

Hopkins University Studies in Historical and Political Science," 15th Series, XII, Baltimore, 1897.

Simpson, Henry, *Lives of Eminent Philadelphians*, Philadelphia, 1859.

S. Slater & Sons, Inc., *The Slater Mills at Webster*, Webster, Mass., 1912.

Smith, W. B., and Cole, A. H., *Fluctuations in American Business, 1790-1860*, " Harvard Economic Studies," L, Cambridge, 1935.

Spencer, Edward, *A Sketch of the History of Manufactures in Maryland*, Baltimore, 1882.

Spencer, R. H., *The Thomas Family of Talbot County, Maryland, and Allied Families*, Baltimore, 1914.

Steiner, Bernard C., *The Life and Correspondence of James McHenry*, Cleveland, 1917.

Stillé, Chas. J., *Pennsylvania and the Declaration of Independence,* [Philadelphia, 1890].

Stone, R. G., *Hezekiah Niles as an Economist*, " Johns Hopkins University Studies in Historical and Political Science," LI, Baltimore, 1933.

Sumner, W. G., *Alexander Hamilton*, New York, 1890.

Taussig, Frank W., *The Tariff History of the United States*, 7th ed., New York and London, 1923.

————, *Protection to Young Industries as Applied in the United States*, New York, 1884.

Tawney, R. H., ed., *Studies in Economic History: The Collected Papers of George Unwin*, London, 1927.

Taylor, George Rogers, *Agrarian Discontent in the Mississippi Valley preceding the War of 1812*, Chicago, 1931.

The Federal Census, Critical Essays by Members of the American Economic Association, " Publications of the American Economic Association," New Series, No. 2, New York, 1899.

Tilghman, Oswald, *History of Talbot County, Maryland, 1661-1861*, 2 vols., Baltimore, 1915.

Tompkins, D. A., *History of Mecklenburg County*, 2 vols., Charlotte, 1903.

Trentiss, H. P., *Timothy Pickering as the Leader of the New England Federalism, 1800-1815*, Evanston, 1932.

Tryon, Rolla M., *Household Manufactures in the United States, 1640-1860*, Chicago, 1917.

Walker, Francis A., *The Making of a Nation, 1783-1817*, New York, 1895.

Ware, Caroline F., *The Early New England Cotton Manufacture*, New York and Boston, 1931.

Watkins, James L., *King Cotton; A Historical and Statistical Review, 1790-1908*, New York, 1908.

Watson, John F., *Annals of Philadelphia*, 2 vols., Philadelphia, 1898.

Weeden, William, *Economic and Social History of New England, 1620-1789*, 2 vols., Boston and New York, 1890.

Wetzell, W. A., *Benjamin Franklin as an Economist*, " Johns Hopkins

University Studies in Historical and Political Science," 13th Series, IX, Baltimore, 1895.
White, George S., *Memoir of Samuel Slater*, 2d ed., Philadelphia, 1836.
Woodbury, Margaret, *Public Opinion in Philadelphia, 1789-1801*, " Smith College Studies in History," V, Northampton, 1920.

ARTICLES

Bourne, Edward G., " Alexander Hamilton and Adam Smith," *Quarterly Journal of Economics* (1893), VIII, 328-344.
Burnet, E. C., " Observations of London Merchants on American Trade, 1783," *American Historical Review* (1913), XVIII, 769-780.
Clark, Victor S., " Colonial Manufactures," *The South in the Building of the Nation* (1909), V, 299-312.
Clement, John, " Coxe Hall," *Proceedings of the New Jersey Historical Society* (1914), Third Series, IX, 27-37.
Daniels, G. W., " American Cotton Trade with Liverpool under the Embargo and Non-Intercourse Acts," *American Historical Review* (1916), XXI, 276-287.
Dawson, Henry B., " The Motley Letter," *Historical Magazine* (1871), Second Series, IX, 157-201.
Day, Clive, " The Early Development of the American Cotton Manufacture," *Quarterly Journal of Economics* (1925), XXXIX, 450-468.
Dunbar, Chas. F., " Economic Science in America, 1776-1876," *North American Review* (1876), CXXII, 124-154.
———, " Some Precedents Followed by Alexander Hamilton," *Quarterly Journal of Economics* (1888), III, 32-59.
" Excerpts from the Day-Book of David Evans, Cabinet-maker, Philadelphia, 1774-1811," *Pennsylvania Magazine of History and Biography* (1903), XXVII, 49-55.
Fisher, W. C., " American Trade Regulations before 1789," *Papers of the American Historical Association* (1889), III, 223-249.
Gerard, James W., " French Spoliations before 1801," *Magazine of American History* (1884), XII, 29-45.
Gillingham, Harrold E., " The Philadelphia Windsor Chair and Its Journeyings," *Pennsylvania Magazine of History and Biography* (1931), LV, 301-332.
Gilpatrick, D. H., " Samuel Slater, Father of American Manufactures," *Proceedings of the South Carolina Historical Association*, 1932, pp. 23-24.
(Gilpin, Joshua), " Journey to Bethlehem," *Pennsylvania Magazine of History and Biography* (1922), XLVI, 122-153.
Herring, Harriet L., " Early Industrial Development in the South," *Annals of the American Academy of Political and Social Science*, (1931), CLIII, 1-10.
Hill, William, " The First Stages of the Tariff Policy of the United States," *Publications of the American Economic Association* (1893), VIII, No. 6, 452-614.

Hill, William, "Protective Purposes of the Tariff Act of 1789," *Journal of Political Economy* (1894), II, 54-76.

——, "Colonial Tariffs," *Quarterly Journal of Economics* (1893), VII, 78-100.

Hunt, Gaillard, "Office-Seeking during Jefferson's Administration," *American Historical Review* (1898), III, 270-291.

——, "Office-Seeking during the Administration of John Adams," *American Historical Review* (1897), II, 241-261.

Jefferys, C. P. B., "The Provincial and Revolutionary History of St. Peter's Church, Philadelphia, 1753-1783," *Pennsylvania Magazine of History and Biography* (1924), XLVIII, 354-362.

Keen, Gregory B., "The Descendants of Jöran Kyn, the Founder of Upland," *Pennsylvania Magazine of History and Biography* (1881), V, 451-461.

Lewton, Fred. L., "Samuel Slater and the Oldest Cotton Machinery in the United States," *Annual Report*, Smithsonian Institution, 1926, Washington, pp. 505-512.

Linglebach, W. E., "Historical Investigation and the Commercial History of the Napoleonic Era," *American Historical Review* (1914), XIX, 257-281.

Melvin, F. E., "Dr. Daniel Coxe and Carolana," *Mississippi Valley Historical Review* (1914), I, 257-262.

Miller, Harry E., "Earlier Theories of Crises and Cycles in the U. S.," *Quarterly Journal of Economics* (1924), XXXVIII, 294-329.

Nussbaum, Fred. L., "American Tobacco and French Politics, 1783-1789," *Political Science Quarterly* (1925), XL, 497-516.

Rantoul, Robt. S., "The First Cotton Mill in America," *Historical Collections of the Essex Institute* (1897), XXXIII, 1-43.

Rezneck, Samuel, "The Depression of 1819-1822, A Social History," *American Historical Review* (1933), XXXIX, 28-47.

——, "The Rise and Early Development of Industrial Consciousness in the United States, 1760-1830," *Journal of Economic and Business History* (1931-1932), IV, 784-811.

Riddell, W. R., "Pre-Revolutionary Pennsylvania and the Slave Trade," *Pennsylvania Magazine of History and Biography* (1928), LII, 1-29.

Scull, G. D., "Biographical Notice of Doctor Daniel Coxe, of London," *Pennsylvania Magazine of History and Biography* (1883), VII, 317-337.

Sears, L. M., "Philadelphia and the Embargo: 1808," *Annual Report of the American Historical Association, 1920*, pp. 253-263.

Smith, W. B., "Wholesale Commodity Prices in the United States, 1795-1824," *Harvard Review of Economic Statistics* (1927), IX, 171-183.

Smith, W. Roy, "Sectionalism in Pennsylvania during the Revolution," *Political Science Quarterly* (1909), XXIV, 208-235.

Taylor, G. R., "Wholesale Commodity Prices at Charleston, South Carolina, 1732-1791," *Journal of Economic and Business History* (1931-1932), IV, 356-377.

Wooster, Harvey A., "A Forgotten Factor in American Industrial History," *American Economic Review* (1920), XVI, 14-27.

INDEX

Act to assist cotton manufactures of Pennsylvania, 151n.

Acts of Congress, 20n., 28n., 123

Acts of Parliament, 116, 147, 152

Adams, John, 16, 17, 38, 39, 40

Adams, John Quincy, 48

Agricultural Adjustment Act, 201

Agriculture: burden on, 79; importance of, 52, 63, 78-79, 81, 82, 90, 107n., 183, 197, 200; improvements in, 80; southern, 71, 110; surplus produce of, 113, 127, 181

Almy, Brown & Slater, 163, 167, 173n.

America: industrial resources of, 79, 190; productive capacity of, 198; self-sustaining, 128

American economy: balance in, 181, 191, 198; diversification of, 192, 197; dominance of agriculture in, 63; importance of manufacturing to, 138ff.

American Museum, 153, 197

American Nationalist School, vii, 197, 198, 201

American navigation: Coxe on, 32ff.

American Revolution: background of, 5-6; Coxe's attitude toward, 6n., 28

American system, 142, 190n.

Ames, Fisher, 29n., 108n., 112n., 118n., 122n.

Annapolis Convention, 10n., 14, 50, 52, 75, 149, 176

Anne Arundel County, 149

Arkwright, Sir Richard, 147, 152, 154, 157, 160, 161, 162, 163

Arkwright mills, 161n., 163

Articles of Confederation, 49, 55, 59, 66, 67

Baltimore Manufacturing Society, 158n.

Bank of England, 12, 26n., 27

Bank of New York, 162

Bank of North America: defended by Coxe, 11-12, 12n., 15; opposition to charter of, 10-12

Bank of Pennsylvania, proposed, 11n., 12n.

Barton, William, 86, 100n.

Berlin Decree, 116, 126

Beverly cotton mill, 158-159, 163, 167, 169n.

Bingham, William, 103n., 155n., 156n., 157

Bond, Phineas, 152n., 154

Boston Manufacturing Company, 173

Bounty: on British exports, 82; on cotton, 144, 169n.; price differential as such, 80; recommended by Coxe, 90, by Hamilton, 101

British West Indies, 125, 193

Brown, Moses, 160, 161, 168, 169n.

Cabot, George, 39, 99n., 159n., 169n.

Canals, 88, 142

Capital, in manufacturing, 27, 87, 93, 113, 120, 155, 158, 172, 191, 195

Carey, Henry Charles, 111n., 197, 198

Carey, Mathew, 44n., 51n., 110n., 111n., 153, 164, 166n., 173n., 181, 197-198

Chalmers, George, 102n.

Chesapeake-Leopard affair, 131, 133

Classicists, 195, 196

Clinton, George, 16, 72, 74n.

221